Feeling Trapped

GENDER AND JUSTICE

Edited by Claire M. Renzetti

This University of California Press series explores how the experiences of offending, victimization, and justice are profoundly influenced by the intersections of gender with other markers of social location. Cross-cultural and comparative, series volumes publish the best new scholarship that seeks to challenge assumptions, highlight inequalities, and transform practice and policy.

Feeling Trapped

Social Class and Violence against Women

James Ptacek

UNIVERSITY OF CALIFORNIA PRESS

University of California Press
Oakland, California

© 2023 by James Ptacek

Library of Congress Cataloging-in-Publication Data

Names: Ptacek, James, author.
Title: Feeling trapped : social class and violence against women /
    James Ptacek.
Other titles: Gender and justice series ; 9.
Description: Oakland, California : University of California Press,
    [2023] I Series: Gender and Justice ; 9 I Includes bibliographical
    references and index.
Identifiers: LCCN 2022024996 (print) I LCCN 2022024997 (ebook)
    I ISBN 9780520381605 (cloth) I ISBN 9780520381612 (paperback)
    I ISBN 9780520381629 (epub)
Subjects: LCSH: Intimate partner violence—United States—Case
    studies. I Social classes—United States—Case studies. I Women—
    Violence against—United States—Case studies.
Classification: LCC HV6626.2 .P795 2023 (print) I LCC HV6626.2
    (ebook) I DDC 362.82/920973—dc23/eng/20220902
LC record available at https://lccn.loc.gov/2022024996
LC ebook record available at https://lccn.loc.gov/2022024997

Manufactured in the United States of America

32 31 30 29 28 27 26 25 24 23
10 9 8 7 6 5 4 3 2 1

*To the sixty survivors who told me their stories
and shared their hopes for social change*

Contents

Preface

Since the beginning of my career as a sociologist, I have wanted to examine how social class affects violence against women. While there are many studies of intimate violence that focus on poverty and the working class, there are not many that address class in a comparative way, in terms of class privilege and class disadvantage. I was fortunate to find sixty women to talk with me about their experiences, including women from all classes.

I hope this book reveals these stories in all their vividness and complexity. I make extensive use of women's reflections in developing a collective account of intimate violence. They offer sharp observations on what is common and what is unique about what they have gone through. Their insights drive the book. I believe the reader will be moved by their words, just as I have been.

I am fortunate to have a rich circle of supportive colleagues. Special thanks go to Donna Coker, Viveka Enander, Walter DeKeseredy, Alesha Durfee, Raquel Kennedy Bergen, Molly Dragiewicz, Leigh Goodmark, Kathleen Daly, Joan Pennell, Kersti Yllö, and Mimi Kim. At Suffolk University, Susan Sered and Felicia Wiltz have been most kind.

For many long discussions during the research process, I must also thank Marta Flanagan, Michele Bograd, Tom Denton, Todd Crosset, Anne Richmond, Janet Meyer, Kendall Dudley, Carol Plaisted, and Pam Pacelli.

This research was inspired by a host of feminist scholars and anti-violence activists, including Linda Gordon, Patricia Hill Collins, Kimberlé Crenshaw, Raewyn Connell, Arlie Hochschild, Judith Herman, Kathleen Ferraro, Audre Lorde, bell hooks, Beth Richie, Andrea Ritchie, Joey Mogul, Kay Whitlock, Hillary Potter, Mary Koss, Melissa Harris-Perry, Angela Davis, Angela Harris, Susan Miller, C. Quince Hopkins, David Adams, Susan Chorley, Ted German, Fernando Mederos, Juan Carlos Areán, Lisa Lachance, Caitlin O'Brien, and Bob Pease. Owing to concerns about confidentiality, several survivors and advocates who contributed to the research cannot be named here.

At the University of California Press, I have been lucky to work with Maura Roessner, Madison Wetzell, and my longtime colleague, Claire Renzetti. They have all been so good to me!

I had many conversations about this work with my life partner, Bonnie Zimmer, who has worked with survivors for many years. I appreciate the support of my son Alex Zimmer, who was eager to comment on my writing.

A version of chapter 5 was previously published as "Rape and the Continuum of Sexual Abuse in Intimate Relationships: Interviews with US Women from Different Social Classes," in *Marital Rape: Consent, Marriage and Social Change in Global Context*, ed. Kersti Yllö and Gabriela Torres (New York: Oxford University Press, 2016). A version of chapter 2 was published as "Hidden Dramas of Masculinity: Women's Perspectives on Intimate Violence in Different Social Classes," *Violence Against Women* 27, no. 5 (April 2021): 666–87.

CHAPTER I

Conversations with Women about Abuse

The physical assault that leads women to [domestic violence] shelters is merely the most immediate manifestation of the subordination they experience. Many women who seek protection are unemployed or underemployed, and a good number of them are poor. Shelters serving these women cannot afford to address only the violence inflicted by the batterer; they must also confront the other multilayered and routinized forms of domination that often converge in these women's lives.

—Kimberlé Crenshaw

What causes women to feel trapped in abusive relationships with men? Consider how four women from different social classes describe this situation. A woman I call Jackie spoke to me about feeling completely dominated by her partner.[1] He punched her repeatedly and threatened her with a knife. A white woman, she was poor and homeless during part of her relationship:

> I was too afraid to leave. I was too afraid to run. I felt like he would come find me no matter where I was, especially after I was pregnant and then after I had my [child] he would come and find me because I had one of his possessions. . . . I was so afraid.

She was fired from her job for being pregnant, which made it even more difficult to survive and protect herself on the streets.

Cheryl, a white woman raised in a working-class community, was regularly hit, kicked, threatened, and sexually assaulted by her partner. He would threaten to kill himself if she didn't do what he wanted. This is how she describes her marriage:

> I was emotionally and spiritually dead. I wasn't allowed to make decisions about what I wanted to eat. . . . I couldn't make any decision. . . . I am a

smart person. . . . The world should have been opened up to me and he had hammered me away into this tight little pine coffin and had buried me six feet under and that's how I lived my life.

Her husband's behavior at her workplace caused her to lose her job, making her even more dependent on him.

Debra, a professional African American woman, talked of her own feelings of despair. She was severely beaten and sexually abused by her husband:

I felt like he had complete control over me and I couldn't do anything about my situation. I had this grief inside me and I felt powerless to him. I felt weak. I'm not that kind of person. . . . I'd get on my knees and pray for God to change him, change me. . . . I tried everything. . . . I felt I was in bondage.

Her status as a highly educated professional did not protect her from abuse; her husband was a professional as well, and his status helped him evade any consequences for his violence. At her workplace, when she talked about the abuse she was told she must be doing something to cause it.

Finally, Beth, a white woman who had substantial investments in her own name, was married to a man who frequently yelled at her, hit her, and threatened to kill her. She had black eyes, cuts, and many bruises from the violence. At one point, she felt so desperate that she spent several days contemplating what would happen if she killed him:

I wanted to figure out how many years I would get in . . . jail if I killed him, because I thought, well, this would be better. You know, like, I was thinking, I don't think I could do it, but I was, like, I thought, well, I wonder how long. . . . Because I thought my parents would feel really bad if he killed me. . . . Maybe they won't feel as bad if I killed him and they could come and visit me in jail. Where does that come from, you know?

Despite having her own money, for a long time she felt unable to protect herself or change her marriage. She didn't kill him; she divorced him. Her awareness of her homicidal feelings helped her to leave. But she suffered for many years before doing so.

These women express feelings of fear, overwhelming depression, powerlessness, and desperation. But they did not remain trapped: they all left their violent partners and changed their lives. Now that they are safe and free from the abuse, it is unsettling for them to recall such feelings. As if to distance herself from such despair, Cheryl asserts that she is "a smart person." Debra says, "I'm not that kind of person." Beth asks where her homicidal feelings came from. There is pain, guilt, and shame in the telling of their stories. This despite having left these men, despite all the things they did to avoid further victimization, and the many efforts they made to change their violent partners.

This is a book about traps and women's resistance to them. Why do so many women feel trapped in abusive relationships with men? And just how does social class affect this feeling? These questions are examined through interviews with sixty women from different social classes. All were abused by their husbands or boyfriends.

In this introductory chapter, I present the theoretical frameworks of the study, describe how I conducted the research, and offer an overview of the book.

MYTHS ABOUT INTIMATE VIOLENCE AND SOCIAL CLASS

The relationship between class and intimate violence is much misunderstood. Two opposing myths about class circulate in public discussions. The first myth is that social class is all that matters, that it is only or mostly poor and working-class women who are victimized. Called the "class myth," perhaps this could be more memorably seen as the Stanley Kowalski myth, after the violent character in Tennessee Williams's play *A Streetcar Named Desire*.[2] After all, the sleeveless undershirt Marlon Brando wore in his film portrayal of the working-class Kowalski has become known, hideously, as a "wife beater." At the program where I worked as a batterers' counselor for eight years, many of the men in the groups were working-class or poor. But the men attending these groups included doctors, lawyers, journalists, scientists, business executives, psychologists, divinity students, and college professors. In trainings with health-care workers and criminal legal officials about violence, I often made note of these occupations. The disbelief this list provokes among professionals is powerful.

The second and opposite myth is that class doesn't matter at all, and that the same levels of violence can be found in every class level. This "universal risk" or "classless intimate violence" myth denies that class status matters for women in the United States.[3] This myth is repeated whenever a celebrity is named in a case of intimate violence. But while violence against women may be found in virtually every neighborhood, poverty and economic hardship increase women's vulnerability to intimate violence. Research indicates that rates of such violence are significantly higher in poor and working-class households than in economically privileged ones.[4] Poverty and racism affect women's trust of the criminal legal system.[5] Intimate violence may further be compounded by women's abuse at the hands of the police or the Border Patrol.[6]

Both of these myths distort the relationship of social class to women's victimization. This study challenges the first of these myths, the notion that intimate violence is only a problem for people in working-class and poor neighborhoods. This idea is clearly false. But while some incidents of battering and rape involving Hollywood celebrities or professional athletes have received widespread attention, such cases are often so extreme and sensationalized that they offer no real understanding of women's experiences in economically privileged communities.

This study also seeks to challenge the second myth, the notion that class has no bearing on violence against women. While it is true that this violence can be found at every class level, social circumstances, especially poverty and racism, significantly affect women's risk of abuse. Following the lead of Patricia Hill Collins, who suggests a "both/and" way of framing social inequalities, it might be said that it is true *both* that intimate violence can be found in virtually every community, *and* that there are social circumstances, such as poverty and racism, that make it difficult for women to resist or escape violence.[7]

Illustrating the power of these myths, one woman explained how she was forced to fit someone's image of a person who was victimized. She has spoken publicly about her experience. On one occasion she had a chance to share her story on local television. But before going on camera, the director of the shoot, a man, insisted that she take off her earrings and change her clothes. He said she was too pretty and too well-dressed to portray a "battered woman." He felt he knew what such a woman looks like, and so he changed her appearance to fit his image.

CLASS AND PRIVILEGE AND CLASS DISADVANTAGE

To explore why it is that women so often feel trapped, I conducted in-depth, semistructured interviews with sixty women, all of whom had been abused in intimate relationships with men. They had all been separated from their abusive partners at the time of the interviews. These conversations explored the meaning, the context, and the dynamics of violence and abuse. The interviews lasted from one to six hours; a number were completed in two parts. I recruited women through flyers sent to shelters, women's advocacy programs, counselors who work with abusive partners, therapists, and community activists. As the term "intimate violence" was in the heading for the flyer, it is likely that women responding to this kind of recruitment would be more severely abused than women contacted through other methods. On the whole, the violence and abuse these women suffered was more extreme than what I had found in a study of women seeking domestic violence restraining orders in the criminal courts.[8] The violence was also more extensive than what I had seen in my time as a group leader in a program for abusive men.

I chose to interview women who had left abusive relationships, hoping that distance from the relationship might offer some perspective on their experiences and shed light on the long-term consequences of abuse. The study flyer invited participants who had been out of abusive relationships for a number of years. The length of time between the separation and the interview varied from one to thirty-two years, but most women had been separated for fewer than ten years. Having had some time away from these abusive relationships gave the women a chance to talk about the separation and the extent to which they had healed from the violence. Of the sixty women, 73 percent (n = 44) were white, 23 percent (n = 14) were Black or African American, one was Asian American, and one identified as Hispanic.

I grouped the women I interviewed into four class categories: poor, working-class, professional, and wealthy. Let me explain these categories. From a Marxist perspective, classes represent deep social divisions formed by domination, exploitation, and social exclusion in capitalist societies.[9] There is much confusion about the number of classes in the United States and how they should be defined. The term "middle class" is particularly troublesome. Social scientists have found that this term lacks either a clear or a consistent definition. Many scholars use "middle class" to refer to professionals, managers, and those credentialed by higher education.[10] But in news articles, government reports, and some academic studies, "middle class" is often used interchangeably with "middle income."[11] This is confusing, because families at the median household income are best seen as part of the working class.[12] For instance, in 2020 the US median household income was $67,521, according to the US Census Bureau.[13] This is not even close to the average income of professionals. In 2019, the average salary for lawyers was over $120,000; for doctors, it was over $200,000.[14]

Both "middle class" and "middle income" obscure the bright line between those with class privilege and those with class disadvantage.

Poverty, the most obvious disadvantage, clearly contributes to why some women feel trapped in abusive relationships. But the difference in life chances between the working class and the professional class is also important to understand. This gap has been growing. Anne Case and Angus Deaton charted the increase in deaths among those without college degrees due to suicide, drug abuse, and alcoholism. They call these "deaths of despair." This increase among working-class people is so significant that in recent years, life expectancy for the US population as a whole has *decreased*.[15]

This book was completed during the COVID-19 pandemic. During this time, the line between the working class and the professional class has been illuminated, in terms of jobs that remain steady and jobs that have disappeared, jobs with health insurance and jobs without any benefits whatsoever. Economically marginalized people and communities of color have been the most harmed by this disease, in terms of the number of cases and the number of fatalities.[16] Deaths among Black, Native American, and Latinx individuals are nearly twice as high as deaths among white and Asian American people.[17]

In the first ten months of the pandemic, women lost significantly more jobs than men; this was especially true for Black women, Latinas, and Asian women.[18] In 2020, 3.5 million mothers of school-aged children left the paid workforce.[19] By early 2021, women's overall labor participation was the lowest it had been in over thirty years.[20] Service sector workers were especially affected. This gendered job loss is related to increased demands upon women for caretaking at home.[21] There is early evidence that the pandemic has increased intimate violence, likely due to increased isolation and economic stress.[22] At the same time, since the start of the pandemic, the wealth of US billionaires has risen by 70 percent.[23] This global crisis has dramatically exposed class, race, and gender divisions in the United States.

In their map of the US class structure, Earl Wysong, Robert Perrucci, and David Wright avoid the term "middle class" entirely and mark the greatest division as between the "privileged class" (which includes the wealthy, along with professionals and managers) and the "working class" (which includes the poor).[24] I also avoid the term "middle class" and all the confusion it represents. Instead, based on their occupations, household income, and investments during the abusive relationships, I have categorized the women's households as poor, working-class, professional, and wealthy. This offers the best way to explore class privilege and class disadvantage.

Women are referred to by the class category they were in during their relationships. Most of those from poor communities reported no regular income. Some were on disability or other forms of state assistance. The occupations of those who were employed included the hotel industry, food service, drug dealing, and prostitution. Most did not have high school diplomas. None were married; most were not raising children. These women's relationships with their abusive partners averaged five years in length.

The working-class group had household incomes generally from $30,000 to $90,000, without significant investments. They worked in the building trades, food service, transportation, and clerical jobs. Unlike the wealthy and professional men, many of the working-class men's jobs were unstable; some men worked on and off, did seasonal labor, or held a variety of minimum-wage jobs. Like many of the wealthy and professional women, working-class women largely worked part-time in order to care for their children. Very few of the men or women had college degrees. Most women were married and had children; the average length of their relationships was less than ten years.

Those in the professional category had household incomes from $100,000 to $300,000, but mostly without substantial investments. Their occupations included higher education, information technology, medicine, and sales. Half of the women worked full-time and half part-time. Most of the women and half of the men had graduated from college, and many had advanced degrees. Most were married, and most also had children. The average length of the marriages or relationships was nineteen years.

The wealthy households had either incomes from $500,000 to several million dollars a year or millions in inheritance or investments. The occupations (largely of the men) included finance, medicine, and business management. Most of the men and women were college graduates, and some held advanced degrees. Most of the women in this category were married, had children, and worked part-time. The average length of the relationships was over fourteen years. Overall, the women in the privileged classes (wealthy and professional) were in much longer relationships than women in working-class and poor communities. Since most women said they felt "trapped" in these relationships, this means that the professional and wealthy women felt trapped for a much longer period of time.

When they were in these relationships, 15 percent (n = 9) of the women's households could be categorized as poor, 43 percent (n = 26) were working-class, 23 percent (n = 14) were professional, and 18 percent (n = 11) were wealthy. But class status can be fleeting, especially for women. Research has shown that recently divorced women are twice as likely to be living in poverty than recently divorced men, and that women are more likely to receive public assistance following divorce than men.[25]

Based on their circumstances at the time of the interviews, most of which took place years after their separation, there was a marked decline in women's economic status. Of the sixty women, 35 percent (n = 21) were now poor, a category that more than doubled in size; 28 percent (n = 17) were working-class; 25 percent (n = 16) had professional status; and 10 percent (n = 6) remained wealthy. Most of the wealthy and professional women did not lose class status, although some certainly did. But many of the formerly working-class women were now poor. At the time of the interviews, almost half of the women who were poor were homeless or had been homeless since separating from their partners. In some cases, women's physical injuries were disabling; in other cases, men had succeeded in damaging their ex-partners financially, both during the relationships and after separation. For a number of women, being single mothers created overwhelming dilemmas around work and their children's needs. Problems with addiction, depression, and other mental health issues in the wake of the abuse were also consequential.

In a capitalist society, social class is part of our identities. Annette Kuhn writes: "Class is not just about the way you talk, or dress, or furnish your home; it is not just about the job you do, or how much money you make doing it. . . . Class is something beneath your clothes, under your skin, in your reflexes, in your psyche, at the very core of your being."[26]

Social class shapes the comparisons we make between ourselves and those in other classes. Class affects our desires and our feelings of envy, contempt, anger, guilt, and shame. Since racism causes poverty, class divisions are racially coded in the United States. In this study, class is examined on three levels. I explore the similarities and differences between the women from different classes. Social class is also addressed as it appears in conflicts within these relationships. And last, class is discussed at the individual level. As I show, class divisions inspired a range of feelings in both the women and their abusive partners. These feelings help to explain men's motives for violence and women's ability to name their experiences as abuse.

THE INTERSECTION OF MULTIPLE INEQUALITIES

The concept of intersectionality addresses the simultaneous operation of privilege and discrimination in people's lives.[27] This term was developed by Kimberlé Crenshaw, whose quote opens this chapter. Since there are many dimensions of identity—including class, race, gender, ethnicity, sexual orientation, age, health, religious affiliation, criminal history, and citizenship status—most people occupy complex social locations in which they are privileged by some parts of their identities while being discriminated against because of other aspects. For those women in the study who had class or racial privilege, this privilege obviously did not prevent them from being physically and sexually abused. In fact, half of the wealthy women had been in more than one abusive relationship. Nonetheless, privilege and discrimination affected women's experiences.

Patricia Hill Collins and Sirma Bilge emphasize that the different forms of inequality—such as gender and class and race—shape one another. "Intersectionality," they write, "examines how power relations are intertwined and mutually constructing." As they put it, "Within intersectional frameworks, there is no pure racism or sexism. Rather, power relations of racism and sexism gain meaning in relation to one another."[28]

This feminist approach inspired the design of this study and the kinds of questions I asked about feeling trapped. The class and racial identities of the women are named in this book to raise this complexity.

THE SOCIAL LOCATION OF THE AUTHOR

A researcher's personal background can both help and hinder the process of the investigation. One report on social-scientific methods states, "Every researcher has a biography that becomes an element in and an aspect of the collection and analysis of data."[29] Like all scholars, I bring strengths and limitations to this project.

In one way or another, I have been engaged with the problem of violence against women since 1981. I worked as a group counselor with abusive men for eight years. I trained hospital, mental health, and criminal legal professionals on intimate violence. I conducted research on men who abuse their partners, on intimate violence and sexual assault on college campuses, and on women seeking domestic violence restraining orders.[30] I explored innovative approaches to violence against women used in Canada, New Zealand, Australia, and the United States.[31] I taught college courses on violence against women for over thirty years. In addition, I have learned much from my life partner, Bonnie Zimmer, who founded and directed a hospital-based program for women who were abused.

Relevant to the matter of social class, while in my twenties I volunteered as a labor union organizer in the taxicab and restaurant industries and also became involved in a newspaper strike. Talking to people about improving their working conditions gave me a vivid understanding of class conflict.

If these are strengths, I certainly have limitations. I am a straight, white, professional-class man with US citizenship. I identify with the gender I was assigned at birth. While I have occasionally encountered angry men on the streets, I actually have no personal experience of being truly terrified, of fearing that someone actually meant to do me serious harm. Most women I know can't say this. Many gay men I know can't say this. But I do have a relevant story. A girlfriend I had in high school had been abused by her former boyfriend. I discovered this during an argument. In the middle of an angry exchange, she suddenly curled up on the sofa and said, "Please don't hit me." I was horrified that a woman would say this to me. At one point I felt the wrath of this former boyfriend quite directly. He snuck up to me at a football game and punched me in the head hard enough to knock me down. Apparently he felt entitled to control who this young woman dated, even after she had broken up with him. When I am asked how I came to study intimate violence, I think about the impact of these experiences.

I was fortunate to have had loving parents who modeled a true partnership while raising five children (three of them boys). My father worked in a factory. My mother was a schoolteacher who marched for the Equal Rights Amendment and walked picket lines for her union. Along with my other privileges, having such parents has at times made me think I am the wrong person to study intimate violence.

I grew up in two overwhelmingly white, Christian cities near Milwaukee, Wisconsin, one working-class and one professional. The second of these cities, Wauwatosa, is a suburb just outside of Milwaukee. When I was growing up, it was said to be a "city of beautiful homes." In practice, what that meant was beautiful homes for white people. The first Black resident bought land in Wauwatosa in 1955. His unfinished home was damaged by vandalism and arson; he received threatening phone calls. The city council repeatedly tried to block construction.[32] Milwaukee is one of the most racially segregated metropolitan areas in the country. Racially segregated cities like Wauwatosa are created intentionally.[33]

I have no history of abusive treatment by the police. I assume that my gender, class position, race, sexual orientation, religious background, and citizenship have generally served to protect me from violence. These are privileges, which operate as the flip side of discrimination.

How does my background affect the research? If I don't have personal experience of being terrified, this creates obstacles to understanding what these women have gone through. I believe my gender made it more difficult for me to find women to interview. My inability to speak Spanish limited the number of Latinas I was able to connect with. Owing to my whiteness, my efforts to find Asian American and Native American women to interview were largely unsuccessful.

While these are surely limitations, I believe that good work on social inequalities can be done if researchers are honest about their backgrounds and make efforts to compensate for their lack of lived experience. I conducted interviews with counselors, antiviolence activists, and women's advocates in preparation for this research, half of whom were women and men of color. I called upon a number of people to offer insights on this study, including women who work with survivors and who have suffered intimate violence themselves.

THE INTERVIEW PROCESS

Consistent with the guidelines of feminist research methods, I gave women an opportunity to tell their stories at length.[34] I sought to express respect, empathy, and support during the interviews. I checked in about the process regularly and encouraged women to take breaks or come back again another day to complete the conversations. A central goal was to avoid doing anything that would cause these women to feel I was shaming them in any way. My questions provoked strong feelings. Shame, a feeling sharply affected by race, class, and gender, is a major obstacle to women's seeking help.[35] I was determined to offer an anti-shaming presence. I believe I generally succeeded, but I know I failed at least once. I was interviewing a white woman who had been married to a wealthy man, and I asked about her income. She was working part-time. When she told me what she earned, I felt the sting of reflected shame on my face. In at least this one case, my question about income somehow evoked this response. In a class-divided society, income is used as a singular measure of individual worth in a most damaging way. A few women declined to talk about what they earned; my classifications are estimates in some cases. For some, questions about money raised more protectiveness than questions about intimate violence.

Before participating in the interviews, some women had not talked about their abusive relationships for many years. Others talked often about their experiences in their roles as advocates or public speakers. Some were shy and nervous, while others possessed self-confidence and a terrific sense of humor. These were emotionally intense conversations. One professional woman had post-traumatic stress disorder (PTSD). She knew the interview would bring back overwhelming feelings about the abuse, and so she made sure to schedule an appointment with her therapist for the following day. During the interview I checked in with her:

> [Are you still doing okay?] Oh, I'm so far gone. It's all right. It's like I'm extremely triggered. I'm really motivated to share my story. There's no other way. . . . I can certainly handle this. But I'm not optimizing my rationality.

Another woman thought she might have difficulty sleeping after our interview, as she hadn't talked about her experience in many years. Yet another woman said she would take a long walk after our conversation to clear her head.

In these conversations, I felt I was able to create good rapport, although this owes as much to the generosity and grace of these individuals as it does to my own skills. They told me about many things that our culture sees as shameful. Women shared details of their own drug and alcohol addiction, of depression and suicide attempts. They talked of losing their children to child protective services and of working in prostitution. They spoke frankly about sex; a few discussed having affairs. This openness convinced me that I had succeeded in making meaningful connections during the interviews. The questions I asked expressed a sense that intimate violence is a serious and highly consequential crime. One question was, "Was your partner held accountable by anyone for his abusive actions?" Another was, "Did anyone acknowledge the injustice of the abuse you experienced?"

At the end of each interview, I asked women how the conversation had gone for them. The feedback I received was very positive about the interview experience. Women felt supported and validated by the conversations, and they appreciated the chance to talk about their experiences. Research indicates that when in-depth interviews are conducted carefully, survivors generally have positive responses to them.[36]

A woman friend who had survived intimate violence advised me that I might not be able to tolerate all the pain I would encounter. She was right. The degradation, sexual abuse, and physical violence women described overwhelmed me. Women often cried as they explained the struggle with their partners and the toll this had taken on their children.

Kate was a white woman who like her husband was raised in a working-class community. She was attacked by her partner at least thirty times; she suffered concussions, extensive bruises, and cuts. Her husband threatened to kill her more times than she could count. At one point in our conversation, the violence Kate described actually took my breath away. She was relating an incident in which her husband punched her in the face so hard that she was lifted off the floor. I looked down and froze as I was trying to take this in. She stopped to ask me, "Are you breathing?"

Following many interviews, I was exhausted and irritable for the rest of the day. One day a woman described being repeatedly raped by her husband. That night, I had nightmares of being captured by the Nazis during World War II. This is how the dreams of a privileged man interpreted such violence. At one point my spirits were so affected from a series of interviews that I sought guidance from my minister. Since she had previously worked in a battered women's shelter, she was able to offer useful ideas about taking walks and finding solace during the research process.

It may sound surprising, but there was actually more laughter than tears in the interviews. Humor creates a friendly bond between strangers. It breaks tension in an emotional conversation. Women would sometimes laugh even while describing extreme violence. One white woman spoke about her avoidance of relationships after she had left an extremely violent man. Their household income had been over $100,000. He "almost strangled me to death," she said. At the time of the interview she was unemployed and had no place to live. "I've stayed away from relationships or dating, just because [of] the situation I'm in, being homeless right now," she told me. "And I don't like men very much. No." At this point she looked directly at me, and as I am a man, she laughed very hard. I laughed with her.

There was a lot of good-natured humor at my expense. One thing I asked about was the division of household labor. For a number of women, this question was oddly funny, in that it appeared remarkably naïve:

I did 99 percent of it [*much laughter*]. He wouldn't do anything, are you kidding? (a white working-class woman)

Housecleaning [*laughter*]? There was no division. (a white professional woman)

[*Much laughter*] You gotta be kidding me! . . . Zip, nothing. [He would say]: "I'm rich. I have money. . . . You do that." (a white wealthy woman)

With their laughter, these women seemed to be saying, "You don't know what it's really like to actually live with an abusive man, do you?" If that is what they meant, they were of course correct.

VIOLENCE AND GENDER INEQUALITY

To explain why most women from every social class felt trapped in these relationships, it is important to examine more than the abuse and its consequences. There are broader dimensions of gender inequality that are relevant to women's experiences of abuse. An understanding of patriarchy is essential here.

In feminist writing, the term "patriarchy" has apparently fallen out of use in recent years. Critics of this term have said that it oversimplifies gender inequality; that it suggests a universal and unchanging type of societal power; and that it fails to address multiple inequalities, and therefore differences among women and men based on race and culture.[37] At the same time, it must be acknowledged that many activists continue to use this language, and that its usage in public conversations seems to be increasing. A look at the number of articles in the *New York Times* containing the word "patriarchy" indicates the growing popularity of this term. Using the *New York Times* archive search engine, there were more than five times as many articles mentioning "patriarchy" in 2020 as in 2010. Over this same time period, there were also increases in articles mentioning "feminism," "feminist," and "violence against women."[38]

There is scholarship that is mindful of these criticisms of patriarchy and that uses the term in careful ways. Patriarchy has been used in many studies of violence against women.[39] Many Black feminist scholars use this concept, often in connection with intersectionality.[40]

The treatment of patriarchy that is most useful to this study was developed by Sylvia Walby.[41] Her work argues that patriarchy cannot be fully understood without attention to class and racial inequalities. Walby sees patriarchy as constantly being challenged and defended, rather than as being universal or fixed. "Women are not passive victims of oppressive structures," she writes. "They have struggled to change both their immediate circumstances and the wider social structures."[42]

Oddly enough, while Walby continues to write on gender inequality, she no longer uses the term "patriarchy" herself. Despite her contributions to clarifying this term, she believes this word is often "misinterpreted" for the aforementioned reasons.[43] Nevertheless, it is my argument that her theory of patriarchy illuminates the sources of women's entrapment in abusive relationships. Her theory highlights the role of violence in creating inequality. Her work further shows where change needs to be made to transform gender inequality. Patriarchy remains a useful concept, so long as its meaning is made clear.[44]

Walby defines patriarchy as "a system of social structures and practices in which men dominate, oppress, and exploit women."[45] Drawing from several different kinds of feminist theory, including Black feminism, Walby sees women's oppression as located in six different sites in Western societies. Discrimination in the paid labor force is one site of inequality. A second site is unpaid domestic labor; as I have shown regarding the COVID-19 pandemic, this has direct consequences for women's ability to do paid work. Sexuality is a third site; inequality in heterosexual relationships is apparent in the sexual double standard and in the denigration of lesbian and gay love. The state is a fourth site, involving the legal system, the government, and welfare assistance. Cultural representations of masculinity and femininity are a fifth site. Central to this study, violence against women is a sixth site of inequality. Walby argues that in the West, this violence is so common and has such predictable consequences that this must be seen as its own basis of women's oppression. These different sites are explored throughout this book.

These six bases are distinct, and yet they are related to one another. The state is involved in violence against women in many ways. The "sexual abuse to prison pipeline" offers one such link, a way of naming the harm the state does to girls. According to a report by the Human Rights Project for Girls, overwhelming numbers of girls in the juvenile justice system have been sexually abused. Some studies found that most girls in detention have been victimized.[46] Instead of addressing this reality, the juvenile detention system criminalizes the ways that girls react to this violence. Common responses to abuse such as running away from home or resisting parental authority are treated as crimes. Girls are then placed in foster care or youth detention, which frequently exposes them to more abuse. Without adequate support, girls make more attempts at coping that are again criminalized, creating a cycle. The sexual abuse to prison pipeline is especially relevant for Native American, Black, and Hispanic girls, who are overrepresented among those detained and committed. Girls who identify themselves as lesbian, gay, bisexual, transgender, or gender nonconforming are also criminalized at high rates.[47]

It is therefore unsurprising that high rates of victimization have been found among women in prisons and jails.[48] Research shows that at least half of women in detention previously suffered some form of trauma, including child sexual abuse, adolescent and adult sexual violence, and physical abuse from intimate partners.[49] Sexual violence committed by correctional officers compounds this trauma.[50] Between 1980 and 2019, the number of women in prisons and jails increased by more than 700 percent.[51] Native American women, Black women, and Latinas are disproportionately confined in prisons and jails.[52] Most women's crimes are nonviolent; they are either drug offenses, property crimes, or violations of public order such as prostitution.[53] What this means is that the crimes these women personally suffer are generally more severe than the crimes they are incarcerated for. Feminists of color and human rights activists have long argued that the US prison system is racially discriminatory, brutal, cruel, and in violation of both the US Constitution and principles of international human rights.[54]

This increase in women's incarceration does not reflect a surge in crime rates. Rather, it is the result of heightened penalties for drug use and difficulties that women encounter when leaving prisons and jails.[55] Larger economic and political matters also contribute to the mass incarceration of men and women. The "prison industrial complex" is a way to name these issues. The activist group Critical Resistance defines this term as follows:

> The prison industrial complex (PIC) is a term we use to describe the overlapping interests of government and industry that use surveillance, policing, and imprisonment as solutions to economic, social and political problems. . . .
>
> This power is . . . maintained by earning huge profits for private companies that deal with prisons and police forces; helping earn political gains for "tough on crime" politicians; increasing the influence of prison guard and police unions; and eliminating social and political dissent by oppressed communities.[56]

Just as the concept of the "military industrial complex" identified a set of shared interests involving the military and private companies, the prison industrial complex is a set of powerful connections between private companies, politicians, and government officials. These relationships shape the expansion of state control in ways that are independent of crime rates.[57]

As Crenshaw indicates in the quote that opens this chapter, race and class operate together with gender in women's experiences of violence. Walby's institutional sites are places where racism is entrenched along with sexism. She says that the state is "patriarchal as well as capitalist and racist."[58] An intersectional analysis of patriarchy informs the investigation in this book.

INTIMATE VIOLENCE AS SOCIAL ENTRAPMENT

Along with a broad theory of gender inequality, this study is guided by a more specific understanding of why women feel trapped in abusive relationships. In my study of women's experiences seeking domestic violence restraining orders in Massachusetts, I argued that intimate violence against women should be seen as a kind of *social entrapment* rather than just as an individual experience.[59] The power that abusive men exert over women lies in more than just physical force. There is a social dimension to the endless dilemmas women face when they are abused by their partners. This perspective was inspired by Linda Gordon. In her history of family violence in Boston, she said, "One assault does not make a battered woman; she becomes that because of her socially determined inability to resist or escape: her lack of economic resources, law enforcement services, and quite likely, self-confidence."[60] To name intimate violence as social entrapment is to connect men's violence and women's suffering to community responses and to institutions such as hospitals and the criminal legal system. How friends and family members act when informed about abuse matters greatly. Nurses and doctors, police, judges, and religious leaders all have opportunities to support women and their children in the wake of violence. These responses can be corrupted by sexism, racism, contempt for the poor, and biases of many kinds. Seeing the experience of intimate violence as social entrapment links private violence to public responses and connects social inequalities to women's victimization. This study seeks to provide a window into both individual women's experiences and the responses of their communities to this violence.

OVERVIEW OF THE BOOK

Every chapter examines why women feel trapped in abusive relationships. Chapter 2 addresses the cultural images of masculinity that are dominant in US society. How are violence and abuse related to the kind of masculinities these men present? How do these abusive partners view themselves as men? How do their abused partners see them? What similarities and differences do women report across social classes? And how do the dramatically different kinds of masculinity these men present in public and in private contribute to women's feelings of entrapment?

Four major dimensions of intimate violence are often identified by activists and researchers: psychological abuse, physical abuse, sexual abuse, and economic abuse. To explore these overlapping dynamics, it is best to start with psychological abuse. Chapter 3 examines the psychological cruelty that women reported, placing this in the context of cultural images of women as "bad wives" and failed women. The verbal degradation experienced by women is explored for their insights into men's motives for the violence and abuse. For many women, the psychological attacks caused the most lasting harm. Such attacks have a lot to do with why women feel trapped.

Chapter 4 details the physical abuse and threats that women suffered, with attention to class similarities and differences. Explanations for the abuse are examined, along with the harm caused by the violence.

Chapter 5 is devoted to sexual abuse. Inspired by Liz Kelly, this topic is developed as a "continuum of sexual abuse" and includes delusional jealousy, surveillance, infidelity, reproductive abuse, the use of pornography, child sexual abuse, and rape.[61] These aspects of sexualized domination form their own dynamic of entrapment.

Chapter 6 focuses on economic dependence and economic abuse. The role of money is investigated at every class level. Economic abuse is key to understanding why many women felt trapped in these relationships.

Women were asked about feelings of love, fear, anger, guilt, and shame in order to map the emotional dynamics of their relationships. This forms the substance of chapter 7. These feelings play an important role in women's entrapment. How did the men seek to control their partners through fear? How did men attempt to create guilt and shame in these women? How did the women manage these feelings? What roles did friends, family, religious leaders, therapists, and feminist activists play? How does social class affect these emotional processes?

All of the women either left, or in a few cases were left by, their abusive partners. Chapter 8 investigates the process of separation, with attention to social class. Since the women had left their partners often many years before the interviews, there is an opportunity to examine the extent to which the women had healed from the violence and abuse since separation. Women were asked what justice would look like in the wake of this abuse, and what they would like to have happen to their ex-partners.

The book's conclusion draws together the many ways that women felt trapped and resisted entrapment. A revised model of social entrapment is presented, and the conclusion ends with a discussion of what this model suggests about a way forward in stopping intimate violence against women.

CHAPTER 2

The Hidden Dramas
of Masculinity

His relations with women . . . lie in a contingent region,
where morality no longer applies. . . . His relations with other
men are based on certain values . . . but with woman—she
was invented for this reason— . . . he is tyrannical, sadistic,
violent or puerile, masochistic or querulous; he tries to satisfy
his obsessions, his manias; he "relaxes," he "lets go" in the
name of rights he has acquired in his public life.

—Simone de Beauvoir

Writing in 1949, Simone de Beauvoir sketched a complex portrait of patriarchal societies, stating that many men present contradictory faces of
masculinity in public and in private. In this passage, the French feminist
and existentialist philosopher argues that men see their private relationships with women as inhabiting a zone of immorality where they can
secretly indulge any desires, needs, or feelings of hostility. For many
women, Beauvoir states, "this drama is a daily reality."[1] In her view, the
dominant positions men hold in the labor force, in politics, and in the
culture at large grant them this license for abusive conduct.

The fluidity of gender is at the heart of contemporary theories of
masculinity. Men who are violent with their intimate partners display
remarkably different kinds of masculinity in public and in private. This
is well known among survivors, researchers, and feminist activists.[2]
Confusion over what is true or false about these men causes women to
feel trapped in abusive relationships.

Studies of masculinity and crime generally draw upon interviews with
men. We clearly need good research that draws upon men's perspectives on their own violence. But I believe that women who have been
abused can offer important insights on masculinities. When I worked as
a group counselor, part of my job was to call the partners of the men
and ask about the levels of violence and abuse. I learned that survivors

remember more and reveal more than their partners about the abuse and its consequences.

Cultural representations of masculinity and femininity are an important dimension of gender inequality, according to Sylvia Walby.[3] In this chapter, I explore such representations through women's perspectives on the masculinities of their violent partners. How are violence and abuse related to the kind of masculinities these men present? How do these abusive partners view themselves as men? How do their abused partners see them? How do these men view women in general? And last, what similarities and differences do women report across social classes?

The theoretical contribution of this chapter unfolds in the following fashion. Following the insights of Beauvoir, I argue that men's intimate violence against women might best be understood as dramas of masculinity, dramas kept hidden from public view. Consistent with the work on masculinities by Raewyn Connell and James Messerschmidt, I detail how violent and abusive men are seeking a kind of masculine recognition though their private actions. Applying insights from Charles Taylor's theory of recognition, I propose that for abusive men, this masculine self-recognition is fused with misogyny. Recognition for the men simultaneously involves the *mis*recognition of their women partners, meaning that rather than being seen as full human beings, the women are viewed with contempt. This concept is examined with attention to the social class circumstances of the men and the women.

MASCULINITIES AS INDIVIDUAL AND COLLECTIVE PROJECTS

Connell and Messerschmidt argue that masculinities are not natural outcomes of biology. In their view, masculinities are not inherent traits or unchanging dimensions of men's lives. Nor are they simply the passive result of socialization. Rather, informed by the existentialist philosophy of Jean-Paul Sartre and Beauvoir, Connell and Messerschmidt see masculinities and femininities as individual and collective "projects."[4] Masculinities and femininities are actively chosen, embraced, and embodied by individuals. They are commitments individuals make about self-identification and self-expression in societies deeply divided by gender.

While these are individual projects, they are shaped by class, culture, and history. As Messerschmidt states, "Although masculinity is always individual and personal, specific forms of masculinity are available, encouraged, and permitted, depending upon one's social class, race, and sexual preference."[5] These projects are focused on how to act as a man, how to relate to women, and how to relate to other men in the context of gender inequality. "Gender is always relational," Connell and Messerschmidt argue, "and patterns of masculinity are socially defined in contradistinction from some model (whether real or imaginary) of femininity."[6] "Imaginary" models of femininity are important to this analysis, as I show.

Because there are multiple ways to "do" masculinity, there are conflicts between men regarding masculinities. Connell has named the kind of masculinity that is most idealized in a culture, by both men and women, "hegemonic masculinity." According to Messerschmidt, "In contemporary Western societies, hegemonic masculinity is defined through work in the paid-labor market, the subordination of women, heterosexism, and the driven and uncontrollable sexuality of men."[7] Hegemonic masculinity legitimates the subordination of women to men. The primacy of whiteness, homophobia, and avoidance of anything seen as "feminine" is important to the kind of masculinity now culturally dominant in the United States. Along with Walby, Connell sees "compulsory heterosexuality" as a key patriarchal practice.[8]

Other ways of doing masculinity that depart from these requirements are seen as inferior, and displaying them can lead to discrimination and abuse. Queer masculinities, the masculinities of men of color, egalitarian or pro-feminist masculinities, and pacifist masculinities challenge the legitimacy of hegemonic masculinity. Hate crimes against lesbian, gay, and transgender individuals and the mistreatment of LGBTQ communities by the criminal legal system indicate the intensity of these gender politics.[9]

"Masculinity is never static, never a finished product," according to Messerschmidt.[10] Rather, masculinities are ongoing, situation-specific practices. "Different types of masculinity exist in the school, the youth group, the street, the family, and the workplace. In other words, men do masculinity according to the social situation in which they find themselves."[11]

The kind of masculinity that is admired and supported in the West is not an openly violent masculinity, according to Connell.[12] And in fact, in the wake of the #MeToo movement, many prominent white celebrities, business executives, professionals, and politicians have lost their positions as a result of credible accusations of sexual harassment and violence.[13] This is one indication of cultural transformations of masculinity occurring in Western societies. However, it must be noted that many women who have publicly named their abusers have received anonymous death threats, have lost their jobs, and have been publicly shamed for coming forward.[14] What this backlash indicates is that many men continue to use violence and hostility to punish and silence women.

As Messerschmidt states, "Crime by men is a form of social practice invoked as a resource, when other resources are unavailable, for accomplishing masculinity."[15] Among men, there is often a private tolerance for and collusion with this kind of hidden, abusive masculinity. This dynamic perspective on masculinities can help to illuminate the multiple faces of masculinity that abusive men present in intimate relationships with women.

THE HIDDEN DRAMAS OF MASCULINITY

Most of the men who had been in relationships with the women I interviewed presented amiable public masculinities, while at the same time engaging in secret, violent masculinities when with their partners. Over half of the women described their ex-partners as either "charming" or "nice" in public. This is the side of their partners that they were initially drawn to. "Charming" in particular seems to name the deliberate, public effort most men made to win admiration from friends and family by being polite, agreeable, and friendly. But while "charming" can mean likable or pleasant, women used this term to mean manipulative or two-faced. "He always put on that charming boyfriend type of thing, acting like he was such a gentleman," a white working-class woman observed. "He was always charming outside of the relationship, very nice to other people," a Black professional woman stated. "People really bought into that."

Even when in private, the men would often shift back and forth between being kind and being cruel. Many men isolated their partners from their friends and relatives out of fear the women would disclose the abuse. Some men threatened to harm or kill their partners if they talked.

Most women said that while the psychological abuse began early on, the physical and sexual abuse didn't start until well into the relationship. It was generally after the marriage or after years of living together that the violent faces of masculinity were fully revealed. In many cases, this was not until women were pregnant or had children. This made it difficult for them to make sense of this violence. The abuse was mostly hidden from public view until the women separated from their partners, thus exposing the men's hidden behavior to their friends, their families, the police, and the courts.

According to the women in this study, the presentations of masculinity by their partners often seemed to be elaborate dramas, just as Beauvoir described. Some women referred to these shifting displays of masculinity in theatrical terms. A Black working-class woman spoke of her partner "trying to throw his weight around" when he was with other men. A white working-class survivor spoke of how "he put on this 'manly manhood' when he was around other people." Another white working-class woman explained that her partner "would put on a façade at the church as a good guy." A white professional woman talked of "chest-puffing" displays by her ex-husband.

A white professional woman described seeing her husband transform from his public to his private face:

> He could turn [his anger] on and off very quickly. . . . If somebody came to our door he could be very charming and pleasant, and then as soon as he shut the door you'd see it in his face that his anger level was up.

This observation reveals how carefully this man fashioned his masculine demeanor for different audiences.

Beauvoir wrote of the "puerile" or childish dimensions of men's private dramas. Some women spoke of "temper tantrums" by their partners. A number of the men who said they would kill their partners did this out of abject dependence on these women, threatening murder if the women left the relationship. Some men threatened suicide if their partners left.

Sometimes these attacks would go on for days. These tirades were apparently so important that some men would force their partners to listen and would not allow them to leave the room, even to use the bathroom. Most women stated that in private their partners were angry either all of the time or a lot of the time. This created a frightening situation. In these dramas, the men tolerated only a narrow range of roles for their partners. Many women were not allowed to express anger. In fact, assertiveness or resistance to men's control was a common reason for the violence and abuse.

ABUSE AND CONTROL, ABUSE AND RECOGNITION

In their intimate relationships, the men sought to frighten and control their partners. This is consistent with a large body of feminist scholarship.[16] The conflicts in these relationships that led to violence often concerned access to money, women's sexual availability, the division of household labor, women's time with their family and friends, and women's desire to leave. These issues appeared similar in every class category.

While they could identify specific issues that led to violent conflicts, most women insisted that the abuse could not be fully understood in terms of individual conflicts. The dramas of masculine control transcended specific incidents:

> He was always angry, every day. Every day he got angry about something. (a Black survivor from a poor community)

> It very much escalated over time. First everything seemed to be okay, but then at the end, it was almost like—it was a constant—all the time, I felt threatened being around this person. And I was like, he'd move, I'd flinch. (a white working-class woman)

> Conflicts . . . just conflicts over everything. What was cooked, how I shopped, what time I came home and if it took five minutes longer than anticipated. Why didn't I answer the phone? . . . There [were] conflicts over everything—everything. (a white professional woman)

> Oh, God—everything was a conflict. If I said the sky was green he'd say it's purple. I mean . . . it was just constant, constant. (a wealthy white survivor)

One white working-class woman said that "the whole relationship was a conflict." In many cases, women didn't understand what their partners were angry about, even in incidents when men were severely violent. A Black professional woman talked of her confusion about this. "He would come home and he would be really upset for no apparent reason." In these cases, the full meaning of the dramas was known only to the men.

In many relationships, the men somehow needed to win all the arguments, regardless of what they were about. This was consistent across the class categories:

> I was always the one to back down. . . . I would say you're right . . . now that I think about it, you're correct and I'm not. If I said I was wrong, he was right, it usually ended. If not, then . . . he would shout and scream. (a white working-class survivor)

> He needed to be the person holding forth. So there was no time or space for me to say anything except yes, or occasionally a clarifying question. And my job became becoming the soothing listener, and trying to find a way to support him so that he didn't get enraged. Because he was always enraged. (a white wealthy woman)

As Connell and Messerschmidt insist, "gender is always relational."[17] These masculinities were accomplished at women's expense.

Along with control, these secret dramas were also about men's identities, in that the abuse communicated men's views of themselves and their rights as men. Messerschmidt speaks of violence as a way of seeking a kind of masculine recognition, both self-recognition and social recognition.[18] The abuse was about controlling women, and at the same time, it affirmed men's views of themselves as powerful, superior, and entitled. Dominating their partners made many of the men feel better about themselves:

> He got off on putting me down. It just made him feel better. . . . He had low self-confidence. (a working-class Asian American survivor)

> I think it made him feel better about himself when I was feeling like shit. When he totally turned me into a wet rag . . . somehow he would start to feel good about himself. (a wealthy white woman)

Connell and Messerschmidt admit that the relationship between masculinities and femininities is underdeveloped.[19] Connell describes the most culturally supported form of femininity in the West: "All forms of femininity in this society are constructed in the context of the overall subordination of women to men. . . . The option of compliance is central to the pattern of femininity which is given most cultural and ideological support at present, called here 'emphasized femininity.'"[20] Connell describes this form of femininity as displaying "sociability rather than technical competence, fragility in mating scenes, compliance with men's desire for titillation and ego-stroking in office relationships, and acceptance of marriage and childcare as a response to labour-market discrimination against women."[21] Emphasized femininity is one of a number of kinds of femininity, many of which resist subordination by men and the whole project of heterosexuality. Multiracial feminisms and the movement for LGBTQ rights disrupt these kinds of femininity.

In the case of straight men who are abusive with their intimate partners, the subordination of women is clearly paramount. Violence and abuse serve as ways of confining women within patriarchal rules of domestic relationships. This is consistent with emphasized femininity. But for these men, degrading women seemed to be essential to the assertion of their masculinities. Judging from their verbal abuse, most of the men viewed their partners as failed women. This appeared to be a stance that men took against their partners, and in fact it was consistent with their views of women in general. This therefore goes in a different direction than the culturally emphasized type of femininity. I propose that men's relationship with femininity in these relationships can be understood as hidden dramas of recognition and misrecognition.

If these hidden dramas are about men's identities, in the sense of self-recognition and social recognition, women's identities are also central in these interactions. At every class level, men degraded their partners with hostile language. Most women said they were shouted or screamed at, called names, and criticized by their partners. If the search for masculine recognition drives this abuse, it must be said that these are also dramas of misrecognition. In his writing on multiculturalism, Taylor introduces "misrecognition": "Our identity is partly shaped by recognition or its absence, often by the misrecognition of others, and so a person or group of people can suffer real damage, real distortion, if the people or society around them mirror back to them a confining or demeaning or contemptible picture of themselves."[22] Taylor's work addresses the politics of social movements around racism, women's rights, and colonialism. He sees that these movements "turn on the need, sometimes the demand, for recognition."[23] This drive for recognition, which he sees as a human need, is sought both in public and in private. While most of his emphasis is on political struggles over dignity and equal treatment in the public realm, he argues that this struggle also occurs in intimate relationships. "On an intimate plane, we are all aware of how identity can be formed or malformed through the course of our contact with significant others," he states.[24] Misrecognition names how identities can be "malformed" in intimate relationships. "Misrecognition shows not just a lack of due respect. It can inflict a grievous wound, saddling its victims with a crippling self-hatred," Taylor claims.[25]

The violence that the women suffered was itself humiliating. But in their verbal attacks, men identified just why their partners were supposed to feel guilty and ashamed. Women reported that they were called bad mothers, bad wives, bad girlfriends, and bad lovers. Many men used hateful, vulgar language to attack their partners. A white working-class woman said, "When he would demand sex . . . and I didn't always oblige, he always wanted to call me a whore and . . . a slut." These verbal weapons are deeply sedimented in sexist societies. According to Sylvia Walby, culture represents its own domain of patriarchy. This is shown by the power this language has to degrade women.[26] There is a particular danger when a woman is labeled with these particular words; to some men, such a woman has no sexual boundaries that can be violated. "I was the whore when it suited his purposes to call me that," a white working-class woman told me. She was repeatedly raped by her partner.

Any source of pride women possessed was used against them. If women felt good about their work, the men said their jobs were worthless, or that because they were African American they didn't deserve their positions. If women felt they were attractive, they were told they were too thin, weighed too much, or were ugly. If women took pride in their education, they were told they were ignorant. As motherhood was central to many women's sense of self, they were told they were terrible mothers. These were efforts to vilify women's identities. In men's chest-puffing displays of masculinity in public, the identities of those in the audience are not necessarily challenged. But in these hidden dramas, savaging women's identities was central to men's performances. The kind of masculinity they presented in private was fused with misogyny. What was affirming to the men was degrading to the women; what was degrading to the women was affirming to the men.

Taylor's work complements Messerschmidt's argument that crime arises out of a search for recognition. Linking recognition to misrecognition illuminates the impact of men's hidden dramas, the psychic injuries that survivors often identify as the most serious harms they suffered.

The men's violence and abuse involved identities and recognition in yet another way. The angry and violent rants often involved scapegoating, or blaming women for things that were out of their control. This scapegoating revealed how efforts at masculine recognition are frequently tied to other forms of entitlement. One white working-class survivor felt she had to manage the man's tirades about his job if she wanted to avoid being scapegoated:

> If he was very angry that day, like if he had a bad day at work, I would just sit there. "Yes, rich people suck, I know it." I would just agree with whatever he was complaining about. I just didn't want to get into that big of an argument 'cause I knew it would end badly for me.

A Black professional woman raised a related form of economic strain. She said the violence arose from class resentment:

> [He] resented the fact that . . . I came from a very comfortable background, and he didn't. He had a really rough life. . . . He hated what I, in his mind, what I represented. I represented what he didn't have, never had in his life.

A wealthy white woman saw her husband's violence as a response to his overall feelings of failure:

> I don't know that it was totally directed at me. I just happened to be there. I just think he was really, really miserable and disappointed with his life.

These dramas of recognition thus involved more than just expressions of gender privilege. They were also connected to economic entitlement, a sense of the financial success the men were owed as men. For some men, the racial privilege in these dramas was clear. A white working-class survivor explained:

> He hated people of color. He hated associating with people of color. He thought he was better than that. And he thought that, as a white man, it was his entitlement to have access to power and money and wealth and privilege, and he was going to ensure that the rest of the world knew that that's who he was and that's how he was going to get by. So, I think he [internalized] those messages of power and dominance as a white man who would have control over those who were under his thumb, and I was that. I was under his thumb.

During their angry rants, white men from a variety of social classes expressed contempt for people allegedly beneath them: disabled people, people of color, and people who were working-class and homeless. For these men, gender, class, and racial entitlement were mutually reinforcing. These different groups of supposedly inferior people served as props in these dramas of white masculine superiority.

Taylor notes a collective dimension to misrecognition. He describes how this is done to "a person or group of people" by "the people or society around them."[27] While the abuse in these relationships was directed against individual women, the men often denounced women as a group while attacking their partners. Men's repeated use of misogynist language illustrates this: these words name negative qualities that supposedly represent inherent characteristics of women. These are the imaginary, contorted models of femininity against which the men defined their masculinities. Men's desires for recognition seemed to require a misrecognition of their women partners, and of women as a collective group.

To explore misrecognition in the interviews, survivors were asked about their ex-partners' feelings about women in general. They had a lot to say about this:

> I think he sees women like a piece of meat, like as a piece of furniture, a punching bag. (a Black survivor from a poor neighborhood)

> I feel like he had this lack of respect for women as a whole. . . . He just had this skewed vision of women. Women were to be seen and not heard. . . . He would often say that, you know, all women . . . were bitches. (a Black working-class woman)

> I honestly believe he views them as a lesser class than the male gender. I also feel that he does have concerns and issues [with] women when they

are in authority or will present themselves as equals. (a white professional woman)

It's not that he just hates women, he sees them as nonpersons and for purposes of serving him, whether sexually, financially, or me building a world for him. We are just objects of exploitation. (a wealthy white woman)

At every class level, most women said their former partners either hated or deeply disrespected women.

In her work on the negative stereotypes of Black women in the United States, Melissa Harris-Perry describes how misrecognition harms individuals. "At its core, shame is an emotional response to misrecognition," she states. And perhaps especially for women, this kind of shame corrodes one's sense of self. "Shame brings a psychological and physical urge to withdraw, submit, or appease others," she observes.[28] Such shame causes women to feel trapped in abusive relationships.

When I worked as a group counselor with abusive men, I was trained to interrupt them when they used derogatory names for women, or even if they identified their partners only using terms such as "my wife," "the wife," "my ex," or "my girlfriend." To challenge men to see women more fully, in ways beyond these limited roles, I would say, "What is her name? Use her name when you talk about her."

To examine how women from different classes viewed these dramas of masculinity, they were asked about their ex-partners' perceptions of themselves as men and about how the men wanted others to see them. Women were further asked about the kind of men they saw their ex-partners as. At every class level, these questions about self-recognition and social recognition elicited rich and multilayered reflections.

MASCULINITIES IN POOR COMMUNITIES

Most of the women from poor neighborhoods were African American; some were white. All of the men from these communities were men of color, mostly African American, but also Cape Verdean, Latinx, and Native American. Most of the men did not earn legitimate incomes. They either were disabled, were unemployed, or worked in the underground economy, where they dealt drugs and committed theft. Most of these men had served time in prison prior to their involvement with the women in this study. Their previous crimes included robbery, gun charges, drug possession, shoplifting, sexual violence, and murder. Most of the women from poor neighborhoods had gone to the emergency room for their injuries; most had been threatened with death. Most women had had weapons used against them. Some showed the scars on their bodies during the interviews. Most women in poor communities said they were raped by their partners.

Like the men from other classes, those from poor communities had dependencies on alcohol, marijuana, cocaine, and heroin. The difference is that poor and working-class men mostly abused drugs, while the wealthy and professional men mostly abused alcohol. Involvement with drugs, likely in combination with racial and class discrimination, caused some of the poor men to do time in prison.[29]

Their sense of themselves as men therefore had many challenges. In a society where racism both creates and concentrates poverty, these men were marked with not only racist stigmas but also the stigmas of being ex-prisoners, drug users, unemployed, and poor.[30] After leaving prison, they had to contend with "invisible punishment," the disqualifications for public housing, welfare benefits, and job opportunities that are the consequences of conviction.[31] These economic consequences have a long-term impact on men and on the women in poor communities. Some men suffered from mental illness and other disabilities, both of which are correlated with poverty.[32] For many different reasons, then, they struggled to survive.

Asked about the kind of men their ex-partners wanted to be seen as, women from poor communities named being a good person, successful, responsible, sexually desirable, a big shot, tough, and violent. Perhaps some of these qualities reflect the attitudes of their friends and family members. A white woman from a poor community said this about the kind of man her ex-partner wanted to be seen as:

> I would think just as a man, as any man. "I work and make money, I pay my bills and does the right thing." I mean he was an addict. Nobody wants to be seen as an addict; [you] try to cover that up, of course.

A Black survivor spoke of how her ex-partner wanted to be seen. He did low-paid service economy work:

> Being successful. You know . . . you want to have a family and take care of your family. . . . He had dreams of—get a house and a car . . . it just didn't work out.

In the context of their economic difficulties, which were simultaneously challenges to their masculinity, some of the poor men sought public status through other means. The physical violence, sexual victimization, and dehumanization that take place in prisons provide the context within which inmates create their masculinities.[33] Violent masculinities developed there affect the communities that men return to after leaving prison. Mirroring masculinities that are dominant in prisons, some of the men wanted to be seen as tough and violent. "He looked scary when we were on the street," a poor white woman said of her ex-partner. "Like this tough rocker look." A Black woman said of her Latino ex-partner, "He wanted people to know that he was tough and he's a big dude, big guy nobody can mess with."

Other men highlighted their sexuality. "He's like, 'I never had a girl tell me that I wasn't sexy. I've never been turned down,'" a white woman said. "He wanted to make sure he looked just right. And he wanted to be getting the ladies and driv[ing] the nice cars."

Some of the men from impoverished neighborhoods acted differently in public than in private. But not all of the poor men kept their dramas hidden; some were openly violent with their partners. "I walked to the bus stop. . . . I was waiting and I saw him coming and he started hitting me in front of everyone," a Black woman told me. "Nobody did anything. He started beating me, brought me back home. Nobody called the police." A second Black woman said, "People knew how he was. It wasn't a secret. No, people knew. And he also didn't hide it." He would attack her when other people were around, and sometimes people would intervene to stop the abuse. But some friends of the abusive boyfriend approved of the violence he used against her.

In the poor neighborhoods, the contrast between how the men wanted to be seen and how the women saw them was sharp. "He liked to paint this picture like he's good to me and he's okay, he don't do no wrong," one Black woman reported. Asked how she saw him, she answered, "violent, vicious, a side that I didn't see until he lived with me. . . . It's hard to see that true person from a distance." He frequently degraded her with coarse language. He choked her and threatened her with a gun. Another Black woman said her ex-partner wanted to be seen as "a drug dealer, a big shot." She saw him as "a fraud. . . . Acting like he's someone else when he's really not." He called her terrible names; she went to the emergency room for injuries he inflicted on her.

MASCULINITIES IN WORKING-CLASS COMMUNITIES

Over half of the working-class women and men were white. Some were African American, Latinx, and Asian American. Just half of the working-class men had full-time jobs. Some were in the construction trades or did skilled factory work. But many were employed in manual labor or unskilled jobs in food service or retail, jobs that lack benefits or steady futures. Many men had a series of part-time or seasonal jobs. Some had spells of unemployment due to alcoholism. Two-thirds of the men abused either drugs, alcohol, or both.

Some had previously been arrested for arson, assault and battery, drug crimes, theft, or drunk driving. Most of the men threatened to kill their partners; many used guns and knives in their assaults. Many of the working-class women went to the hospital due to the violence. Like the women from poor neighborhoods, most working-class women said they were raped by their partners.

Working-class women reported that their partners felt unhappy and insecure about their status as men. Some men were depressed and even threatened suicide. One man was worried that people would think he was weak and not sufficiently in control of his wife, because she would often argue intensely with him. For many of the men, their insecurities were focused around money. Some men were upset that their partners made more money than they did or had more education. One African American woman spoke of her partner's sense of failure:

> He definitely felt emasculated. He didn't like the fact that you know, I had all the money. He didn't want to go out and get a job to get money, but . . . he also had an issue with the fact that I have all the money. . . . He wanted people to think he was successful, or a winner, that's his favorite word, winner. . . . He didn't feel like he had the level of success that he should have had at his age.

When asked what kinds of men their partners wanted to be seen as, working-class women named being strong, hard-working, successful, loving, tough, powerful, and superior to women. A number of women described images of a friendly, loving family man. "He's this outgoing, wonderful person on the outside just like his dad was," a white woman related. "And when you get home he's a persecuting, better than thou, control guy." Another white woman spoke of her partner's public image as "just very lighthearted, funny, good-natured . . . nurturing, somebody who really cared about like kids and animals." Men's physical strength was also a common theme as a source of masculine pride. "I think he saw himself as a macho man. . . . He was pretty strong . . . he had pretty big arms," a white woman stated.

Survivors from working-class communities played roles in men's public displays of masculinity:

> I think he wanted others to see he had it all. A good job, a woman who did everything he wanted her to do, whether it was cook, clean, whatever and just like take care of herself, nice outfits, makeup, skin, that type of thing. (a white woman from a working-class neighborhood)

Public appearances mattered to the men in working-class communities. Most were well-mannered with their friends and relatives. "To other people, he was a completely different person," one white woman reported. Offering a memorable phrase, she said, "It was street angel, house devil." An African American woman claimed, "He was Mr. Nice Guy in front of everybody in the public." Another white woman insisted, "All of my friends loved him . . . loved him. He was very charming."

In their private dramas, some of the working-class men asserted their status as the "man of the house." This was especially true of the married men. A working-class Latina stated:

> He would tell me that just because I'm the one that works and I'm the one that pays the bills does not mean that I'm in control of the house. He is a man so he is the man of the house.

The public masculinities these men presented were so convincing that when women finally disclosed the violence and abuse, their friends and family members denied that it was true. A Black woman explained, "Nobody believed when I finally left him and told them, nobody believed that he was that kind of person." She was forced to have sex and was repeatedly bruised by his assaults. A white woman insisted, "Nobody, nobody would believe me. I could gather all my friends, I could show them written documents, photographs . . . and they wouldn't believe me." She was physically abused when she was pregnant. Another white woman asserted: "I would swear to you if he were to walk in the door right now you would think he was the greatest guy ever." She said that he raped her, beat her severely, and caused her to lose her pregnancy.

As with the women from poor communities, working-class women's views of their partners were often jarring in light of how the men wanted to be seen. A white man who wanted to be seen as good and friendly and generous was seen by his wife as "a pathetic, sad excuse for a human being." He called her hideous names. She said he raped her. An African American man who wanted to be seen as a family man and a caregiver was viewed by his wife as "a coward and fake because he would act one way, but I saw the real person every day." He used hurtful words against her and said she was worthless and stupid. He threatened to kill her if she left him.

MASCULINITIES IN PROFESSIONAL COMMUNITIES

The professional men, who like their partners were mostly white, worked in a variety of occupations, including medicine, higher education, government, management, and information technology. These were full-time, well-paid positions. Only a few had histories of trouble with the law; their offenses involved drunk driving and domestic violence complaints from previous partners. Just under half of the men had problems with alcohol. Most of the professional men had threatened to kill their partners; many had threatened the women with weapons. Most women from professional communities reported forced sex.

Despite their professional status, some of the men had a history of being fired from their jobs or of having abusive relationships with women at work. Some men were described as insecure, unhappy, and afraid of being alone. A couple of women thought their partners were either effeminate or gay. In a society that remains profoundly heterosexist, this posed serious challenges to both their public and private statuses as men.

Conflicts over money were just as common in professional relationships as in working-class or poor relationships. Money represented status to the professional men. "He measures everything by finances. What's your income?," one white survivor stated. "The only value is on how much do you make." For some men, being well dressed served as a measure of social standing.

Professional women said their partners wanted to be seen by others as loving, honest, trustworthy, strong, good providers, and in control of their worlds. "He saw himself as . . . having good common sense, of being very courteous, of being very loving, of having a good, healthy relationship with his mother," said one white woman.

Keeping their abusive behavior hidden was important to the professional men; privacy protected their careers and reputations. The public faces of masculinity they presented had little in common with how they acted in their hidden dramas. A white woman explained:

> In public, we'd attend fundraisers and different things and he would pretend that the wife on his arm was like his queen.

An African American survivor revealed:

> When we would be around other people, he was like a different person. I mean, the nicest guy. . . . Some people would come up to me say, "Oh, you are so lucky to have [him] as a boyfriend." So, that stayed with me, too, I'm

like, "He can't be that bad, if everybody else thinks that he's a wonderful person."

When the abuse was going on, the split between the public and private masculinities was perplexing to the professional women, and for some, this dissonance made it difficult to name their experience as abuse. One white professional woman spoke of being thrown down on the ground and attacked by her partner after they had been together for over a year:

> It seemed so out of character for him. I was just really, really, really confused, you know. He . . . comes off as such a nice guy, you know, so, so outgoing and charming, and you know, has this—this persona of being very protective of women. . . . So, it was just like very, you know, confusing and terrifying and like, I almost had to sort of repress it, because it just didn't fit into my overall perception of him.

In hindsight, however, professional women identified the contrast between these public and private masculinities. A white woman indicated her husband wanted to be seen as "strong, caring, concerned, compassionate. . . . He's very involved in the church." She saw him as a bigot and a misogynist; he said she was stupid and compared her to excrement. He beat her repeatedly, leaving broken bones and extensive bruises. Another white woman said her husband wanted to be seen as "a good provider. . . . He thinks his morals are politically correct. He does a lot for nonprofits. He feels that he is a very giving person." She stated he was "a very manipulative, abusive and conniving individual." In his hidden dramas, he criticized "all aspects" of her life, threatened to kill her, and repeatedly forced her to have sex.

MASCULINITIES IN WEALTHY COMMUNITIES

Almost all of the wealthy men and women were white. The men had jobs in finance, medicine, business, education, and the arts. Most had no previous experience with the police. Over half of the men had problems with alcohol or drugs. Most of the wealthy women had bruises or black eyes from the violence; many of the men threatened to kill their wives or girlfriends. Most women felt pressured to have sex; some said they were forced to have sex.

Despite their wealth, a couple of the men lost their jobs at some point. Several of the men struggled with depression. A number of the wealthy women explained their partners' abusiveness by saying they were narcissists. Some wondered if their partners were gay.

Asked how their ex-partners wanted to be seen as men, women identified their wanting to be seen as charming, sexually attractive, talented, intelligent, hard working, caring, and rich. Some of the women agreed that the men appeared like parts of this list. A white woman admitted that early on in their relationship, "He was a handsome man. . . . Like, I could get giddy thinking about how handsome he was." One white woman said her husband wanted to be seen as "kind, thoughtful, caring, smart. . . . He liked to see himself as better than other people."

Some men displayed their status with expensive clothing and cars. Half of the wealthy men had affairs, indicating their sense of sexual entitlement. Like most of the working-class and professional men, those from wealthy neighborhoods sought to portray themselves as charming and cultured in public:

> He would just give off this impression to everybody that he was perfect. . . . We would get in the car to go somewhere—he would be raging all the way from the house to whatever our engagement was for the evening. He would get out of the car, smile, escort me as if nothing was wrong. In the meantime I'd be wiping my eyes, trying to fix my makeup. (a wealthy white woman)

> He was very calculating. . . . He wouldn't let anybody see it, because he was this nice, perfect guy. And I would hear all the time [what] a great guy he was. . . . Whenever I went to a social function with him, he was always on his best behavior. (a wealthy white woman)

Women's assessments of the kind of men their partners were in private ran in different directions. One white woman described what it was like to live with these contrasting, unpredictable presentations of masculinity:

> I was always upset. . . . I was always on edge. I never knew who was coming in the back door. I never knew who was going to show up that day. I never knew if it was going to be this charming individual who could be very loving, or if it was going to be this monster who I didn't recognize.

Women from different classes spoke of this dissonance in terms of Dr. Jekyll and Mr. Hyde, the duplicitous character created in a short story by Robert Louis Stevenson.[34] Wealthy women referred to Jekyll and Hyde the most frequently. Depending on how it is understood, this can be an insightful metaphor for the conflicting faces of masculinity that abusive men present. As it turns out, the inspiration for this epic tale may have been one of Stevenson's friends, a seemingly cultured man who was convicted of and executed for poisoning his wife.[35] It must be remembered, however, that Mr. Hyde was not a distinct personality living inside of Dr. Jekyll, but was rather an invention of the doctor to facilitate his violence and avoid consequences for his actions. In other words, in this famous story, there really was no Mr. Hyde, only a Dr. Jekyll.[36]

One wealthy white woman explained that her partner wanted to be seen as "intelligent, conservative, loyal, dependable, trustworthy. Masculine. Capable." How did she see him?

> Handsome. Loyal. Definitely masculine. Smart, committed. Disrespectful. Cruel. Hurtful, abusive, loving, unloving, caring, and very uncaring, and . . . a lot of both sides, all the time, consistently.

Her partner shouted at her and frequently called her horrible names. He was sexually abusive and threatening. He was angry almost all the time. Another wealthy white survivor said:

> He was everything that was supposed to be good about a person. He was very intelligent, very articulate, handsome, he could be charming. . . . I think he thought of himself as a very caring father. I think he probably thought of himself as a caring husband.

She said that he hated women. In his hidden dramas, he shouted and screamed at her, said she was stupid, useless, and a bad mother. He abused her physically and sexually.

INDIVIDUAL AND COLLECTIVE MASCULINITIES

When I worked as a group counselor with abusive men, I mentioned to other counselors that the things men said and did were so eerily similar that it seemed as if they had all learned these tactics in a classroom somewhere. But the truth is, no classroom is needed. There are multiple places where men learn and rehearse hostility toward women. According to the women in this study, nearly half of the men were raised in abusive households, where it was mostly their fathers who were violent. This was as common among the economically privileged men as among the working-class and poor men. Over a third of the men were abused themselves as children. Violence and abuse toward women was commonplace among the men's relatives and friends as well. "All his friends were like that with their partners," a Black woman from a poor neighborhood stated. A white working-class woman said that in the man's family, "any woman that pisses them off that's out in public is a fucking bitch whore." Another white working-class woman said, "He was just so steeped in that culture that men are everything and women are nothing."

Some men spent family money on pornography, strip clubs, and women in the sex trade, where the degradation of women is the main draw. Some bonded with other men at work around their views of women. A white working-class woman described how her husband's colleagues would talk:

> They're all rated on a I'd-like-to-fuck it scale. . . . It was all about, you know, these girls I would fuck, these girls I would like to fuck, they'll never fuck me, and these girls are too fat, I would never fuck them.

This is consistent with male peer support theory.[37] This theory argues that all-male groups legitimate and encourage violence against women. Such groups can be face-to-face groups, as in bars and strip clubs, or virtual groups that share internet pornography.[38]

Tyrannical masculinities therefore represent collective projects. While they are mostly hidden from public view, they are learned from and at times displayed for other men. Many people around these abusive men had supported their ways of doing masculinity. Most women had called the police at some point, and many, including women who were economically disadvantaged, had had supportive encounters with them. In several cases, the police had saved their lives. But women from every class reported that the police had ridiculed and laughed at them, refused to intervene even when injuries were visible, and discouraged them from filing charges. In these ways, police officers colluded with men's abusiveness and violence.

A number of women said that divorce was seen by others as a greater wrong than intimate violence. The mother of a Black working-class woman urged her to give her husband another chance, for the sake of their children. A white working-class woman said her mother told her, "Well, you know, you got married, now it's your problem." Violent masculinities are therefore collective projects, involving the support of friends, relatives, coworkers, online communities, and in some cases the police.

In Messerschmidt's analysis, crime is a way to "do" masculinity "when other resources are unavailable."[39] This may help explain the intimate violence of poor and working-class men. Clearly, poverty and economic hardship increase women's vulnerability to intimate violence. And yet intimate violence against women also occurs in professional and wealthy communities. These men possessed substantial privileges. Most of them were white. They had the steady, well-paying jobs that the poor and working-class men lacked. They had the social esteem generated by these privileges. What, then, are we to make of men who possess such privileges and yet still pursue patriarchal masculinities in private?

While Messerschmidt's approach is a deficit theory of masculinity and crime, focusing as it does on failed or "damaged" masculinities, he himself raises cautions about theories that focus only on deficits.[40] He argues that researchers should not be limited by the stereotype that violence is only committed by men who are objectively powerless or who feel powerless.[41] Following Messerschmidt's lead, and consistent with the concept of intersectionality, it is important to ask: If gender privilege is central to men's crimes against women, what role does class privilege play? How might class privilege inspire or facilitate men's violence against women?

Messerschmidt relates crime not just to lower-class masculinities, but also to corporate masculinities. Corporate cultures may play a role in intimate violence. If the prison was a key institution for the poor men, the corporation may have been important for the professional and wealthy men, most of whom had positions in corporations. Messerschmidt quotes Joan Acker: "Today, corporations are lean, mean, aggressive, goal oriented, efficient, and competitive but rarely empathetic, supportive, kind, and caring. Organizational participants actively create these images in their efforts to construct organizational cultures that contribute to competitive success."[42] Many corporations embody these elements and foster cultures that glorify profits over all else. Corporate crime, including violent corporate crime, is one predictable outcome. In *Crime and the American Dream*, Steven Messner and Richard Rosenfeld identify a "by any means necessary" ethos in corporate crime in the United States.[43] While they do not address this in terms of masculinities, their analysis is that US society lionizes economic success, regardless of the means used to achieve it. This creates a tolerance for corporate lawbreaking.

Some of the economically privileged men worked in the tech sector. Leaders of Silicon Valley corporations may be no less ruthless than the robber barons of the late nineteenth century.[44] In the wake of the #MeToo movement, reports of sexual harassment in the tech industry made headlines.[45] One survey of people who had left technology-related jobs reported high levels of sexist mistreatment, bullying of LGBTQ employees, and racial discrimination.[46] The tech sector is more dominated by white people and by men than private industries in general.[47] "By any means necessary" corporate cultures apparently foster abuse and discrimination of many different kinds.

The ruthlessness of the wealthy and professional men toward their intimate partners is clear. In a sense, many privileged men viewed their partners as economic competitors: they insisted on controlling all the assets, refused to share financial information, put their partners on allowances, spent money secretly on their mistresses, and hid their assets from divorce courts and the Internal Revenue Service. Interpersonal crimes by white upper-class men might be inspired by such aggressive, masculine corporate cultures.

SUMMARY

Men who abuse women present an extreme example of how malleable masculinities can be. Consistent with the description by Beauvoir, these men presented themselves as good-natured, modern men in public, yet as violent and cruel in private.

Class privilege and class discrimination shaped the contrasting faces of masculinity the men displayed. The men from poor communities lacked the ability to gain status through paid labor. While some wanted to be seen as successful and responsible in public, in their private dramas they sought dominance over the women in their lives. The poor men seemed to reenact the violence and exploitation of prison masculinities in their intimate relationships. The racism and brutality of the prison system have been deeply destructive to poor communities of color.[48]

The working-class men felt strained due to the difficulty of maintaining stable, full-time employment. In public many wanted to be seen as friendly and hard-working family men, and they succeeded in achieving this. Contrasting with their public personas, in private they sought to demonstrate their superior status as men through violence and abuse. Some men claimed entitlement as the "man of the house." In their hidden displays of masculine identity, they scapegoated their partners for their own money problems and undermined the women's work and schooling, which only made the money problems worse.

The professional and wealthy men had access to remarkable economic resources, and yet conflicts with women over money were just as common as in the other classes. If getting hold of economic resources was the goal of the poor and working-class men, hoarding the household money was the goal of the professional and wealthy men. Some of the economically privileged men seemed obsessed with money as a measure of status. They succeeded in portraying themselves in public as charming, cultured, and agreeable. They won the esteem of their families and friends, and some were even admired as important members of their communities. Yet this was somehow not enough recognition. They engaged in hidden dramas of violence and abuse in order to achieve a special kind of masculine affirmation.

The contrasting faces of masculinity that abusive men presented helped to conceal the abuse and caused women to feel trapped in abusive relationships. Extending Messerschmidt's theory of masculinities and crime, men's intimate violence against women might best be seen as hidden dramas of masculinity. These are dramas of masculine recognition and at the same time dramas of misrecognition, in which men view and act toward their intimate partners through a prism of failed womanhood. As Connell states, "'Masculinity' does not exist except in contrast with 'femininity.'"[49] For these men, the contrast between their hidden masculinities and their hostile, imaginary views of femininity is extreme.

If the kinds of abuse that men commit appear similar across social classes, the masculinities they present are nonetheless shaped by social class, and the ways that women feel trapped are also affected by class status.

CHAPTER 3

Failed Femininity and Psychological Cruelty

The etymology of "misogyny" is "hatred of women." But the Greek word *gynê* means, more specifically, "wife." The household, perhaps even more than the state, remains a bastion of patriarchy. The "bad wife" is one that fails to cede authority to her husband, usurping or intruding upon spheres that traditionally fall under his control—money, sex, business, speech. . . .The culturally sanctioned idea of the "bad wife" provides easy provocation for the violent misogynist who feels his masculine authority has been jeopardized.

—Stephanie McCarter

To address the overlapping forms of abuse that the women experienced, it is useful to begin with psychological cruelty. Many women named this as the first kind of abuse they suffered from their partners. Women reported that their husbands and boyfriends attacked them verbally with humiliating language, shouted at them, isolated them from their families and friends, and threatened to take their children away. Studies indicate that many women who suffer intimate abuse say that the psychological attacks cause the most lasting harm.[1]

I argue that the verbal degradation reveals men's justifications for their violence. After examining men's criticism of their partners as "bad wives," "bad mothers," and "bad girlfriends," I relate verbal abuse to women's childhood experiences and other forms of psychological cruelty. The dynamic of social entrapment becomes visible in the ways that these men sought to disgrace and disempower their partners.

FAILED FEMININITY: BAD WIVES, BAD GIRLFRIENDS, AND BAD MOTHERS

In the quote at the beginning of this chapter, Stephanie McCarter argues that the image of the "bad wife" remains a powerful way of policing women's behavior. As she sees it, the cultural image of the "bad wife" is called upon by abusive men to justify their actions. Much feminist work has been dedicated to challenging the ways that women are misrepresented. In *The Second Sex*, Simone de Beauvoir describes the myths that have been created in Western patriarchal cultures to restrict women's freedom:

> Woman knows and chooses herself not as she exists for herself but as man defines her. . . .
> Woman is both Eve and the Virgin Mary. She is an idol, a servant, source of life, power of darkness; she is the elementary silence of truth, she is artifice, gossip, and lies; she is the medicine woman and the witch; she is man's prey; she is his downfall, she is everything he is not and wants to have, his negation and his raison d'être.[2]

As indicated by Beauvoir, such myths about women have long histories. McCarter traces both the word "misogyny" and the image of the "bad wife" to ancient Greece. These images continue to have consequences in women's lives today.

Contemporary feminist work has moved beyond the universal claims made by Beauvoir to focus on myths created for particular groups of women. Patricia Hill Collins traces what she calls "controlling images" of Black women to slavery and its aftermath. "Portraying African-American women as stereotypical mammies, matriarchs, welfare recipients, and hot mommas helps justify U.S. Black women's oppression," she argues. "Even when the initial conditions that foster controlling images disappear, such images prove remarkably tenacious."[3] These intentionally distorted images of Black women are dehumanizing. Other scholars have identified controlling images of Native American women, Asian American women, and Latinas, originating in colonialism, war, and the racist politics of labor migration.[4]

Controlling images of women of color have powerful consequences. Many scholars have seen the misrepresentation of Black women as central to the shift in public support concerning antipoverty policies in the 1990s.[5] The goal of the 1996 "welfare reform" law was clear: President Bill Clinton sought not to end poverty but to "end welfare as we know it."[6] The idea that poverty was caused by class conflict or racism or sexism was replaced by an individual explanation: poor people, meaning Black women, have caused their own suffering and must be held accountable for it. This is clear in the very name of the 1996 law: the

Personal Responsibility and Work Opportunity Reconciliation Act. The law transformed the system of cash benefits for poor families that had existed for sixty years. It transferred the management of family support to the states and required that women seeking cash assistance find jobs to create their own economic independence. It also sought to limit pregnancies and pressure women to get married.[7]

Dorothy Roberts describes the controlling images of Black women that relate to this law: "Dominant U.S. culture defines Black sexuality as inherently and essentially immoral and treats the Black female body as representing innate promiscuity. This racialized sexual mythology is reinforced by a corollary belief that Black women procreate recklessly and pass on a depraved lifestyle to their offspring."[8] As Roberts puts it, "Welfare ceased being an entitlement and became instead a behavior modification program to control the sexual and reproductive decisions of cash-poor mothers."[9] Since the law's passage, almost all states have sharply curtailed cash assistance to families. Fewer low-income families are served by this program, and as a result many are unable to meet their most basic needs.[10] Studies indicate that most women receiving welfare have been victimized by intimate partners.[11] Restricting cash assistance to poor families greatly reduces women's options to escape violence.

Narratives of the "bad wife," the "bad mother," and the "bad girl" affect the operation of the criminal legal system and can even lead to wrongful convictions of women.[12] Joey Mogul, Andrea Ritchie, and Kay Whitlock argue that negative myths about lesbian, gay, and transgender individuals are so deeply entrenched that they are best seen as "archetypes."[13] They chronicle the ways that these archetypes have led to the unjust treatment of queer individuals by the criminal legal system. In a separate work, Ritchie chronicles how racist and sexist controlling images facilitate the killing and sexual abuse of women by police officers.[14]

These are all examples of misrecognition; these are ways that people are viewed with contempt and discriminated against. In chapter 2 I argued that in abusive relationships, seeking masculine recognition seems to require the misrecognition of men's partners; these are two sides of the same coin. Seeing women as failures helps abusive men feel superior. The women interviewed for this study reveal how images of "bad wives," "bad mothers," and "bad girlfriends" were called upon by their abusive partners in their verbal attacks. These negative caricatures became weapons that did real harm.

WHAT VERBAL DEGRADATION
REVEALS ABOUT THE MEN

Within every class category, almost all of the women interviewed said they were called names and criticized by their partners. Most women indicated they were shouted or screamed at. When asked how often this verbal abuse occurred, many women laughed at the question. It happened so often that it was impossible for many of them to say. Women said this happened "all the time," "many times a week," an "infinite number of times," "almost daily," "hundreds of times," and even a "gazillion times" to indicate how relentless this abuse was.

At times the use of profanity seemed indiscriminate; men appeared to seize on anything and everything they could think of to denounce their partners. According to a Black working-class survivor, "He said I was stupid or I was a bitch or I was a horrible mother." These words nonetheless have specific meanings that give them their potency. They express different justifications for abuse and evoke different kinds of guilt and shame in women.

As I show, these are terribly familiar slurs and criticisms. But while the words used here are commonplace, the reader should imagine the impact of these words when used repeatedly by a husband or boyfriend. Expressions of misogyny were constant in many of these relationships. These words were often shouted at them. There were no obvious differences between the kinds of dehumanizing names and criticisms reported by women from different social classes.

Through their verbal abuse, these men attacked women's identities. The goal of this abuse appears to have been to demonstrate dominance by humiliating and disempowering the women. The men wanted their partners to feel guilt and shame. If examined carefully, these words and criticisms illuminate the men's justifications for their abusiveness. Five themes appeared in the women's testimony. These themes show how the men sought to define their partners' character and worth, drawing upon widespread negative images in our culture. Each makes a demand on these women.

Men Said Their Partners Are Too Assertive; Women Are Supposed to Be Submissive to Men

The word "bitch" was the most frequently named insult. This word is often used to demand a woman's obedience or to silence her, and her anger in particular. A Black survivor from a working-class community said, "In front of his friends he would be, 'bitch, go get me something to drink.'" A number of the Black women in this study were called this name by their partners. Sometimes this was made even more personal by linking it to a particular ethnicity. Placing "Dominican" or "Cuban" before this word draws specific cultural meanings into it. The image of the "angry Black woman" has its own history. In her work on Black women and shame, Melissa Harris-Perry writes of "a powerful stereotype of black women: one that characterizes them as shrill, loud, argumentative, irrationally angry, and verbally abusive."[15] Men can draw upon this controlling image to press Black women into a diminished posture.

This curse word was used during physical attacks. A poor white survivor reported, "He pulled out all the phone cords in the house. . . . He was like, 'you can't call the cops bitch.' He grabbed me and then he started punching me while I was on the floor."

This is such a frequently heard invective that one feminist magazine has attempted to defy it by reclaiming it. The magazine is called *Bitch*, and this is how its founders justify such a controversial name:

> The writer Rebecca West said, "People call me a feminist whenever I express sentiments that differentiate me from a doormat." We'd argue that the word "bitch" is usually deployed for the same purpose. When it's being used as an insult, "bitch" is an epithet hurled at women who speak their minds, who have opinions and don't shy away from expressing them, and who don't sit by and smile uncomfortably if they're bothered or offended. If being an outspoken woman means being a bitch, we'll take that as a compliment. . . . If we choose to reappropriate the word, it loses its power to hurt us.[16]

This publication seeks to confront this term head on and defuse its power over women. The editors name the motivation for using this word. Drawing from this perspective, these men sought to silence their partners and overcome their resistance to being mistreated.

Men Judged Their Partners as Unattractive; Women Are Supposed to Conform to Men's Definitions of Beauty

Many of men's criticisms degraded women's identities by attacking their physical appearance. The men called their wives or girlfriends "ugly," "fat," and "unattractive" and criticized their bodies, their hair, their skin, their clothing, and their makeup. In our sexist society these words can be used to shame any woman, regardless of how she looks. A white survivor who worked in retail said, "I was a knockout when we got married. . . . And he still managed to make me feel ugly." Another white working-class woman, who described herself as skinny, was told she was fat.

Men Shamed Their Partners as Being Too Sexual and Therefore Immoral, Deceitful, and Untrustworthy; Women Are Supposed to Be Modest and Faithful

Sexualized language appeared at every class level. "He put me down a lot of the time," a white women told me. She worked as a nurse. What did he say? " 'You're not going to find anybody better than me.' 'I know you're cheating on me.' 'I know you're a liar.' 'You're a ho,' or many other different names." A white professional woman reported, "He always wanted to call me a whore and a bitch and a slut." Some men used an obscenity that reduces women to nothing but a sexual body part.

The difference between men's definitions of what is "attractive" and what is "too sexual" was often difficult to follow. A white working-class woman spoke of her partner's rules about her appearance. "He never allowed me to wear makeup because he thought it was slutty and he didn't want me to look like a slut. Although he often called me a slut and a whore. The only time he allowed me to wear makeup was when I was covering up bruises that he had put on my face." A working-class Latina said her boyfriend picked out a short skirt for her, and after she put it on, called her a sexually degrading name. A white professional man made his wife dress in ways that she considered "sluttish."

Men Said Their Partners Were Failures in Their Roles as Women: They Were Bad Wives, Bad Girlfriends, Bad Mothers, Bad Lovers, and Bad Cooks; Women Are Supposed to Meet Men's Needs in All These Areas

Many of the women said that every aspect of their identities and behaviors was criticized, including their lovemaking, their parenting, and their housework.

Most women who had children were told they were bad mothers, precisely because it was so harmful. A white professional woman stated, "One of his favorite things to do would be to criticize me about my parenting because that's one of my most sensitive areas." A Black professional woman said her partner would criticize her to the police when they came to the door. He would tell them, "This girl is an unfit mother. . . . She wants to run off with bad friends, don't want to stay home, take care of the baby." He hoped to draw sympathy from the police during their many visits to the household. A wealthy white woman said, "It was like a knife in my heart, because he knows this about me. That being a mom, being a parent, was something I took very seriously."

Trying to live up to men's definitions of the good wife, the good girlfriend, or the good mother was exhausting. Women described how men's expectations constrained them:

> I did everything he told me to do. . . . A lot of the time I prevented myself from getting hurt either psychologically or physically by just complying to this man. . . . I never, ever placed any demands on him. It was him putting demands on me. I did everything I could to keep myself safe. Most of the time it would work. (a white survivor from a poor community)

This woman was coerced into being the "good girlfriend." Her boyfriend threatened her regularly. Managing his anger and violence was a daily effort for her.

A white woman in a professional household talked about her work to conform with the "good wife" image:

> I tried to be more agreeable and compliant as far as what he wanted in the bedroom. And then I finally just quit, just quit. I just gave up trying to be what he wanted from me. Couldn't do it anymore.

The violence intensified, and she left the marriage. The amount of effort that she and other women spent on fulfilling these expectations was remarkable.

Men Attacked Women as Losers; Women Are Supposed to Recognize Their Inferiority to Men

Along with men's attacks on their assertiveness, appearance, sexual morality, and other alleged failures as women, there were judgments of a different kind. A number of the men used the terms "loser," "idiot," "stupid," "useless," "worthless," "shit," and "trash" to disparage their partners. This is yet another kind of cruel misrecognition, another kind of dehumanization. In my view, this focus on women's intelligence, achievement, and overall worth combines woman hating with the ruthless competitiveness of the US capitalist system. There may be projection in these verbal attacks; the women described many of the men as insecure about their economic status. These men did more than degrade them as "losers"; most deliberately undermined their wives and partners economically, seemingly in an effort to make them into "losers." This is taken up in greater detail in chapter 6.

Each of these five themes offers justifications for abuse. The men resented their partners' assertiveness and attacked them for it. They judged their partners as either not sexual enough or too sexual, thus justifying their control over how their partners dressed, whether they wore makeup, who they went out with, whose numbers were on their cellphones, and who their friends were. The men castigated these women as failures as wives, mothers, and girlfriends, thus justifying their punishment. The men said their partners were losers, were worthless, and would never amount to anything, and then made these criticisms a self-fulfilling prophecy by undermining the women's education or causing them to lose their jobs.

I believe these names and criticisms tell us nothing about the women. But they reveal a great deal about these men. These are the hostile, dehumanizing images through which the men viewed their partners. They sought masculine self-recognition by viewing women with contempt. Since some of these slurs are meant to shame all women, their use further underscores the men's hostility toward women in general. As shown in chapter 2, most women said their partners disrespected or hated women.

CHILDHOOD EXPERIENCES OF EMOTIONAL ABUSE

Most women reported emotional abuse or neglect in their childhoods. There was no obvious class pattern to these reports. This was a living history; the abuse left many with feelings of unworthiness, guilt, and shame. Most women brought up their childhoods when talking about the abuse by their husbands or boyfriends. These experiences of degradation felt similar to them. Here is how a Black working-class survivor made the connection between childhood abuse and her marriage:

> [How did this abuse affect you?] It really had an adverse affect on me because growing up, before I even got involved with him. . . . There was abuse in the home . . . verbal abuse, I was always called names, you know, "you're a stupid cow," "you'll never amount to anything." I never really heard anything positive about myself. . . . My aunt had a problem with me. And now my husband has a problem with me. And I just can't seem to get it right. And you know, so I felt guilty about not being whatever it is that people said I was supposed to be.

The childhood abuse seemed to mark her and make her expect judgment as an adult. From a very different class position, a wealthy white woman made a related observation:

> He would just constantly talk about how ugly I was, or how ridiculous I looked, or something. Always. In front of people. But . . . I'd grown up with that, so to me it was normal.

The legacy of childhood abuse seemed to form a continuous line from the past to the present. One white working-class survivor described the emotional scars of childhood as "like walking around with glass shards in your stomach." She said, "I was open and ready for this idea that I still was unworthy."

ISOLATION: RESTRICTING WOMEN'S RELATIONSHIPS

Over half of the women reported feeling isolated while in their abusive relationships, including most women in every class category. Undermining women's relationships is a common tactic of control. Some men were jealous of women's friendships and sought to diminish these bonds. Other men feared that their partners would talk about the abuse to their families and friends, and so they sought to keep them quiet. Women who visited their families were subjected to numerous phone calls from their partners as a form of monitoring their behavior. Some women were told they couldn't answer the phone when the men were at home, enabling their partners to screen who was calling them. Men's reasons for isolating their partners seemed similar across the class categories.

In these ways, the men imposed one-sided rules about who their partners could see, rules that had the effect of disempowering the women. This is how women described these constraints:

> I couldn't talk to any friends or family. Nobody could come over. . . . That was his rule, that was his way. . . . Friends or family would have [told] me to leave him. And I think that was a fear. (a Black woman from a poor neighborhood)

> I'd given up any hope of having friends because he would just pout and carry on every time I wanted to go out with my girlfriends so I didn't really have any friends anymore. (a white professional woman)

These rules damaged women's connections with their friends and their roles as sisters, daughters, aunts, and nieces. Most of the isolation that women experienced was imposed upon them by their abusive partners. But there were other forms of isolation. Some women were already disconnected from their families. In some cases, their parents sided with their abusers. For others, isolation was the result of geographic distance from their families of origin.

Women also isolated themselves from their families or friends to hide the abuse. One Black woman from a poor community said, "I didn't want to see my family because I didn't want them to see me like that." They didn't want anyone to see their bruises or their depression. A professional Black woman spoke of her conversations with family members:

> They would constantly call me, asking me how I was doing, and I'm like, "Oh, I'm doing great! It's going really well!" So I put this façade for them, because I didn't want—I did not want them to know that I was in a bad relationship. You know, that was not an option. Not an option.

All of these forms of isolation undermined women's strength and thus their ability to resist the abuse or leave these relationships.

CHILDREN: REASONS TO STAY, REASONS TO LEAVE

Children played a complex role in women's entrapment. Being pregnant or having children was part of what made women feel stuck in the relationships. At the same time, the abuse of their children caused some women to leave.

Most of the men who were fathers abused their children. Psychological abuse was the most common form. Men would scream at their children and call them awful names, just as they did with their partners. In fact, men used some of the same anti-woman names listed previously in this chapter against their daughters. Often children witnessed their mothers being degraded and physically abused. Some men were neglectful, failing to take care of their children while they were drunk or high on drugs. A number of the men were physically abusive, hitting their children and threatening them. Many children were afraid of their fathers, even long after they grew up and left home. A few men abused their children sexually, one of the most upsetting kinds of abuse that women reported.

For the women who were mothers, which was most of them, a singularly powerful form of psychological abuse was to threaten to take their children away. Most of the fathers made these threats. Again, there were no substantive differences across class categories. Threats to take the children were another way to make women afraid and submissive. At times these threats were made to make women remain in the relationships. One white working-class woman had already had her children taken away for a period by the child protective agency:

> He'd say, if you don't do what I want you to do, I will call [child protective services] . . . and you'll never see your kids again.

Economically privileged women received the same kinds of threats for resisting their partner's abusiveness:

> I would try to get strong at times, and he would threaten to take our son away. (a white professional woman)

> He told me that if I left him that he would win custody of the kids. (a white wealthy woman)

This threat against women's identities as mothers was often one threat among others, including men's threats to leave or to sleep with someone else if the women wouldn't do what they wanted. But the threat of having their children taken away was uniquely painful. During and even after divorce, there were bitter fights over custody of the children, involving repeated trips to court. Most but not all of the men seeking custody failed to obtain it. One abusive man was granted sole custody, and another forced child protective services to briefly take a child into state custody. Some women were investigated by state officials and lost custody due to the intervention of family members or neighbors.

The thought of losing their children was pivotal for mothers in deciding whether to stay or leave. For some women, threats involving their children caused them to remain with abusive men. One poor white mother feared what would happen if she left:

> He made me afraid they were gonna take my baby away. He made me afraid that he was gonna kill me. He made me afraid that if I didn't comply with his demands that this would happen. . . . After the baby came that's when he came in and grabbed for control because he knew that this child was the most important thing to me ever in my life.

A white woman in a relationship with a wealthy man felt trapped when she unexpectedly became pregnant:

> When I was pregnant, lying on my back in bed, I felt that now I'm pregnant and I can't even date anybody else to get out of this mess. . . . I felt pregnant and trapped.

If motherhood caused some women to feel trapped, with no clear way out, concern for their children caused many women to leave the relationship. A white working-class woman talked about threats to take her daughter:

> [Did he ever try to control you . . . by using your daughter?] Yes, absolutely, yeah. . . . He did that even before she was born . . . by saying when she's born, I'm going to take her and you're not going to have her. And then of course after she was born, you know, he used some of the same tactics. . . . She was way more important to me than he was, so that's what drove my plan B. . . . I wanted to get out of there sooner rather than later so that I didn't have to share her with him.

Abuse of the children made some women develop plans to leave. A severe threat to kill her and her child was the turning point for one working-class Black woman. Her husband threatened them with a gun. For others, the physical or sexual abuse of their children was decisive. "My . . . daughter was like the turning point that helped me to change my life," a white professional woman said. Her husband degraded her child, and she began to see the effects of this on her daughter. The indifference of some men toward their children spurred other women to separate.

Some children intervened in their fathers' abuse of their mothers, and this forced a redefinition of what they were experiencing. One white working-class woman described how her son had challenged his father:

> It was never a particular incident when I said enough is enough until . . . my son . . . got in between us one day and said, "Dad you can't talk to my mom like that. You've got to stop calling her those names." And then I made a plan.

For a white professional woman, her daughter's college class in women's studies made her rethink her husband's abusiveness. She had numerous bruises and black eyes from the violence:

> She would come to me but I always felt like there was contempt for me from her as she was becoming more and more aware of women's issues. Now, I don't know whether it was her contempt, or my contempt for me.

There were women who fell into both categories: having children at first made them feel trapped, but seeing the effects of the abuse on their children made them leave.

CLASS EXPECTATIONS OF WOMEN

Women's class position posed challenges to their gendered duties as wives, mothers, and girlfriends. Many poor and working-class women witnessed family instability and disabling illnesses growing up. Both the women and the men had high rates of alcoholism and drug use. They were more likely than economically privileged women to be exposed to homicide and incarceration in their communities.

One of the key reasons that many couples don't get married has to do with a lack of financial stability.[17] Research on marriage and divorce finds that women without college degrees are less likely to be married than professional and wealthy women and are more likely to get divorced.[18]

Most of the poor women were mothers, but none were married. It was difficult for the poor women to sustain emotional bonds with family members. The average length of the relationships was five years. The circumstances of one poor white woman illustrate some of these disadvantages. Like other women in poor communities, she had suffered terribly as a child. She lost her father at a young age, and her mother was unable to care for her due to mental illness. This affected her relationship with a violent man and her sense of her role as a partner and a mother. Her partner was homeless:

> I had a borderline mother who would have a revolving door of boyfriends. I didn't have any models of healthy anything. I didn't know what a healthy relationship was. I had a bleeding heart. I had empathy. I had hope that people could change. I had more than enough hope that people could change because I was so neglected when I was a kid that I identified with that pain he had had.

She had a child with this man. It was not her plan to raise a child on her own, although this is what happened after she left him. She said, "I always struggle with that shame of being a single mother because it has always been stigmatized within my family, because my mother is the only single mother in her family." Her partner's violence and neglect of the child made her tell him to leave. His violence in response to this led her to call the police. They put her in contact with child protective services. She welcomed this assistance and found it supportive, especially in a culture that blames poor women for their own suffering.

Another white woman from a poor neighborhood had a cocaine habit. Like some other women, her drug dependency overwhelmed her life and strained her ability to care for her children. She was incarcerated for a time for drug possession. At one point, she gave custody of her children to her parents. She did this so she could work in prostitution and support her addiction. She got involved with a man who used drugs and had served time for a violent crime. She showed me scars on her body from being stabbed by him; he was convicted for an attack that almost killed her. At the time of the interview, she was no longer using hard drugs and was in a new relationship that she felt good about.

A Black woman from a poor community also struggled with drug dependency. She and her partner both used drugs, and he had served time in jail. She was arrested, along with her partner, for hitting back after he attacked her in public. The police put her child in foster care, and her mother took custody of her child for an extended period of time. She eventually regained custody after getting clean.

Most of the working-class men and women had jobs, but there was substantial economic strain. Many men had unstable jobs or did seasonal work; some women worked part-time. Many of the men had problems with alcohol or drugs. A number of the men had been charged with crimes, and some had served time. Over half of the working-class women were married and had children. The average length of their relationships was nine and a half years.

For the working-class women, expectations of being a "good wife" and "good mother" constrained their choices about their relationships. Along with economic dependency, these internalized cultural rules made it hard for them to leave their abusive relationships. One Latina talked of the shame of divorce. She did clerical work:

> I got married. I had a lot of pride. I knew that it was the wrong thing to do. I knew I shouldn't have been with him. I didn't want people to look at me like, "oh, she got married to this man and she's divorcing him a week later or months later," so I stayed in the relationship hoping that . . . things would change, and they didn't, they just got worse.

She wanted to have a long marriage like her parents had:

> My parents were married . . . and I wanted to be married. I wanted my husband. I had my son and I didn't want my son not to have a father. I wanted that American Dream, that's what I wanted. Unfortunately . . . my ex-husband was addicted to drugs and he beat women and I thought I could change it and I couldn't. . . . I just wanted a good life.

Her husband called her a bad mother "all the time." This was compounded by the stigma of divorce in her community and her attempts to avoid this judgment.

A white working-class survivor was taken in by her parents after leaving her severely abusive partner. She was pregnant. While they were supportive in some ways, they judged her harshly about being a single mother:

> It was great they were being supportive financially and materially, but the whole time my mom was saying, "Nobody's ever gonna want to date you being an unwed mother." "You're a disgrace to the family." "You're the first person who has ever had a child out of wedlock in our family."

She said that in her family, a child is "supposed to have a mother and father and anything less is just not okay." She ended up returning to her severely violent partner, marrying him, and living with him for a number of years before leaving him. Her husband repeatedly called her a bad mother, as well as a number of other vicious names.

A white working-class woman divorced her husband after many years of abuse. He abused her and their children. They lived in a religious community. She described the costs of divorce to her social relationships:

> I've lost a lot of friends, telling me that God hates divorce, I shouldn't divorce him. . . . [Who would tell you this?] Very close friends of ours. . . . And they knew we were having trouble. . . . I mean, everybody saw us fighting. Nobody even thought our marriage would last this long. . . . They flat out wanted to have nothing to do with me. They remained friends with him. [You lost friendships around this?] Oh, I've lost a community, I've lost reputation, I've lost his family, my family, they all hate me. . . . It's because of the divorce.

In different ways, each of these working-class women grappled with the images of the "bad wife" and "bad mother." They were judged by their partners as failed women. But they also felt judged by their communities and by the rules of the culture at large.

Research on intimate violence in professional and wealthy neighborhoods speaks of a "culture of affluence" that affects women's resistance to abuse. In their study of intimate violence in a white, economically privileged midwestern community, Megan Haselschwerdt and Jennifer Hardesty found the following:

> Families were expected to appear "perfect" despite the implicit understanding that this was not the reality. Perfection was measured by having a nuclear

family structure, attractive physical appearance, material and monetary wealth, and successful careers and children. In addition, the appearance of a "happy family" was the community standard, and there was enormous pressure, especially on the mothers, to conform to this standard.[19]

While they don't use this language, Haselschwerdt and Hardesty are describing the rules of femininity in a white suburban neighborhood. The culture in this community stigmatized divorce and promoted silence, secrecy, and shame around violence. This is femininity in the service of class and racial privilege. This kind of femininity covers women in shame for violating these rules.

The women I interviewed talked about their hopes for an idealized kind of family. While women from all classes spoke of such hopes, in white, economically privileged neighborhoods divorce and intimate violence marked the difference between the "haves" and the "have nots." Class status is always relational; it raises the self-image of one kind of community in comparison to another. The status of professional and wealthy white communities depends on contrasts, real and imagined, with less privileged communities.

Almost all of the professional women were married, and most had children. Some women worked full-time outside the home, some part-time. Most of the professional men made significantly more money than their partners. While there was strain in some relationships around men's unemployment or job changes, most women were economically secure—so long as they stayed in the relationships. When they spoke of feeling trapped, they were focused on their children and the fear of becoming single mothers. Like many working-class women, their fear of divorce, of being the "bad wife" and "bad mother," made it difficult to resist or escape the abuse. Professional woman worried about the effects of being divorced on their families and their standing in the community:

> I was trapped because I couldn't fail at my marriage. I was trapped because he was the father of my child. Divorce doesn't run rampant in my family at all. I felt like I had something to live up to, that they raised me better. (a white woman who worked part-time in social services)

> Every time I thought about leaving I didn't because of the shame of divorce. I was thinking of the impact it would have on my [child]. (a Black professional woman)

Along with friends, children played a role in reinforcing these class- and race-based cultural rules.

What happened after women divorced their professional partners? The stigmas of failed femininity haunted some of them. Survivors explained what it was like after they left their husbands:

> I lived in the suburbs. I went to church, there were families. I went to the grocery store, there were families. In the city, you can get lost. You know, there's lot of single people. Everywhere I went [after the divorce], it was in my face, and it, it was like, it was like I had an A, adulteress or something because friends who were, you know, married friends seemed to kind of move away. (a white survivor who worked in business management)

> I can remember having enough problems coping with the word "single," okay, and because I thought that was such a bad connotation, "single" or "divorced" was horrendous. I never in my wildest estimation pictured myself as a divorced woman. . . . Do you see what I'm saying? All the stuff that was inside of me. And I can remember once having a conversation with my son on the phone and he goes, "Just how do you think it is to cope with having a single mother?" (a white professional woman)

The culture of affluence weighed heavily on these women's feelings about separation.

Like the professionals, women in wealthy relationships worried about not having enough money for their children. Perhaps especially because the abuse made them feel so bad about themselves, they poured their energies into being what they saw as class-appropriate good mothers:

> Once we had children . . . I just decided that I had to do whatever it took to keep that relationship alive and healthy. Even if that meant shutting up and just enabling. I wouldn't have used that word then, but that's what I was doing. (a wealthy white woman who went from full-time work to being a stay-at-home mother)

> I never wanted my children to be without a father. . . . We were living in an affluent suburb. . . . I just didn't know how I'd take care of them. I think if I had a trust fund I would have been out of there in a heartbeat. I think of myself as someone who is strong, not weak, but I felt very helpless in that situation. (a wealthy white survivor who worked part-time in the medical field)

At every class level, men's attacks on their partners' femininity drew their power from the cultural images of "bad wives," "bad mothers," and "bad girlfriends." Women made choices about their lives within the constraints presented by these negative images and within the gendered and racialized expectations of their social classes. They feared being judged in these ways by their extended families and their communities. This fear of judgment made many of them feel trapped in their abusive relationships. After leaving, some women were indeed judged and even shunned for leaving.

THE IMPACT OF PSYCHOLOGICAL ABUSE

There are psychological consequences to all forms of abuse, including physical, sexual, and economic abuse. But a number of women spoke directly about how the verbal attacks made them feel. A Black college student from a poor community spoke about her self-image in the wake of the abuse. Her partner told her, "you're nothing" and "you will never be anything":

> [How did this abuse make you feel?] I was like a piece of trash. I was not worthy. I couldn't do anything good in my life.

For some, the verbal degradation was seen as more consequential than any other form of abuse. One white woman who worked in food service was repeatedly punched by her husband, leaving many bruises and bloody lips. And yet she describes the verbal abuse she suffered this way:

> I used to almost pray that he'd hit me. Because the pain would go away from that. But the emotional—the pain would never go away. I can still hear it in my head. . . . I can still see his face and I can still hear it.

She was saying this fifteen years after leaving her marriage.

A white woman who worked in management was badly injured after a physical attack by her husband. But she, too, emphasized the harm from the verbal attacks:

> With a broken bone or a black eye or some kind of damage to your body, that heals. . . . The black eye goes away. But when you have verbal abuse, what your brain does is you record every single word and phrase and look, and at least for me, I gained this horrible shame about myself as a person, because I was being criticized for everything that I did.

She is describing an attack on her identity that lingers eight years after her divorce.

A Black professional woman was told she was "stupid" and worth "nothing" by her husband. "He managed to make me feel unworthy and inferior. It killed my morale," she reported.

A married wealthy white woman talked of the effects of the abuse on her self-esteem:

I was definitely very physically attracted to this man, although I didn't want to have any part of him because he made me feel so terrible about myself.

Most women spoke of depression; it is as if this woman hating became internalized. One white working-class woman said, "[He] is the only person who could make me completely break down into a mass of jelly, sobbing on the floor in the corner." Ten women had either thought about suicide or attempted to take their own lives. Research indicates a strong connection between intimate violence, depression, and suicide among women.[20]

SUMMARY

Men's psychological cruelty has been framed here as an attack on women's identities. The men viewed their wives and girlfriends as failing the culturally elevated expectations of femininity. Illustrating the power of patriarchal culture, the language of bad wives, bad girlfriends, and bad mothers caused feelings of guilt, shame, and depression in the women. This is the flip side of men's efforts at masculine self-recognition; they sought to demonstrate that they were superior to their partners. This harsh language justified their other forms of abuse. In the men's eyes, their partners deserved it.

Women reported other injuries to their identities from their childhoods. Most women had been neglected or emotionally abused in childhood, which intensified the power of their partners' psychological cruelty. Coerced isolation further harmed women's relational identities as friends, sisters, aunts, daughters, and nieces.

Economic deprivation posed challenges to the women's ability to fulfill ideas of the "good woman." In professional and wealthy neighborhoods, sexism, combined with class and racial privilege, presented its own constraints about women's choices. The harm from the psychological abuse was extensive, and as I show, long-lasting.

CHAPTER 4

Terror, Fear, and Caution

Physical Violence and Threats

The causes and consequences of gender inequality and
women's lack of safety are interrelated, and multifaceted.
Fear of violence affects the everyday lives of women and
girls—restricting their freedom and use of the city and public
space. Women and girls living in poverty, or belonging to
socially excluded or stigmatized groups—whether based on
age, race, religion, ability, or disability—often bear the brunt
of risks and dangers.

—Lakshmi Puri

Violence remains a serious obstacle to the freedom of women and girls
worldwide. In the preceding statement, UN Women deputy executive
director Lakshmi Puri relates this widespread violence to gender inequality, poverty, and social stigmas. Violence is both a cause and a
consequence of inequality, in Puri's view. Research demonstrates that
rates of violence against women and girls are substantial in all regions
of the world.[1]

In the United States, women are more likely to be assaulted and
killed by people they know than by strangers.[2] According to the Centers
for Disease Control and Prevention (CDC), homicides of women are
strongly related to intimate violence: "Nearly half of victims are killed
by a current or former male intimate partner." Non-Hispanic Black
women and American Indian/Alaska Native women are killed at rates
nearly three times higher than that for white women.[3] Unfortunately,
federal data don't generally address issues of race and social class simultaneously. Since racism is deeply related to poverty, reporting data
on race by itself creates misunderstandings about violence. Research
that does address social class shows that poverty and economic stress
are closely tied to homicide and to intimate violence against women.[4]

Violence must be understood as a common feature of family life. Writing in 1936, three years after fleeing Nazi Germany, the Jewish philosopher and sociologist Max Horkheimer stated: "The role of coercion, which marks not only the origin but also the development of all States, can indeed be hardly overestimated when we try to explain social life in history up to the present." In a project focused on authority in the family, Horkheimer discussed violence against women and children. He argued that threats of violence within families have become both deeply internalized and suppressed. He asserted, "Terror has changed into fear and fear into caution."[5]

This sentence captures the effects of violence on the women in this study. They spoke of terror and fear, but many women described a constant, everyday feeling of caution. For many women, sharp feelings of fear were suppressed over time. And yet the possibility of physical violence loomed behind the women's interactions with their partners. The phrase that many women used to express this was "walking on eggshells":

> I had to walk on eggshells around him, make sure I did everything right. (a Black woman from a poor community)

> There's a lot of walking on eggshells, because you never know what you're gonna say or what you're gonna do that's gonna set him off. And it could be anything, anytime. (a white woman from a wealthy neighborhood)

This has become such a common way of describing the experience of being abused that there is a book on leaving such relationships that has "walking on eggshells" as its title.[6]

This chapter examines a number of dimensions of physical violence. What kinds of physical violence and threats did these women suffer? What were the men's histories of violence? What was the context of this violence in the different social classes? How did the women and their partners explain the violence? What did the women do to try to stop it? And last, what was the impact of the violence on the women?

FORMS OF VIOLENCE

Women reported many types of physical abuse. They spoke of being pushed and grabbed; slapped and punched; choked; and threatened with guns, knives, and other weapons. For some women, physical violence was rare or intermittent. A few women preferred to see their experience as mostly psychological abuse, although even these women were at times afraid of their partners or reported some acts of violence. But this is overall a group of women who suffered many kinds of violence on many occasions. Most women in every social class reported being pushed, grabbed, or shoved, as well as being slapped, hit, and punched. Most women said they were kicked by their partners. Some women experienced every single form of violence they were asked about. For some there was physical abuse on a monthly, weekly, or almost daily basis. Many said that the abuse increased over time.

The violence was often extreme. Sexual violence, which is the focus of the next chapter, was extensive. More than half the women said they had been choked by their partners, something that is recognized as a major risk factor for homicide.[7] Fully two-thirds of the women said their husbands or boyfriends had threatened to kill them, and for many women this was a frequent threat. Some men threatened to have other people kill their partners. Over half of the women were either threatened or attacked with guns, knives, or other potentially lethal weapons. Two women had knives held to their throats. Two women had guns put to their heads; one had a gun put into her mouth. Another woman was shot at. Severe violence was identified by women from every social class.

Men were also violent and abusive toward their children. Two-thirds of the women had children, and half of their partners were either physically, psychologically, or in several cases sexually, abusive of the children. There were no apparent differences in child abuse across social class.

There were class differences in the reports of violence against women. Poor and working-class women were more likely to be slapped, hit, or punched; threatened with a knife, gun, or other weapon; kicked; and choked. Poor and working-class men were more likely to threaten to kill their partners. Poor and working-class women also reported more frequent violence than professional and wealthy women. But fear was prevalent at every class level. References to "walking on eggshells" were common in every social class.

MEN'S HISTORIES OF VIOLENCE

Many of the men had experienced abuse in their families growing up, just like the women. Physical abuse was named most often concerning men's childhoods; some men were emotionally abused and some sexually abused. Many women said they didn't know their partners' childhood histories. Some of the abuse was by their mothers and some by their fathers; in cases of child sexual abuse, some involved men outside of the families. Child abuse of some kind was reported by men of every social class.

Many men had witnessed abuse growing up. This included seeing their mothers abused by their fathers or seeing their siblings abused. Some men had alcoholic or drug-dependent parents. Some women saw these histories as influencing their partners' violence.

Over a quarter of the women knew of intimate violence among the men's relatives. Over 40 percent knew of intimate violence among the men's friends. Half of the men abused people other than their partners. Demonstrating a commitment to violent masculinity, there were eighteen men who had abused previous wives or girlfriends; they included men from all social classes. Of these eighteen men, half had abused more than one woman. Some men went on to abuse other partners after separating from the women in the study.

Men were violent with their brothers, sisters, mothers, neighbors, and strangers at bars. The professional and wealthy men largely confined their violence to family members.

PHYSICAL VIOLENCE IN CLASS CONTEXTS

Examining the situations in which the violence and threats arose is important to seeing the dynamic of fear and coercion in these relationships. Women's accounts of violence are discussed within each class category.

Physical Violence in Poor Communities

As most of the poor men had criminal records, their access to housing, jobs, and economic assistance was greatly reduced. Many were further burdened by drug addiction. The need for money was a common catalyst of violence for the poor men, often in connection with drug use and alcoholism. One Black woman, who worked part-time for low wages, described the abuse she suffered. Her partner was violent early on in their relationship, and this made her afraid. He worked, but he had trouble supporting his drug habit:

> I didn't have no more money and he went to get some more drugs and he got mad and he smashed my head up against the wall. . . . I'd always have to be on my p's and q's not to make him mad. That was a job, trying to keep him calm.

She had a serious head injury from the attack, requiring numerous trips to the hospital.

Another Black woman talked of how drug use was the common source of violent conflicts. She was unemployed. Drug dependency overwhelmed her relationship:

> Well he was using drugs. I was using, so it was constantly . . . you know, it was based on the drug using. [Really, how so?] Not having any, him having some not wanting to give me any, me having some not wanting to share with him, not letting him know I had it . . . him going somewhere else doing it with somebody else, I'd get upset, or me going somewhere doing it with someone else, he'd get upset.

She eventually got treatment for her own addiction, and left him.

Men's possessiveness was also a source of conflicts leading to violence. This sometimes involved fear that their partners were sleeping with other people, and at other times involved insecurity about women's contacts with their friends and families. A Black woman from a poor neighborhood described this situation:

> The last experience was I was over at my friend's house. . . . He was coming to pick me up. . . . I went to the door and as soon as I got outside, he punched me . . . with a closed fist he punched me in my face. And he kept punching me and blood was coming out. He dragged me. . . . I thought he was going to kill me. . . . He was just jealous that I was over at my friend's house and not with him. He was really jealous. He didn't want me to be with nobody but him.

She was terrified of this man. She sought help from a women's shelter at one point in the relationship. In order to escape him, she had to leave town.

The men's fear that the women would leave them was another important context. A Black survivor from a poor neighborhood spoke about this. Her partner would threaten to kill her if she left him:

> He used to beat me up for trying to leave him, but he stopped because I threatened him with jail, and he didn't want to go back to jail so he left me alone.

But he eventually did abuse her again. The last time, she was beaten so badly that her girlfriend encouraged her to go to the police. Her friend was in tears when she saw the injuries. The man was prosecuted for the abuse and spent time in jail. When I interviewed the woman she had been out of this relationship for three years, but she was still afraid of him.

Physical Violence in Working-Class Communities

Women from working-class communities also talked of money issues as a source of violence. One Black woman came home from work to find her boyfriend drunk. She wanted to know where the money that she had hidden was. They got into an argument, and he struck her in the head with a heavy object, severely injuring her and resulting in her going to the hospital. A white woman who worked in the service industry got into an argument about money with her live-in boyfriend. They were in a financial crisis, and he didn't like her ideas to solve it:

> He grabbed me around the throat and he started strangling me and he pulled me up and he started punching me and then, of course, I fell to the floor. . . . I was getting beaten up pretty badly by him and I was on the floor and he was kicking me.

She somehow found a way to leave and find safety.

Men's demands for sex were common in working-class relationships. One white woman who worked part-time felt sexual pressure constantly from her husband. Her felt entitled to sex on demand:

> He held a knife to my throat in bed once. . . . It was kind of like one of the reasons I was like I've had enough. . . . He wanted me to have sex with him and I didn't want to, and it was because he was being abusive verbally and physically too around the same time and I was just . . . I was really sick of it. . . . You know, he was forceful with the sex . . . very, very pushy about having sex. . . . I was fighting him off a lot.

She decided to leave her marriage after the knife incident.

Sometimes the women's resistance to their partners of any kind was met with violence:

> We would have these horrendous arguments when I would press him to tell me about why nothing was changing in our relationship. And I would be angry, and I would be lashing out because I was hurt, and there were some of these arguments that became violent during that period of time. . . . He would go berserk if I said I am going in the bathroom now because I do not want to argue anymore. He would kick the door in on me. . . . He would get livid if I tried to leave his presence during an argument. (a white working-class woman)

A Black working-class woman said she didn't always know why her husband got angry. But fear that she wanted to leave the relationship seemed to underlie many of his violent threats. He worked on and off, and she was a homemaker:

It just seemed to be something almost every day. . . . I couldn't do anything right. He said . . . if I left he would track me down and kill me. If I ever tried to be with anyone else, he would kill them, too. Or he would take my [children] and go away, I would never see them again. So it was always some kind of threat.

He hit her every week. She had black eyes and broken bones from the abuse. She was constantly threatened. I asked her about fear:

[Were you continuously afraid of him?] I would say yes. . . . [How did you cope with the feelings of fear?] I pretty much cried all the time. In the beginning I didn't sleep because I thought he would wake up in the middle of the night and decide to do something to me.

When she told him to leave, he threatened to kill her and himself with a gun. It took two years before he finally listened to her and left. Her fear that "no matter what I did, he would find me" made her feel trapped in this marriage.

Physical Violence in Professional Communities

Similar to the poor and working-class women, those in professional communities also named money issues as a key feature in violent conflicts. One incident seemed more like a drunken attack than a conflict. A professional white man lost his job, got drunk, came home, and beat his wife severely. She was six months pregnant at that time. She had broken bones as a result of his attack. She was scapegoated for his work problems; his violence and abuse would increase when he was unemployed. Another professional white woman made a similar observation. Her husband would grab her, shake her, and hit her:

[The abuse] definitely increased the last few years and especially once we moved to [state] . . . It increased . . . because we had no income coming in. He was very, very controlled by money. . . . The abuse definitely got worse.

This woman first became afraid of her husband following a fight early on in their marriage. "He raped me after the fight," she said. "I didn't know it was rape at the time." Nonetheless, the fear caused by this violence "was just under the surface" for the rest of the long marriage. As a mother, her financial dependence on her husband made her feel trapped.

Men's sexual entitlement was the basis for violence against a number of professional women. Over half said their partners physically forced them to have sex. Most of them agreed that the term "rape" matched their experiences. Some women were abused for raising evidence of their husbands' affairs. These matters are detailed more fully in chapter 5, on sexual abuse.

Violence caused by women's efforts to leave was raised by half of the professional women. Taking about separation was clearly dangerous for women of all classes. During the beginning of a period of separation, one man threatened to shoot his wife if she wouldn't let him back in their home. Another professional man threatened his wife with a sharp object after she talked about leaving, leading to the end of their marriage. A third professional man threatened to kill his wife in retaliation for the divorce. After separating, a fourth man choked his ex-girlfriend when she got up to leave during a visit.

A professional Black woman talked of a violent assault after she raised money issues and her desire to leave. "[The] circumstance was I was just plain tired of the drinking and not paying the bills," she explained. Her partner beat her up and stabbed her. She bled so much that she passed out and was taken to the hospital.

There were other minor forms of resistance that seemed to incite men's violence. Some men became enraged and violent when their partners challenged their driving directions or changed their choice of music or the radio station. These dramas seemed to be symbolic of men's control of the relationship. One white professional woman identified a pattern between abuse and finding her voice during a long marriage:

> [What was the first incident?] . . . Isolating me from my friends, and then eventually my family, and spending all my time with him, [his] making all the decisions about where we go, where we would go, it may sound weird but not having sex, and then having it his way or no way. And then it escalated over the years and then I started being very good. I just was very compliant . . . but what was happening, I was sort of dying inside. And then about a year before I left, I realized that I couldn't live like that any longer, and I started . . . voicing my opinions, and to him that was very challenging, and so the physical abuse started again . . . and I knew then that I was never going to allow [it] to happen, and I left.

She aptly described the web of control in which she was living and the diminished role that was forced upon her.

Physical Violence in Wealthy Communities

Similar to the survivors in the other classes, women in wealthy relationships reported being pushed, hit, kicked, choked, and threatened with weapons. A number of the wealthy men threatened to kill their partners.

Once again, conflicts over money and work were common in the wealthy relationships. One wealthy white woman was repeatedly hit and had cuts and many bruises from the abuse. She didn't always understand what her husband became wildly angry about, but she observed two patterns. "When things went wrong with his life, he took it out on me. But when he was working, he was fine." Again reflecting scapegoating, his spells of unemployment were the times he was most violent and abusive. The other pattern had to do with separation; they would often travel apart from one another, and he would go "crazy" when that was about to happen. He threatened to kill her; like some other men, he made this threat in connection with a threat to kill himself. In fact, most of the men who threatened suicide made threats to kill their partners. Men's suicide threats in abusive relationships are associated with more severe violence and are a risk marker for femicide.[8]

Men's jealousy was a common source of tension in all classes. One white woman who was involved with a wealthy man described her partner's reaction after she briefly spoke to a man at a bar. On the way home in the car, he berated her for talking to the man:

> By the time he got home he pulled me out of the car, shoved me down on the floor in the garage and he got on top of me with his knee on my chest and it hurt. . . . A real hard shove.

They had a child together. She first started being fearful after raising money issues with her partner about their child. "Anything to do with money . . . was a really scary thing."

According to one wealthy white woman, the major conflicts in her marriage initially had to do with household tasks, such as shopping, cooking, and the laundry. Her husband assumed she would take care of all this, even though she had her own career outside the home. He was angry on a regular basis. I asked her what his anger was about:

> I was asking him to do something that he didn't want to do. That I was impinging on his—his freedom to not do those things. And he, you know, more and more, I think, saw it as directed against his career.

Toward the end of the marriage, the conflicts shifted to whether to get divorced. During this time the violence increased:

That's when I got hit. Either kicked or hit with fists. . . . He hit me to try to get me to shut up and lie down and do what he wanted me to do, and I was fighting back.

She had difficulty ending the relationship:

I think I could not accept that a twenty-plus-year marriage was going to end, and one that I had compromised so much in, and our children at that time were [still young], and I just, I believed that, you know, nothing was more important than keeping the family together, is what, what [I] was thinking.

One white woman who lived with a wealthy man described an argument about her career and his lack of support for it. In reaction to this argument, he choked her and beat her. Looking back on this incident, she took pride in her assertiveness in this argument, despite the violence:

[I was] standing up for myself in a very smartass way, if you see what I mean, not just walking away but just going . . . you know what? You're an asshole, I've had enough.

Her face and neck were so visibly bruised from the violence that her friends and coworkers were horrified. She initially moved out and sought help from the courts. But she began to blame herself for the violence, saying, "It takes two to tango." The relationship continued for a number of years.

The circumstances in which the men became violent were similar across the social classes. As has been shown, the men were violent in conflicts over money, jealousy, sex, women's efforts to leave, drugs and alcohol, and the household division of labor. These conflicts are best seen as part of an overall pattern of coercion. From this broader perspective, the violence reflected men's attempts to control their partners, often when women were seen as resisting their power. The other theme in these dramas of masculinity is once again scapegoating, ways that men blamed women for things that were beyond their control. Scapegoating is really about strains within the men about their own lives, strains that were somehow blamed on the women.

EXPLAINING THE VIOLENCE

Men's Explanations

According to the women, the men gave a number of explanations for why they were violent and abusive. But the most common one was that it was all the women's fault. The women were failures in some sense, as wives, lovers, or mothers. The reason was usually about their obligations to the men. It was essentially the same explanation from men of every class:

> "See, you can't be making me mad like that." (a Black woman from a poor neighborhood)

> It was always me. "You made me do this." (a white woman from a working-class community)

> "If you hadn't provoked me . . . ." (a white professional woman)

> He was being forced to behave this way, because I was so inadequate, or I was so stupid. (a white wealthy woman)

One white woman from a working-class community explained:

> He would say it was me. Like I provoked it somehow. By looking a certain way, or doing a certain thing, or by challenging him. That was our biggest thing. Because . . . I'm not very submissive. So I didn't fit into the role very well. The more abuse I got, the more submissive I was, up until the end. . . . Basically he wanted me to be this little person that he came home to, that just basically, you know, waited on him hand and foot, and gave into his every whim. Made whatever. And I wasn't.

Some men claimed they were entitled to abuse their partners:

> [Did he try to explain why he was abusive to you?] No. Women deserve it, is what he said one time. We must like it. (a white working-class woman)

> How did he explain what he did? Did he try to give reasons? "I'm a man. It's my right." (a white wealthy woman)

Drugs and alcohol were blamed by some men for their violence and abuse. "He used to apologize afterwards, saying he was drunk," said a Black woman from a poor neighborhood. "He would use that excuse all the time," a white wealthy woman stated. "Oh, I don't remember." "Oh, I was drunk." A few men claimed the problem was that they had bad tempers.

Economic strain was raised by some men as an explanation. One Black man from a working-class community felt he was blamed by his wife for being out of work; this is why he was violent, he told her. A professional Black man blamed the poverty and abuse in his childhood for his abusiveness.

Women's Explanations

With the benefit of hindsight, at the time of the interviews most women saw the violence as a way for men to control them and make themselves feel superior. As a white working-class woman said, "You'd think things were going well and hunky dory, and obviously he needed a control fix." But while they were in the relationships, the violence was more difficult to understand. Most men blamed their partners for the violence and abuse; most women felt guilty as a result. The verbal degradation and the constant criticism made women feel guilty and ashamed. This made it difficult to see what was happening as abuse. This psychological abuse caused many women to feel trapped in these relationships.

Women talked of how guilt affected their perceptions of the abuse. For a number of women, self-blame was connected to feelings of worthlessness. One white woman from a poor household explained this. She had multiple surgeries, and became permanently disabled, after being stabbed with a knife:

> I feel as though I might have antagonized it. I might have said something smart to hurt his feelings or push his buttons at a bad time and it escalated to where what happened, happened. . . . I literally felt like I was what [he] told me I was, nothing. I didn't deserve nothing so I was with men who treated me like nothing. . . . I felt like that's what I deserved I guess at that time. Not today though.

A white woman who worked in food service spoke of how she explained the violence. Her partner hit her repeatedly, kicked her, and threatened her with a knife. She had many bruises and lost teeth as a result of her partner's attacks:

> I think the more he degraded and the more he abused me—I think he—he like, I don't know if there's a word, maybe got off on the control? Because it made him feel like more of a man?. . . . [Did you see it that way when it was going on?] Oh, no. [How did you see it when it was happening?] It was me, I needed it. It was my fault. I asked for it. [You believed that?] Oh, yeah, I did. For years.

During her marriage, a Black professional woman went through a change in how she explained the violence:

> Initially I was thinking okay well maybe I'm doing something wrong so let me stop doing that and not make him angry. Even when I didn't do those things he was angry. He was always looking for something. I rationalized his

behavior to myself. . . . With time I saw that it was unfair, it was wrong. He would beat me. The anger was coming out.

She had many bruises and cuts from her husband's violence and went to the hospital for her injuries.

A wealthy white woman talked of her guilt feelings. She had bruises and cuts, was often threatened, and developed PTSD from the abuse:

> It was so hard for me to talk about myself, and how I felt—pretty bad—and what I thought, my thoughts, just my thoughts and my feelings were irrelevant for the longest time. . . . He would do something, and I would think it was my fault. . . . You know, "Is it plausible that it could be me?" You know, like that's how I fit into the equation. So I didn't even have a right any more to my own thoughts or feelings because it was all about him and his problems. . . . My problems were irrelevant.

Self-blame and sexist rules blocked an awareness of the injustice of what the women were suffering.

At the time of the abuse, women from all classes saw the issue as caused by alcohol and drugs. A white working-class woman put it this way:

> I think part of the reason must have been the drugs and the alcohol, I would think. I'd like to think that. I mean, I don't really want to think that he hated me that much to be that vindictive, to treat me like that.

A wealthy white woman gave an explanation that many shared:

> I don't really know if I understood that I was abused. I just thought he was drunk, a drunk that drank too much and that's when . . . he did these things. I didn't really categorize him at the time as being a domestically violent man. I really didn't think of that, I thought he had an alcohol problem.

Other women focused on psychological issues as the cause of the violence. They saw the abuse as largely the result of their partners' having a bad temper, being depressed, being insecure, or being stressed from work. Professional and wealthy women were most likely to call their partners narcissists or sociopaths. While there are things that are relevant to the violence concerning these terms, they serve more as descriptions of the men's behavior than as explanations for it. On their own, such individualistic, psychological diagnoses conceal the gendered aspects of this violence, in terms of both men's motives and why women are so frequently made the targets of men's distress.

The family backgrounds of the men were also seen as a cause of the violence and abuse. As discussed previously, many men were abused as children, and even more witnessed abuse in their families growing up. Some of the men used these experiences themselves as explanations for their violence. One Black professional women was involved with a Black man who came from a lower class. He had experienced abuse growing up. Class and racial empathy made it difficult for her to recognize herself as abused:

> He had had a really hard life growing up as a child, and I was trying to be very understanding, and coming from where I was coming from, you know, kind of caring about him in some ways because he didn't have the things that I had. And I think also that's what kept me, kept me with him for, for the time that it did. I felt bad for him . . . . And used anything to, to come up with excuses for his behavior. And I completely bought into that. I really fed into that.

She decided to leave when the violence became life threatening.

WOMEN'S EFFORTS TO STOP THE VIOLENCE

Given the extensiveness of this hostility and brutality, it is important to see how survivors resisted the violence. Most women fought back, both verbally and physically. Consistent with the work of Hillary Potter, the Black women, across the class categories, were more likely to fight back physically than were white women. Potter explains this by saying that Black women's resistance to intimate violence is part of a historical legacy: "Battered Black women typically fight back because they know that they, and all the Black women before them, have labored and persisted through an expansive assortment of struggles, starting with slavery and through present times." Intimate violence is "another form of domination they must fight off on a regular basis."[9] Unfortunately, while this resistance is important, only a very few women said that fighting back either verbally or physically reduced the violence.

There were class differences in fighting back. More than two-thirds of poor and working-class women fought back physically; only a third of the professional and wealthy women did. A few women did say that their physical resistance made a difference. One Black woman from a poor community explained what had happened to her. When her partner got upset, at first he would call her names, then push and grab her. This escalated to hitting. At one point they were in a fight in which they both drew knives. She had cuts and bruises from the violence and once went to the emergency room for an injury. Surprisingly, she said she was not afraid of her partner:

[Were you ever afraid of him?] No. . . . He gave me a black eye one time. [Okay, and you fought back, but you were never afraid of him?] No. [So he couldn't really scare you?] No, because before, remember now I've been in two previous relationships before and it was violent. So no, I wasn't afraid. I had fought my way through those two so I was not afraid.

One white woman who worked in retail also fought back:

When he pinned me up against the hallway I let loose. I clobbered him. And he never physically touched me again.

In her case, while his physical attacks stopped, the threats, sexual abuse, and psychological abuse continued. Another white working-class woman feared that fighting back would make things worse:

He would say all the time if I fought back—I would just put my hands up to protect my face and he'd be like "You're trying to punch me?" "Don't forget this Miss, if you punch me as hard as you can it gives me every right to punch you back as hard as I can." I'd be like "I'm not trying to punch you." But he made it very clear that if I tried any kind of emotional or physical force to be in defense of myself he was gonna give it back like larger or bigger than I gave it to him. I already know how big he could give it to me.

A number of other women also felt that fighting back would be dangerous for them. But one working-class Black woman insisted that fighting back mattered, even if it did lead to more violence:

That particular day, I remember going back into the house and I asked him, I said, what did you do that for? And we got into this argument. And he went to hit me—and that's when I started fighting back. Because I just thought, you know what? I've had enough. And if he's going to hit me, I just need to hit him back. I just was fed up at that point. [Would that stop the fight, or would that escalate the fight?] It would just escalate the fight. But at that point I just really didn't care. . . . Because, at some point he really started to back off, because I was just like screaming and yelling and crying. It was like, "I'm not taking this anymore. I don't understand why you're doing this. If you are going to hit me," I said, "I'm going to hit you back."

While most fought back in some fashion, this is by no means all that the women did to stop the abuse. Lisa Goodman and her colleagues developed an Intimate Partner Strategies Index, a way of identifying how women respond to intimate violence.[10] I made a check sheet listing the various strategies they found and asked the women to identify the ones that they had used. After they filled it out, I asked them to go back and circle the strategies that actually reduced the violence.

After the violence started, most sought mental health counseling; this was true of most women in all categories except those who were poor. Many sought assistance from domestic violence programs. Nearly half of the women tried to find counseling for their partners for the violence. Some women tried to get their partners into substance abuse counseling. A number of women spoke about the violence to doctors or nurses, which makes sense given the extensive injuries that women reported. Fewer women, mostly working-class and poor women, stayed in shelters.

Just over half the women called the police. Nearly as many sought restraining orders from the courts. This was similar across the class categories. A third of the women filed criminal charges; this was most common for women who were poor.

Half of the women stayed with their families or friends or talked with their families or friends about protecting themselves. Since the men's violence was mostly hidden, many women sought to have other people around as a way to find safety.

A number of women left home to find safety and tried to end the relationship.

Finally, Goodman and her colleagues named a number of what they called "placating" strategies. These included keeping things quiet for their partners, doing whatever their partners wanted to stop the abuse, trying not to cry, avoiding arguments, and avoiding their partners altogether. These were some of the most common things that women did, across all classes.

When asked directly what they did to try to prevent further abuse, the women talked a lot about placating strategies. They described how they tried to accommodate their partners. They sought to do whatever they could to keep the men from becoming angry; almost a quarter of the women talked of "walking on eggshells." One white working-class woman said, "I would do whatever I could to appease him." Women also spoke of self-silencing. Many women felt that they had to stifle their anger and opinions:

> I had to be quiet, even if he was sitting there, like being the most antagonistic, I couldn't say anything back. (a white woman from a working-class community)

> The best way to avoid it was not to say anything. . . . As long as I never said a word about anything negative towards him I never had a problem. (a Black professional woman)

Feminist research has found that self-silencing, accommodating to men, and repressing anger are at the root of women's depression.[11]

Survivors also discussed other ways of trying to be a "good wife" or "good girlfriend":

> I did everything in my power to lessen the violence. I keep a very clean house. I'd do things that he wanted. I'd try to cook dinners that he liked. Or I'd try, you know . . . to plan things that he liked to do. . . . The more I tried to make things right the worse things got. (a white woman from a working-class neighborhood)

> I did things like, I'm not real fond of cooking, but I tried to make meals every night. . . . I started doing the housecleaning myself. (a white professional woman)

This is a whole lot of activity aimed at stopping the violence. Which of these strategies worked? Calling the police and getting restraining orders were more effective than many other actions, but even these didn't work for most women; less than half of those who called the police or got court orders said they helped to reduce the violence. Contacting domestic violence programs was more effective than most other strategies; seeking mental health counseling was less so.

Of strategies involving women's social networks, making sure that other people were around was useful for most who did this. Leaving home and ending or trying to end the relationship worked for most women who used these strategies. But even here, many women who did these things didn't believe they completely worked; violence and threats continued for many women even after separation. These strategies are discussed further in chapter 8.

As advocates know all too well, many of the placating strategies were largely unsuccessful. The women's attempts to be the "good wife," "good mother," and "good girlfriend" weren't enough for these men. When they did work, it was only for a period of time. Preventing men from becoming angry appeared to be a never-ending task in the women's accounts.

THE IMPACT OF PHYSICAL VIOLENCE

In the United States, intimate violence is the major cause of injuries to women.[12] In this study, men's violence caused serious and long-lasting injuries. Three-quarters of the women were bruised, often many, many times. Close to half of them had black eyes; this was true for most working-class and poor women. Most poor, working-class, and professional women sustained cuts from the violence. A third of them had broken jaws, noses, ribs, or other bones. Nearly a quarter of the women had concussions, including women from every social class. Almost a quarter of the women, mostly poor and working-class, reported permanent injuries, such as hearing loss, chronic pain, and damage to their backs or internal organs. Most women sought treatment from hospitals; most of the poor women were seen in the emergency room.

Women spoke of fear and its psychic impact. The fear was clearly a central goal of the violence. Even when women would try to suppress it, the constant feeling of fear had a corrosive effect upon them. It shaped how they thought about and interacted with their partners on a daily basis. It affected their sleep and their dreams. Many women were traumatized by the violence. Fifteen of the sixty women were diagnosed with PTSD; other women also had panic disorders or exhibited symptoms of trauma.

Four women with PTSD talked of the consequences of the violence. One white woman said that fear of her partner is what trapped her in her relationship. She was from a poor community. She was hit, chocked, and threatened with a knife. Her partner threatened to kill her "all the time." She was homeless and lived on the street for a time while in the relationship. I asked her about fear:

> [How dangerous is it to live on the streets?] . . . Extremely. . . . The women that I knew, most of them were HIV positive. Most of them were in silent abusive relationships, worse than me. Like bottles were smashed on their heads. They had lacerations all over them. It was just brutal. The domestic violence on the street is just the most brutal hell and I witnessed it almost every day 'cause I had—you know, we had a community.

She was diagnosed with PTSD from the violence and is on disability. Two years after leaving this man, she remains "deathly afraid" of running into him on the street.

A white working-class woman described being hit numerous times. Her husband would at times threaten her with a knife, and she feared for her life. At first, she channeled her fear into getting involved in her work. But the violence escalated:

> You just never knew what would set him off. I didn't know if I would be running or hiding or what I'd be doing. I can't even describe the living in terror all the time. . . . It got to the point—and I know this is kind of gross—it got to the point where he would look at me and I would wet myself.

She left her husband a year before the interview, after an extremely violent attack. But the legacy of the violence has been profound:

I hide in the house, have PTSD. I have anxiety so bad I can't even go to the store. I don't see people. I don't like to talk to people. I have trouble articulating myself when I'm in public because I'm so panic stricken. A shadow of my former self would be a good way of putting it.

A white professional woman explained how an escalation of the violence terrified her. This happened late in her long and abusive marriage:

Really it was not until he raped me that I realized how—how scary things were that I woke up enough to realize. I had been diagnosed with PTSD and anxiety and I was on all kinds of medications. . . . I was so numb. And then he raped me. And I was just so shocked that it completely ripped me right out of that drug-induced fog. And I thought he could really, really, really hurt me you know beyond what has been done. If he could rape me, he could kill me.

She was still very afraid of her ex-husband two years after their divorce. He continues to threaten her.

A white wealthy woman talked of how she has felt since divorcing her husband:

I was barely a functioning human being. The fear I lived with every day impeded every . . . thought. . . . I couldn't sleep at night. . . . I'd be exhausted and have to take naps. . . . I [still] get very upset very easily to the point where it can ruin my whole day. . . . It's like I'm still fighting the battle everyday. . . . Like I'm still emotionally and physically and mentally exhausted.

He hit her and threatened to kill her and did many things that made her believe he was capable of this. She spoke with me six years after her divorce. Leaving did not end her feelings of fear.

Some harms were reproduced across generations. One white professional woman spoke of the scars on her children. They witnessed their fathers' violence against her and were themselves abused by him. Nonetheless, her children could not forgive her for divorcing their father. One son physically attacked her and was violent with his own wife:

I still have this power and control going on in the dynamic of my entire family. . . . I just see it in them. . . . They certainly sided with their dad during the divorce. And they didn't talk to me for some time. . . . They still, to this day, are very bitter and angry. . . . My grandchildren to this day pick up the disrespect from my children towards me. . . . I just wish there were some way . . . that somebody could show me before I die how to get this anger out of my kids [voice shaking, crying].

This was the most upsetting point in the interview for this woman. The bonds holding her family together are badly damaged. She believes her children and grandchildren are following in her abusive husband's footsteps. She talked with me eight years after leaving her abusive husband.

SUMMARY

In the quote at the beginning of this chapter, Lakshmi Puri argued that gender inequality is both a cause and a consequence of violence against women. It is clear that contempt for women underlies men's violence, and that the consequences of this violence serve to disempower women. The power of this violence is measured in both physical injuries and in the ways that it leaves a psychic impact on women in terms of ongoing fear. Terror became fear, and fear became a kind of caution that shaped daily life for these women.

Much of the violence detailed here is severe by any measure. Most men threatened to kill their partners. Choking, which was reported by most women, can easily cause death. There were class differences apparent in the severity and frequency of violence, in injuries, and in men's violence against people other than their partners. But there was terror and fear at every class level. There were remarkable similarities in the kinds of conflicts that led to men's violence across classes.

Most men blamed their partners for the violence, and most women felt guilty and somehow responsible for the attacks. This made it difficult for many women to identify what men did as abuse.

It is important to see the many, many things that women did to stop the violence; to get help for their partners; and to seek assistance from their families, legal authorities, and community agencies. Most of these efforts were unsuccessful in stopping the violence; things that were successful are further discussed in chapter 8, on separation.

The constant fear of violence deformed these relationships and blocked the ability of the women to have a meaningful voice in their households. Even after leaving, many women felt unsafe and still carried the physical and psychic scars of the violence.

CHAPTER 5

The Continuum of Sexual Abuse

Sexual violence ... is a major factor limiting women's options
and choices. Heterosexual relationships and encounters
are the site where many women experience patriarchal
oppression most directly and intensely; they are also
a site of resistance and struggle.

—Liz Kelly

Sexual violence is a terribly common occurrence for women. According
to the CDC, 46.3 percent of women in the United States have reported
some form of "contact sexual violence" in their lifetimes. Contact sexual violence includes rape, unwanted sexual contact, and sexual coercion (sexual penetration that takes place after nonphysical pressure).
More than one in five US women (21.3%) have experienced either completed or attempted rape.[1] According to one CDC study, more than half
(51.1%) of women who reported rape were victimized by their intimate
partners.[2]

Like Sylvia Walby, Liz Kelly sees sexuality as an important site of gender inequality.[3] Kelly argues that sexual violence—and the fear of such
violence—greatly constrains women's lives. Most of the sixty women in
this study reported that their partners either threatened or used physical
force to make them have sex. Nearly half said that the term "rape" fit
their experiences. These experiences of forced sex were part of a wide
range of sexually abusive behaviors. Women spoke of sexualized verbal
degradation, delusional jealousy, infidelity, reproductive abuse, attacks
on the sexual parts of their bodies, pornography, the sexual abuse of
their children, and rape. These acts might best be understood as representing a continuum of sexual abuse.

This idea of a continuum comes from Kelly.[4] She states that sexual
violence, in all of its manifestations, operates "as a form of social control
by denying women freedom and autonomy."[5] Seeing sexual violence as

a continuum identifies a "common character" beneath all of these acts, the "abuse, intimidation, coercion, intrusion, threat, and force men use to control women."[6] Kelly claims that even allegedly "minor" forms of sexual abuse, such as obscene phone calls, draw their impact from "the explicit or implicit threat of further assault."[7] The threat of violence thus underlies women's experiences with all forms of sexual abuse, according to Kelly. Women know that sexual abuse is a common occurrence. The 60 women Kelly interviewed in her study "knew of 435 other women who had experienced either rape, domestic violence, or incest."[8] The 60 women I interviewed knew of more than 250 other women who had been either physically or sexually abused as adults. This included their mothers, grandmothers, other relatives, and friends. Poor and working-class women knew of more women who were abused than did the economically privileged women.

I do not follow Kelly's definition of sexual violence precisely or the specific contents of her continuum. She combines physical and sexual aspects of abuse; in her view, sexual violence is the umbrella term for all forms of violence against women. While they surely overlap, I have separated the categories of physical and sexual abuse. I also use the term "abuse" rather than "violence." In this study, I learned that for many women "abuse" better describes the range of their experiences than does "violence," which prioritizes physical suffering. This echoes conversations with advocates working in domestic abuse programs and rape crisis centers that were part of the preliminary research for the study. Recent scholarship has emphasized that prioritizing physical violence over psychological, economic, and other forms of abuse obscures the web of coercive control that traps women in abusive relationships.[9] But like Kelly, I argue that these sexually abusive behaviors are interrelated, and that seeing them as part of a continuum helps explain their impact on women.

In addition to the violence in their intimate relationships, women also reported sexual abuse in their families of origin, in school, in the workplace, and on the street. For Kelly, this is all part of the continuum. Such abuse can create a generalized fear of men's aggression through which new experiences are interpreted. Over a third of the women were sexually abused as children; more working-class and poor women than economically privileged women reported this. Half of the women said they suffered violence and abuse from teachers, bosses, coworkers, fellow students, or strangers. This abuse was frequently sexual in nature. Seven women revealed rape or attempted rape by acquaintances or strangers;

two were gang raped. Most women in every social class stated they were the target of abusive sexual remarks in public, such as sexual propositions and comments on their appearance. Sexual abuse is an important way for men to achieve a kind of masculine self-recognition, a sense of themselves as superior to their partners and to women in general.

Just over half of the women had suffered abuse in previous relationships with men; this abuse was often sexual. Five women, most of whom were from working-class communities, said they were raped in previous relationships. An experience of rape at gunpoint by one boyfriend greatly affected the next relationship that one woman had. "[My ex-boyfriend] had put a gun to my head and so when somebody requested sex I thought I'd better do it or else somebody will shoot me," she said. She is a white woman with an advanced degree. One survivor said that her previous experiences made her feel that this was "just the way life was." Others said they came to fear all men. Seeing sexual abuse as a continuum highlights the consequences one abusive event may have for later experiences.

This chapter examines eight forms of sexual abuse that were emphasized by the women I spoke with. The interconnections between these forms of violence and abuse will become clear. Following this, women's thoughts about naming and not naming their experiences as rape are discussed, along with the consequences of the sexual abuse.

VERBAL DEGRADATION

Some of the forms of verbal abuse detailed in chapter 3 were sexual in nature. In their angry tirades, men called their wives and partners ugly sexualized names. In previous chapters, I have discussed these common insults as forms of misrecognition, as "confining or demeaning or contemptible" images that cause women great harm.[10] Along with accusations of deceit and promiscuity, there was harsh criticism of their bodies, hair, clothing, and makeup. Men told their partners that they were unattractive, and that no one would ever want them. Many men, seeing their partners as failed women, sought to control their appearance. There was not much difference in this degradation across the class categories:

> [Did he ever attempt to degrade or humiliate you in any way?] Yeah. You know, you're a liar. You're a piece of shit. You're a dirty human being. (a poor white woman)

There were other things about my body, you know like breast size and . . . I didn't have large breasts and he would remind me all the time of that. . . . He preferred a more feminine look apparently. (a white working-class survivor)

[He] told me I didn't dress good enough, said he would not pick me again. I wasn't good enough. (a wealthy white woman)

This was an ongoing source of humiliation for many women.

There is remarkable hypocrisy beneath these verbal assaults. In many cases, these men condemned their partners for the very characteristics that they themselves possessed. They alleged that these women were somehow immoral. Yet it is the men's sexual violence that is criminal. They accused their partners of being excessively sexual and deceptive, yet according to the women, as I show, many of these men were having multiple affairs or seeing women working in prostitution.

DELUSIONAL JEALOUSY AND MONITORING

A number of the women said that the first abuse they recalled involved what can only be called delusional jealousy. This is the suspicion of cheating or the feeling that there is a threat to one's relationship that is so exaggerated as to be out of touch with reality. Fully three-quarters of the women indicated their husbands or partners checked up on them or monitored their phone calls or their whereabouts. Some of this was motivated by men's fears that their partners would tell other people about the abuse. But much of this was connected to jealousy and possessiveness. There was little difference across the class categories. Women's partners would call them at home to make sure they weren't out with someone else, listen in on their phone conversations, review calls on their phones to see whom they had contacted, check to see that they were at work by repeatedly texting them or looking for their cars, time them when they went grocery shopping, and even look under the bed and in the closets for hidden lovers.

For many women, this was a relentless form of abuse. Asked to indicate on a check sheet how many times their partner had acted this way, some women wrote "often," "a lot," "every day," "always," "daily," "100's" of times, and "too numerous to count." Consistent with the kinds of names the women were called, the misogynist assumptions here are that women are somehow by nature both sexually insatiable and dishonest. Women were accused of having sex with ministers, doctors, neighbors, mail carriers, colleagues, friends, and grocery clerks. "When he'd drink, to him I was always doing something," one Black woman said. "I was cheating, I was seeing people. I didn't understand that." She worked part-time in food service for poverty-level wages. A white woman described the behavior of her partner, whose income was in the millions of dollars. "He would get upset if I wasn't home and say, 'Well, where were you? Are you screwing around on me?'"

Out of jealousy and remarkable insecurity, some men policed what their partners wore when leaving the house. Several women said they could not wear makeup, because their partners were fearful that this would attract too much sexual attention. One white working-class woman said her partner constantly accused her of cheating. "I know you're cheating on me, I know you're a liar," he would shout. "Perfume—I wasn't allowed to wear it. Putting on makeup—I was accused of, you know, seeing other guys, or dressing up for other guys." An African American working-class woman described how she dressed in clothes that were too big for her in order to follow her partner's rules. "My clothes were baggy because he didn't want anybody looking at me and I just kind of got used to going in the store and buying a big size." The rules that men set out were at times difficult to follow. "What I wore was a problem, I tell you," another white working-class woman said. "You know, very jealous, very jealous. . . . 'I saw you looking at that guy.' But yet . . . when we went out, he wanted me to dress like skimpy, but then he'd complain if people looked at me."

One white survivor described an extreme case of controlling behavior. Her partner ordered her not to look at other men. She worked in health care:

> I used to have to keep my head down. . . . Keep my head down and not look—if I was riding a bus or a train, I would pretend like I was sleeping, I would put hoodies over my head because he would accuse me of looking at somebody.

This possessiveness extended to undermining women's relationships with their friends and family members. A wealthy white woman said, "He hated my friends because they took me away from my focus on him and the family. . . . He was jealous of my attention and my deep love for my family and my friends." Many men set out rules that their partners couldn't talk to other people on the phone, couldn't visit their families, couldn't have male friends, and couldn't even see their girlfriends.

Even the women's children became a focus of competition for women's attention. One white working-class woman described her partner's behavior:

> For the time I was with him if [my daughter] would cry he would immediately put up his own fuss that made it very clear that I had to attend to his needs first. . . . Or else I was getting pushed around or shoved.

Women described how jealousy escalated into rage and violence. A white working-class woman recalled:

> He and I were in the grocery store and he perceived me as checking out another guy, you know? Looking at another guy as if I wanted to, as if I was interested in the other guy. But I wasn't. . . . He was very paranoid and suspicious. . . . He yelled and screamed at me.

What did this jealousy and monitoring accomplish? Through these hidden dramas, these men controlled whom their partners talked to, visited, and went out with. The men's rules about clothing and makeup imposed their views of femininity on these women. The jealousy and possessiveness isolated women from their social networks and supportive resources. In the context of underlying threats, this also served to keep the men's violence a secret.

THE THREAT OF MEN'S AFFAIRS

Infidelity was seen by many women as a form of abuse, as an attempt to control and punish them. One-third of the men were unfaithful. Of the forty-five men who checked up on or monitored their partner's whereabouts, twelve were themselves having sex with women outside of the relationship. Women from all class categories reported infidelity; the highest rate was among wealthy men. "I would say that you know having an affair was another kind of abuse," one wealthy white woman said. "Another way to try to control what I did, which was, I should shut up, I should do what he wanted." A white woman married to a business executive spoke to her therapist about her husband. She was worried he might be having affairs. As she later learned, he was indeed sleeping with other women. Given the power of his social position, her therapist advised her to "be more accommodating, and . . . go along, to make peace. . . . I just didn't know how to handle high-powered men, basically is what she said." A married white working-class woman stated, "He goes around saying [the baby's] not his, and that I'm a slut and a cheater. And now I know it's really because he is."

Men would blame their partners for their own affairs, and as a result some women felt like failures as wives and lovers. One white working-class survivor blamed herself for her husband's repeated infidelity:

> I felt like my identity as a woman and as a wife was shredded. . . . I can't even tell you. My identity as a woman, I just—[*crying*]—to find out . . . that he'd been with other women. . . . You know, I lost all my bearings as a woman, and I felt so ashamed that I wasn't enough. That was my first reaction [*crying*]. I'm so ashamed that my husband was a cheater. So ashamed.

After divorcing her husband, she has helped other women who are struggling with shame from abusive relationships. A wealthy white woman was told by her husband that she was a bad lover, as an explanation for his having affairs. This devastated her, causing her to contemplate suicide:

> That for me was worse than any beating. It stripped me to the core and why I'm still here I don't know. Because it felt like the bottom.

Violence was used to defend men's self-appointed entitlement to have affairs. Two survivors, both living in professional communities, were physically assaulted for objecting to their husbands' infidelities.

REPRODUCTIVE ABUSE

The terms "pregnancy coercion" and "reproductive coercion" have been used to identify how, especially in the context of intimate violence, men force women to get pregnant or sabotage their contraceptive practices.[11] Other research focuses on violence and abuse during pregnancy.[12] For the women I interviewed, the forms of abuse relating to reproduction were more likely to involve violence during pregnancy and attempts to force miscarriages. For this reason, I use the term "reproductive abuse" to include both violations of reproductive rights (by either coercing pregnancy or coercing abortion) and violations of reproductive health. Over a quarter of the women gave accounts of this kind of abuse, mostly working-class and professional women.

Some of the women described behavior consistent with coerced pregnancy. One white woman, who was poor despite working in food service, was in an economically exploitative relationship with an unemployed man. She felt that her partner sought to get her pregnant because this would somehow bring more money into their relationship.

A married white working-class woman said her husband admitted he tried to get her pregnant so that she couldn't leave him. Both women ended up as single mothers. One white woman with an advanced degree talked about a coerced abortion, which was a turning point in her relationship with her husband.

A number of men abused their partners severely while they were pregnant. "He beat me black and blue," said an African American professional woman. The doctors who treated her were upset about her extensive bruises. Two men pushed their pregnant partners down the stairs. Two women were kicked in the stomach; one was punched hard enough to break her ribs. One white professional woman reported that early in her pregnancy, "He beat me from head to toe. I was bruised everywhere. . . . He didn't want any more children." She was so upset by this that she had an abortion rather than bring another child into her violent home.

In their hidden dramas, two men beat their partners so badly that the women lost their pregnancies. One almost died from her injuries. That assault began with an accusation that she was lying about her whereabouts. Two other men attempted to cause miscarriages. One denied he was the father and accused his partner of cheating on him. Such allegations of women's dishonesty ran through women's accounts.

ATTACKS ON THE SEXUAL PARTS OF WOMEN'S BODIES

Asked about the kinds of abuse they suffered, one-quarter of the women indicated that their partners would physically attack the sexual parts of their bodies. This was reported by women in all class categories except the wealthy women. "I mean every time sex took place, there was abuse. Every time, every time," one white professional woman told me. Many women identified spankings as one form that this took, and most of these women said that it happened repeatedly. As with the reproductive abuse, violent dramas of this kind represent a debasement of all things feminine. While it is not completely clear where the men learned such abusive behavior, half of the men who used pornography committed these acts, according to the women.

PORNOGRAPHY

Ten women described their partner's use of pornography as abusive. "He would try to coerce me to do things," one wealthy white woman said. "You know, whether it was, 'Oh, you know, let's watch this you know pornography tape and you know reenact various things.'" This was most common among poor and working-class men.

A white survivor who worked in retail reported, "It got to the point where he would not have sex without a pornographic movie playing. . . . He would make me do what they were doing. He didn't care if it was painful or humiliating." Another white working-class woman said that toward the end of their decades-long marriage, "the porn he was looking at, at that point, was rape, public humiliation, violence against women." She felt this encouraged him to become more aggressive in their sexual activity, which frightened her. This caused her to divorce him. In recent years, there has been a dramatic increase in extremely violent and degrading pornography. In an analysis of this increase and its relationship to violence against women, Walter DeKeseredy and Marilyn Corsianos argue that "pornography and misogyny are inextricably linked."[13] These women are describing more forms of misrecognition, of being objectified and not seen as full human beings.

THE SEXUAL ABUSE OF CHILDREN

Four women had reasons to suspect their partners of sexually assaulting their children, and while each case was investigated by authorities, no charges were ever filed. This was extremely distressing for these women. The four mothers couldn't get the investigators to take their concerns seriously. "He abused my daughter because he knew that was the only way to hurt me," one woman reported. This took place after they separated. She said this was the worst form of abuse she suffered. Another woman stated, "He would demean her. Call her a slut. . . . She hadn't been penetrated. But there had been some sexual abuse going on." She remains extremely upset about this, although she couldn't prove her partner was responsible. One white working-class woman said her partner showed pornography to their child and attempted to hide this action. She hates pornography and was worried how such degrading images could harm their child's development.

RAPE

Nearly two-thirds of the women indicated their partners either used or threatened physical force to have sex. While almost half of the wealthy and professional women reported forced sex, most of the working-class and poor women did so. Unmarried women had virtually the same rate as married women. Since state and federal laws on rape turn on the threat or use of physical force, these responses are consistent with the legal definition of rape in the United States.[14]

Feminist research has established that marital rape is no less brutal or traumatic or than other kinds of rape.[15] This is clear in the women's accounts. Three women were assaulted anally; one was raped at gunpoint, and another at knifepoint; and one was sexually assaulted with a sharp metal object. One woman was gang raped by her boyfriend and some of his friends.

For seven women, rape was an exceptional event that caused them to leave the relationship. One married white working-class survivor described how the violence changed everything for her:

> That night he would not allow me to go to sleep until I had made love to him. So he raped me and I was just lying there. I just realized I didn't feel anything for him anymore, just fear. I didn't feel any care, concern, or whatever for him.

She left her marriage shortly afterward. For some women, forced sex was a turning point, the beginning of a plan to leave. But for many women, sexual assault was a common, ongoing part of their experience. Sixteen women reported they were *often* physically forced to have sex or were threatened with physical force. Some said they were assaulted "weekly," "monthly," or "almost daily." Some described being so afraid after being raped that they sought to placate their partners to avoid more violence:

> I tried to appease him. So, I tried to do everything he had requested of me including—including sexual activities that I found demeaning. So, rather than being raped, I would do what he asked. Although, of course, now I can say that this was actually rape as well. . . . And they were not really given, they were given as a mechanism to avoid worse damage and injury. (a white working-class woman)

> He raped me that night . . . [*crying*]. Things just went downhill from there. From that point in time I did not have one consensual sexual encounter with him. (a white working-class survivor)

While they were in these relationships, it was difficult for most women to name their partner's actions as abusive:

> It confused me. I didn't understand why he did that. I mean, we were in the process of just having sex normally and then he just started getting really

violent and—and raped me anally and I didn't consent to that. I had never experienced that before. It was nothing gentle; nothing loving; nothing patient; nothing slow or easy. It was just vicious. . . . I screamed out in agony and nobody heard me. And it was just really hard for me to try to make sense of it afterward, so I didn't try. (a white woman from a working-class neighborhood)

We had a huge fight, I can't remember what it was about, and he raped me after that fight. I didn't know it was rape at the time. . . . I didn't realize I'd been sexually abused until I got to [a domestic violence advocacy center] and was going through some questionnaires for intake information. I had no idea I was being sexually abused. (a white professional woman)

For many women, how they defined their experiences changed over time, especially after seeking help from women's advocacy programs. In her study of wife rape, Raquel Kennedy Bergen found that naming is important; if women didn't name what happened as rape, they were less likely to end the relationship or seek help.[16]

NAMING AND NOT NAMING RAPE

Kelly observes that from women's perspectives, what is "typical" and what is "aberrant" behavior by men "shade into one another."[17] In these narratives, the women often struggled with how to name these forms of abuse. A number of obstacles became apparent that prevented women from seeing their experiences of forced sex as rape.

Social Support for Men's Sexual Entitlement

In the United States, rape in marriage became a crime in all fifty states only in 1993.[18] The United Nations reports that as of 2018, only 77 countries (out of 185) have explicitly made rape in marriage a crime.[19] Even within the United States, the laws on marital rape are uneven from state to state. A 2019 review of state legislation showed that in seventeen states, a spouse cannot be convicted of rape if their partner was unconscious, drugged, or incapacitated.[20] There remains an unwillingness in some US state legislatures to regard this as a crime that is as serious as other forms of rape.

Public perceptions also reflect a reluctance to take marital rape seriously. In a review of research on attitudes toward marital rape, Kersti Yllö found that "marital rape is viewed as less serious and less damaging both physically and emotionally than other forms of rape."[21] In studies using vignettes of sexual assault, subjects' perceptions of the seriousness of rape decreased as the closeness of the perpetrator and survivor increased. So stranger rape is viewed as more harmful than acquaintance rape, which in turn is seen as more harmful than marital rape. This pattern holds even when the particulars of the acts are the same and the descriptions of the injuries are the same. Women who are married are seen in these studies as more blameworthy than unmarried women.[22]

Long-standing patriarchal rules about sexuality and women's duties to their partners affect how both men and women perceive violence and attribute blame. It is understandable that many of the women who were interviewed felt confused about this themselves. They talked of their feelings of obligation concerning their husbands:

> I lived in a [religious community] where people said, "There's no such thing as marital rape. He's your husband. He's the head of the house, he can take what he wants, when he wants." (a white survivor from a working-class community)

> Somebody brought up the question of marital rape and I was still way too brainwashed and I was like . . . "What, what are you talking about? I was his wife. He could do whatever he wanted with me." . . . It took me a long time to realize that I had the right to say no, and that if I didn't have that right nothing was a real yes. (a white woman with inherited wealth)

Just over half of the women were married. But many unmarried women seemed to feel the same obligations toward their partners:

> It was difficult . . . to really like see it, you know, as that [rape] at the time because it felt like such a gray area. Because it was someone I was like, you know, already sexually involved with. But, you know, at the same time. . . . He would be physically forcing me to do stuff when I didn't want to, and it wasn't until I was later . . . trained as a counselor with [a rape crisis center], that you know, I realized that that . . . totally fits the definition of sexual assault. . . . I always thought that I was doing something, something wrong, you know, I wasn't a good girlfriend, or it was kind of what I deserved. (a white woman from a working-class community)

Even when women did seek help, they were sometimes told it was their duty to submit to their partners. "I remember telling my mother once, talking to her about it," one white woman related. She was from a working-class neighborhood. "She said, 'Well you just don't give him enough which is why he has to take it that way. Give him more sex and he will be happier.' That didn't work."

Rape Culture

Sarah Ullman offers a useful definition of "rape culture": "This term refers to the fact that US society often holds women responsible for being raped, frequently ignores or excuses rapists, and fails to support victims afterward."[23] Men's blaming of women for being abused draws upon rape culture. Research consistently finds that men support rape myths much more than women do.[24]

A 2018 survey found that 56 percent of men agreed that "false accusations of sexual assault against men are very common."[25] What is more upsetting is that this survey found that 51 percent of *women* also agreed with this statement. There is no sound empirical evidence that false accusations by women are "very common"; this is a rape myth.[26] Research on false allegations of rape has found that such allegations are uncommon, and that the real problem is that women vastly *underreport* rather than overreport rape.[27]

The culture in the United States blames women for rape as well as for problems in intimate relationships.[28] This is compounded by the legacy of racist images of women. In their national study of Black women, Charisse Jones and Kumea Shorter-Gooden charge:

> We have yet to eradicate the prejudices and discrimination relentlessly directed toward African American women. . . . In response to this unrelenting oppression many Black women in American today find they must spend significant time, thought, and emotional energy watching every step they take, managing an array of feelings, and altering their behavior in order to cope with it all.[29]

According to Ullman, "racism is part of the 'rape culture' that spawns rape."[30] What Patricia Hill Collins calls "controlling images" of Black women as "overly sexual" arose under slavery to justify the rape of Black women by slave owners.[31] These images continue to be common forms of misrecognition, and they shape police responses and even the responses of rape crisis centers to Black women.[32]

The weight of racist images was evident in one survivor's reflections on guilt. She is a Black woman from a poor community. "Yeah I felt guilty about it, I have," she said, reflecting on the rape—at gunpoint—that made her leave the relationship:

> It's one of those things when you're growing up, and I don't know about every culture, but being a Black woman, it's like you carry yourself a certain way and you try to do that. And I try to make sure I carry myself a certain way and don't do certain things. But then there's that question in the back

of my head like was there something I did. . . . You start to question yourself and the things that you did that may have led them to do or feel comfortable with doing what they did. . . . I felt guilty, but I also felt very violated.

In this explanation of her victimization, this woman has to negotiate powerful gendered and racialized ideas of a woman's sexual responsibilities.

The Stigma of Being a "Victim"

For many women, the term "victim" is a stigmatizing, discrediting identity. Most of the women who were interviewed disliked or even hated the term; for them it was shameful and worth avoiding. A white woman who worked in a restaurant told me, "Automatically, I think of something negative when I hear 'victim.'" A Black woman who was in college during her relationship said, "If I say, 'Oh, I was a victim,' I feel like people think, 'Well, you kind of asked for it,' or 'you probably deserved it.'"

A white woman with a PhD was annoyed that I had even used the term during the interview. "I don't like that word. I noticed you used it. . . . And I'm like why does he use that word?" Advocates at women's shelters and rape crisis centers are told to avoid the term "victim" and instead to use "survivor," a word that many interviewees preferred. Many said they perhaps were victims at one point, but now they are survivors. Some wanted something that goes beyond being a "survivor" and liked the word "thriver."

For many of these women, "victim" is a one-dimensional label associated with people who are helpless and weak, who whine and complain, and who somehow deserve to be abused. It is another form of misrecognition. A Black woman who was poor, but who now works with survivors, talked about her problems with this word:

> I think victim is so demeaning. . . . "Victim" makes it sound like you did that to yourself. It's victimizing. . . . When I see clients who are in the relationship, an abusive relationship, I don't like to use the word "victim" because I think they're more than that.

This level of discomfort with the word "victim" may be another reason why it is difficult for many women to acknowledge that they were raped. To say one has suffered rape is to relate oneself to a most horrible kind of victimization. Rape is itself "a highly stigmatized experience," according to Prachi Bhuptani and Terri Messman-Moore. They say, "No other groups of trauma victims are blamed for their ordeal as frequently as sexual assault survivors."[33]

Early in the interview, I asked women to fill out a checklist from an abusive behavior survey.[34] This list of check-off items includes being threatened with physical force to have sex and being physically forced to have sex; the word "rape" does not appear. Near the end of the interview, I asked women about a number of different terms that might be used to describe their experiences. The terms included victim and survivor, as well as rape. I asked these questions apologetically, stating that the words we have to describe the range of women's experiences are too few in number and too crude. Even coming toward the end of a long conversation about abuse, a direct question using "rape" was painful for many women to consider. Often there would be a long pause before a response. Of the thirty-eight women who reported they were either threatened with force or physically forced to have sex, thirteen used the term "rape" themselves even before I got to these questions. After I asked about it, an additional sixteen women agreed that the word "rape" described their experiences. Thus a total of twenty-nine survivors explicitly named what they suffered as rape. Nine women who had reported a threat of physical force or use of physical force to have sex did not identify with this word. Perhaps owing to class stigmas, wealthy women were least likely to name the forced sex that they suffered as rape.

A white working-class woman revealed her complex thoughts on the term "rape":

> [You don't seem to have described much in terms of like sexual abuse or sexual violence. Either of those words fit?] You know, it never occurred to me while we were dating. I don't think it did until I started working [as a domestic violence advocate]. Because to me sexual abuse has a stigma attached to it. It has to be this violent rape, and I now know that it doesn't. . . . On more than one occasion, I had to—I don't want to say had to, I—he made me feel like I had to have sex or do things that I didn't want to do. Not things I didn't want to do, it's not that it was an act I didn't want to do, it was—if I didn't want to have sex, I had to because I was afraid of what would happen if I didn't. [Well, does the term "sexual abuse" fit that for you?] Yes. ["Rape"? Does that word work for you to describe your experience?] Um, I think for me, like I said, it has some stigma attached to it. But I would say no.

In her response, this woman reveals how stigmatizing the term "rape" is, even for a domestic violence advocate. The stigma of the term "rape" involves more than misunderstandings about rape. It's about identity: it involves being shamed, marked, and discredited for suffering this kind of violation.

THE IMPACT OF SEXUAL ABUSE

Sexual violence is a primary cause of trauma in women's lives. In 2013, the definition of a traumatic event was changed by mental health professionals to include sexual violation.[35] The DSM-5, the basic handbook of mental health disorders, expanded the criteria for post-traumatic stress disorder (PTSD) to include "exposure to actual or threatened death, serious injury, or sexual violence."[36] This expanded definition gave examples of many different kinds of sexual violation, such as "forced sexual penetration, alcohol/drug-facilitated sexual penetration, abusive sexual contact, noncontact sexual abuse, [and] sexual trafficking."[37]

Research indicates that the impact of rape and attempted rape can differ greatly among survivors. A range of psychological consequences appears across studies of women and sexual violence. Short-term effects can include fear, anxiety, shock, confusion, and symptoms of PTSD. Longer-term impacts involve depression, suicidal thoughts, substance abuse, sexual distress, distorted body image, and difficulty forming trusting relationships.[38]

As indicated in chapter 3, most of the sixty women interviewed had periods of depression. Some reported either suicide attempts or suicidal thoughts. One white working-class survivor talked of being sexually assaulted by more than one boyfriend. She worked full-time in medical care:

> [I felt] suicidal—constantly. And I've had more than just this one [relationship]. I've had a pattern in my life. . . . I've been seen by people, been in and out of hospitals because of these men. And wanted to die myself because of how they made me feel. [And how did they make you feel?] Unworthy.

A white professional woman described the consequences of her abuse:

> I was always hit during sex. . . . [This sounds horrible. How did this abuse affect you?] Severe depression. Severe anxiety. I was paralyzed, absolutely paralyzed with fear.

Rebecca Campbell finds that the consequences of sexual assault are cumulative, in that the more assaults a survivor suffers, the greater the harm. She states that the responses of women's social worlds matter as well, and that these effects are also cumulative. Negative reactions can be experienced as a "second rape." Self-blame is common among survivors, but Campbell insists that this needs to be seen as shaped by rape myths and inadequate institutional responses.[39] We have already seen how racism and poverty can affect women's experience of sexual violation.[40]

Some recent studies address differences between the impact of physical violence and sexual violence in intimate relationships. Research has found that in abusive relationships, sexual violence may be more traumatic than the physical violence itself.[41] Feelings of betrayal and distrust due to sexual violation appear to cause higher levels of anxiety, depression, and mistrust.[42] Comparing women assaulted by their boyfriends with women assaulted by their husbands, sexual violence against married women is more likely to involve weapons and cause physical injuries.[43]

This research helps to make sense of the impact of sexual violence on the lives of the women I interviewed. Both the short-term and long-term consequences—especially fear, self-blame, and depression—undermine women's abilities to resist and escape violence.

SUMMARY

In her map of patriarchy presented in chapter 1, Walby sees sexuality as a key site of women's oppression.[44] This chapter details the many ways that women are sexually abused in intimate relationships. These stories were painful to hear and difficult to write about. They can't be easy to read. It is worth restating that these women resisted sexual violence, fought back, and separated from their abusive partners.

Ylló has wondered why sexual violence in marriage has never received the kind of public attention that physical violence against women has, or that child sexual abuse has.[45] She suggests that there is something uniquely upsetting about this form of violence. "It contains a cultural contradiction inherent in no other form of violence and it goes to the very heart of marriage."[46] Rape in marriage presents a threat to the institution of the family. "It just seems too intimate, and the violation of that intimacy is precisely the core of wife rape," she argues.[47] Even researchers who study intimate violence have shied away from documenting marital rape.[48] As disturbing as these stories are, it is important that we sit with them. They reveal much about the dynamics of sexual abuse.

There are many interconnections between the elements of this continuum. The verbal degradation displayed the malicious and controlling attitudes that were expressed in the other forms of sexual abuse. In these hidden dramas of masculinity, men's sense that their partners were somehow failures as women was central to the verbal abuse. Delusional jealousy motivated men's attempts to cause miscarriages in cases where men denied they were the fathers. Men's infidelities were seen by the women as sexually demeaning and controlling, consistent with the verbal degradation they endured. Men's use of pornography was experienced as further debasement. Pornography has been memorably defined by Andrea Dworkin as the "graphic depiction of whores," and some women felt they were being pressed into this role.[49] The sexual abuse of children, which involved pornography in some cases, is an extension of the sexual entitlement and control men assumed over their partners.

The threat of both physical and sexual violence lies beneath this continuum. In the context of a physically abusive relationship, shouting and screaming is itself frightening. The acts of delusional jealousy often led to yelling and violence. Women were assaulted for objecting to men's infidelities. Pornography that represented rape and sexual humiliation scared women, and men who used this kind of pornography brought this abusiveness into their sexuality. The forced sex that most women reported represents the culmination of this degradation and objectification.

There are some class differences in the extensiveness of the violence and abuse, with poor and working-class women reporting more sexual abuse as children, pornography, attacks on the sexual parts of their bodies, and forced sex. But there are more similarities than differences across the class categories.

The forms of sexual abuse detailed here all serve to degrade, threaten, and constrain women. As in the case of physical violence, the escalation of sexual violence made some women leave the relationships. But for many women, the constant verbal abuse, monitoring, and coerced sex made them fearful and depressed. In a culture that blames women for sexual assaults and fails to hold abusive men responsible, many women felt guilty and ashamed in the aftermath of sexual abuse. This served to isolate these women and cause them to feel trapped in these relationships. Seeing this as a continuum clarifies how these words and actions operate as a pattern of control.

CHAPTER 6

Economic Abuse

Control, Sabotage, and Exploitation

I would argue that housewives (both full-time and part-time)
are a class exploited by their husbands who also constitute
a class.

—Sylvia Walby

Many examinations of intimate violence minimize economic abuse or
ignore it entirely.[1] Under the definition of intimate partner violence,
the current website of the National Institute of Justice lists physical,
sexual, and psychological/emotional dimensions of abuse. There is one
reference to "denying access to money or other basic resources" under
psychological aspects.[2] The website of the Office of Violence Against
Women is even more limited in its focus, emphasizing only felonies and
misdemeanors.[3] But many aspects of intimate violence, especially psychological and economic abuse, escape the legal definition of crimes.

Economic abuse is a central feature of intimate violence. A recent
study of survivors in eleven states found that 66 percent reported educational sabotage and 83 percent reported employment sabotage. Most
survivors also reported theft or control of their money, theft or destruc-
tion of their property, and damage to their credit scores.[4]

Economic forms of abuse were common and highly consequential
for the sixty women interviewed for this study. In the passage that begins this chapter, Sylvia Walby states that when women provide unpaid
household labor to men in a marriage, husbands and wives represent
social classes, and that this is a relationship of exploitation. She is not
saying that men and women are classes; rather, she is saying that husbands and wives are. This can be extended to unmarried heterosexual
couples. Recall that in chapter 3 on psychological cruelty, many of the
men debased their partners with terms such as "loser," "idiot," "stupid,"

"useless," "worthless," and "trash." A winner needs to have a loser. In their hidden dramas of masculinity, as I show, many men sought to make the women into economic losers so that they could pose as winners.

Feminists have long criticized theorists of social class for ignoring women. They have contended that the economic conflict that occurs between social classes also occurs between men and women in family households.[5] Some have argued that the domination, economic exploitation, and exclusion that produce social classes are both gendered and racialized processes.[6] These processes create economic vulnerabilities for women in ways that are distinct for different classes and racial groups. More recently, the class literature has been further criticized for neglecting to address men and masculinities.[7]

Walby proposes that patriarchy is comprised of six distinct elements.[8] Two are most pertinent here. She sees women's paid work and unpaid work in the household as important dimensions of gender inequality. Both of these contribute to women's entrapment in abusive relationships.

The language of economic control, sabotage, and exploitation is part of the "Scale of Economic Abuse" that is widely used in research on intimate violence.[9] However, Judy Postmus and her colleagues use the term "exploitation" in this scale in a more limited sense than Walby does. Nonetheless, following an examination of paid and unpaid work, I use the language of economic control, sabotage, and exploitation to further explore the abuse that women reported. The chapter also addresses the impact of economic abuse and the experiences of women who had economic privilege.

GENDER INEQUALITY IN THE PAID LABOR FORCE

Gendered discrimination in the labor market creates inequality and economic dependency in heterosexual households. Based on 2018 data from the US Census Bureau, the gender wage gap in the United States remains significant. Comparing year-round, full-time workers, overall women earned an average of 82 cents for every dollar earned by men. There are even larger differences when this is broken down by race. Compared to white men, white women made 79 cents for every dollar; Black women made 62 cents; Latinas made 54 cents; American Indian and Alaska Native women earned 57 cents; and Asian American women earned 90 cents.[10] Multiple forms of discrimination are reflected here. This is the background against which women form families and negotiate resources for daily life.

There were many women who had high levels of education. At the time of the interviews, twenty-four of the sixty women had college degrees or higher education: six had PhDs, two had master's degrees, and one was an MD. Women had more education than their partners in every class category. But despite an overall advantage in education, most women in wealthy, professional, and working-class communities earned less income. A common pattern was for women who were mothers to work only part-time outside of the home. This reflects the choices women are given in a labor force that is not designed for working parents, and where few jobs have day care or maternity or paternity leave.[11] Even where it exists, parental leave in the United States is unpaid. This places the United States well outside the norm of Western industrial societies, all of which have paid parental leave.[12] Some men pressured the women to stay home or leave work. Most of the women, therefore, were economically dependent on their partners. Only in poor communities did women have more money; often as a result of incarceration, more men than women in these communities were out of the labor force entirely. Even though most men had more income, the majority of them sought even greater economic leverage through abusive actions.

WOMEN'S UNPAID LABOR IN THE HOUSEHOLD

Households are economic units, and shopping, cooking, cleaning, and childcare are essential tasks. Arlene Daniels calls this sphere of women's lives "invisible work."[13] In households where both partners are in the paid labor force, Arlie Hochschild identifies this as the "second shift."[14] When women have little choice about performing these duties, which are still today considered "women's work," it affects their economic dependence on men. Following divorce or separation, this unpaid work can leave women with bitter dilemmas about economic survival, especially if they have children. Even in heterosexual relationships that are free of violence, men spend much less time on housework than women.[15] This gendered privilege favors men in important ways: it allows them to focus their time on paid work or education that can increase their earning abilities, which further intensifies their economic power over their partners.

Nearly a quarter of the women accepted this gendered division of household labor. A few said they didn't trust their partners to take care of their children, due to alcoholism, drug use, and general irresponsibility. But some women took pride in this work:

[How about like housecleaning, cooking, shopping. Did you split these tasks up?] I am a clean freak. [So you did the cleaning?] I'm like that now. [Who did the cooking and shopping?] I did. . . . I love to cook and clean. I don't like to eat too many people's food. He cooked sometimes but dinner was always made. [Was that okay with you?] Yeah even now. (a Black woman from a poor community)

I'm an amazing cook, I clean the house, I take care of the kids. That was fine with me. [So you did all the shopping, childcare, cooking, and house-cleaning?] Yeah. I took care of it all. (a white survivor from a working-class neighborhood)

I did it all. . . . [How did you feel about this division of labor?] I'm not really one that's big on confrontations and I am pretty much ambitious. I love to cook and I love to clean so the division of labor I think I never expected from him. (a white professional woman)

One wealthy white woman saw housework as her responsibility, based on her partner's economic status. Bur she had mixed feelings about this:

The day-to-day stuff in the house was mine, because he was never around. The raising of the kids was mine, because he was never around. He was around sometimes on weekends. . . . So the running of the house, and that was pretty much mine, because he was never there. [How did you feel about that?] Lonely. I mean, I, I accepted it as a way of life for being an executive and what he chose to do. . . . But I understand now that that traveling was something he did because that's what he does to escape all responsibility. (a white woman from a wealthy neighborhood)

There were some relationships in which the division of labor was nego-tiated fairly:

Now, see, the odd thing is and the hard thing to deal with him is his—when he was good he was awesome, and when he was bad he was awful. So he did all the dishes, he did all the grocery shopping, he did all the laundry. (a white working-class survivor)

However, most men in this study refused to do housework or childcare; this was most pronounced in the wealthy and professional relationships. This is exploitation, in the sense described by Walby. Three-quarters of all women were angry or resentful about this. This included most women in every class:

[How were decisions made in your relationship about buying things, about dinners . . . things like this?] A lot of times it was his decision. . . . [How did you feel about this?] I thought it sucked. I mean I thought it should be mutual, 50/50. We both should have had a say in that. [How did you divide household tasks like cleaning, cooking?] I did 99 percent of it. (a white survivor from a working-class neighborhood)

A white woman who was with a wealthy man described a conflict around cleaning:

> I said to him "Help me bring in the dishes." He goes, "What do you mean?" I said "Can you grab the plates and I'll rinse them off." He goes, "I'm not just grabbing the plates. I don't do that. I'm a wealthy man. I don't clear the plates." . . . My mother came in. . . . She looked at me and she said "My dear, he's a wealthy man, he's not gonna be bringing in the plates." . . . I looked at her and I said, "I don't care how much money he has I'm not gonna be his servant." . . . Both my mom and dad said, "Well if you're gonna be asking for that you're just gonna be alone."

This offers evidence of class and gender entitlement in one white community.

One white survivor from a working-class community felt she couldn't manage all the housework and childcare. "I would beg him, I would beg him for help. I was overwhelmed, I was homeschooling, I was exhausted. I just felt like there was no end to it," she said. "Well, he would never help, no matter what I said."

Women said that conflicts over housework and childcare could lead to violence. Two-thirds reported that their partners got very upset when housework was not completed or done to their standards. This was as true for the privileged men as for those who were poor or working-class. For most women, this division of labor was coerced: fear undermined any rational discussion of these responsibilities. "I didn't like it," one Black woman said of her responsibilities for housework. She lived in a working-class neighborhood. "But I didn't feel like I had a choice." I asked a white professional woman about the arrangement around housework with her husband. "This was no cooperation," she insisted. "This was an abusive relationship."

ECONOMIC CONTROL, SABOTAGE, AND EXPLOITATION

Postmus and her colleagues distinguish between economic control, economic sabotage, and economic exploitation.[16] Control concerns the limits men place on women's access to economic resources, such as the household money. Sabotage is the restricting of women's access to employment opportunities. I expand this to subverting women's education. Exploitation is the unjust depletion of household resources, such as by stealing the women's money, refusing to pay the bills, or creating debt for women. Each of these is examined in turn.

Economic Control

The women reported that most men in every class controlled the household money in coercive ways. This was an important measure of their power in the relationship:

> He controlled all the money. He didn't want me to work. He wanted me to stay home. (a white working-class survivor)

> [He] was controlling with money. . . . I would have to chase him, and it was always, "You're always asking for money." And I would be put through this sort of gauntlet before I was able to get some money for him. That pervaded our entire married life. (a white wealthy woman)

The control over the household finances was so complete that one woman felt forced to shoplift to provide for her child:

> Once he had me hooked by marriage he refused to spend any money on [my child]. . . . If his [relatives] didn't give it to us I was shoplifting for it sometimes with my [child] with me and that put us at tremendous risk. I think now what would have happened . . . if I had been caught. It had potentially devastating consequences all of its own. (a white working-class survivor)

Some 45 percent of the women were put on allowances by their partners. This would seem more appropriate for children than adults. This was even more common for the women in the privileged classes than for the working-class and poor women. One Black professional woman revealed the coercion beneath this kind of economic control:

> Anytime I expressed my displeasure I got hit. Because of that, sometimes. . . . I had to swallow some of it because I didn't want to lose my allowance.

Many working-class women said their partners monitored their spending on food and clothing. Hiding the amount of the household's money was another way of limiting women's access to money. This was a common tactic for professional and wealthy men:

> There were some investments and financial things that were hidden from me. He took control of all the investments and it was not open for discussion. (a white professional woman)

> He controlled—you know—paid all the bills and he really controlled the purse strings so I never really knew what we had or what we didn't have, but

I knew what my limits were. I knew I could go [to] the store and get groceries, but even [with] clothing [for the children] I had to sort of be careful. (a white wealthy survivor)

For a number of men, keeping the financial information secret gave them an unfair advantage in their divorce settlements.

Sabotaging Women's Employment and Education

Over half of the men sabotaged their partners' jobs or participation in school. While this was common in all classes, it was more prevalent in poor and working-class relationships. This would seem counterintuitive, given the economic hardship experienced by these men. It makes sense, however, as a means of controlling and disempowering women. Sabotaging their partners was apparently more important to poor and working-class men than their own economic stability.

Over a quarter of the women either left their paid work or lost educational opportunities because of their partners. Some were forced out of their jobs because of the violence and abuse:

I got fired from a job because of him. [Really? What was he doing?] He kept coming to my job and harassing me so they fired me. (a Black survivor from a poor neighborhood)

I would just call in sick a lot, but when I showed up they could see that I had a busted leg or a black eye. . . . Maybe [my boss] could have called me up and said . . . "[You] came to work like four times [in] the last six months with black eyes and a busted leg. What's going on in your life? Do you need some help?" . . . You know . . . no one did that. [Then they fired you?] Yeah. (a Black working-class woman)

Two white working-class women lost their jobs, one after her boyfriend continuously stalked her at her job and the other after her boyfriend physically prevented her from going to work. A professional white woman was fired from an executive position after her husband came to her office drunk and made a scene. He had threatened to ruin her career, and he succeeded.

Undermining women's education was another common form of sabotage by the men. Poor and working-class women were deterred from attending college:

Because of him, I had to leave school. He didn't want me to pursue it. [So he made you drop out of school?] Yes. (an African American woman from a poor community)

Once we got married it was, you know, the roles had [been] defined. . . . There was, you know, "That's woman's work. What do you expect? You're a woman." . . . One of the things he's very insecure about . . . [was] that I was smarter than he was. So he sabotaged any time I was in college. So I—I couldn't do my homework, I couldn't study. (a white working-class survivor)

Despite their efforts, neither of these women had completed college at the time of their interviews, although one was back in school. Another white working-class woman explained how depression affected her schooling even after she left her abuser:

For a while I lost myself. It was very hard for me to move on. . . . Even after the relationship. . . . It affected my grades for a while. I ended up failing a couple of classes. . . . In a way I'm still feeling the ripple effects of this relationship just because I ended up having to drop out of college.

Some professional and wealthy women were either pressured into leaving or prevented from attending graduate school. A white woman from a wealthy community saw the educational sabotage this way: "I . . . understand now he didn't want me to have more power than he had."

Economic Exploitation

Women described a number of forms of economic exploitation, of ways their partners seized or spent their money or caused them to carry debt. In the context of their unstable work histories, poor and working-class men stole money from their partners. The money was often used for drugs or alcohol.

This connects to another form of exploitation, spending the household money in irresponsible ways. A quarter of the men were reportedly doing this, and this involved men from all classes. One working-class white woman explained her predicament:

He was drinking too much, running around . . . you know . . . going to strip joints . . . gambling. . . . By the time we'd get to pay our rent and other bills he'd be sitting there trying to balance the checkbook and couldn't. . . . He'd expect my paycheck to cover everything while he blew all his money. It was very frustrating because then he'd get mad at me and be very abusive.

Professional men would take household money set aside for bills and use it for drugs or for their mistresses. Wealthy men spent lavishly on expensive clothes and cars, while restricting spending by their partners.

To ensure their total control, some men made women sign over their disability checks or paychecks or property to their partners. Some had women deposit their paychecks directly into their partners' accounts, depriving the women of any access to their own funds. These tactics were reported in all classes.

Some men destroyed their partners' property to punish them. In a tactic that expresses woman hatred, several men cut up the women's clothing. In some cases, this was done to prevent women from leaving the house. Men damaged furniture, slashed women's car tires, smashed car windows, and shredded family photos. This maliciousness was deeply disturbing to the women.

Following separation, economic abuse continued for many women in the form of failure to pay child support. This forced women to go to court again and again to file claims of nonpayment. One working-class man wouldn't pay support because he claimed the baby was not his.

According to some of the survivors, especially women who were poor, the economic exploitation was so important to the men that the relationship appeared to be predatory; they were basically preying on the women's resources. One white woman, who had been in love with her partner, said he was out to get her disability check every month. He was unemployed. She feels now that he was a "dirtbag who leeches off of women." A Black survivor from a poor neighborhood described how the man she had been seeing stole everything of value that she had. This ended their relationship.

For some of the wealthy women, there was a different pattern of exploitation. This could be called a "bait-and-switch" tactic: women were encouraged to sacrifice their jobs for an expectation that was not fulfilled. Some wealthy men insisted that their partners leave their jobs in order to work directly for them. But then later, the women were denied any assets or any decision-making over the household finances, despite their labor. In one way or another, they were told that this money was not theirs. This is another kind of "invisible labor" that isn't seen as valuable and doesn't fully register in divorce proceedings. Women who weren't married left these relationships with nothing at all. This is both sabotage and exploitation. Reflecting on her separation, one white woman said, "I resent the fact that he can just go about his business like nothing ever happened, and he has the home that I do not have." Another white woman was told to reduce her hours on her job so that her unmarried partner could spend more time with her. He said, "You don't need to have that income, and I'll take care of things." She cut back on her hours. But he never really did take care of things, and instead he ran up bills that he refused to pay.

THE IMPACT OF ECONOMIC ABUSE

For the poor women, the economically predatory aspect of many of the relationships meant that leaving their partners did not necessarily add more strain. Few of them depended on their partners for economic support, as the men were unemployed or without legitimate jobs. But for many working-class, professional, and wealthy women, the end of their relationships exposed the precariousness of their economic circumstances.

Of the nine women who were poor when they were in their abusive relationships, all but one remained poor at the time of the interviews. For all of them, it had been years since the relationship had ended. Three women were homeless, two of whom were in transitional housing. Four women were on disability. In some cases, this was due to chronic illness or problems with mental health that predated their relationships. Most of the poor women had been to the hospital emergency room as a result of the men's violence; a third of them reported permanent injuries. One white woman was permanently disabled after being stabbed by her partner. In the interview she revealed the wounds on her body.

Breaking this pattern of poverty, one Black woman was no longer poor. She had a solid and fulfilling job as a domestic violence advocate.

Of the fifty-one women who were not already poor, nearly 40 percent lost class status after separating from their partners. Nine of the twenty-six women who had previously been in working-class households were now poor. Most had worked outside the home while in the abusive relationships, either full-time or part-time. But now all nine of the women were unemployed. Three were homeless or had been homeless since leaving their partners. Four were on disability due to illnesses.

Some survivors fled the relationships after severely violent attacks and left with very few belongings. One white working-class survivor described what it was like to suddenly leave her marriage with her children after increasingly violent threats by her husband:

> We were homeless when we left. We had nothing and I had $20 in my pocket. We lived on people's couches. We lived with my friend . . . and to give her a break in her tiny house, [we] would go to another friend's house . . . an even smaller house. We might stay there for an overnight or a couple of days in the afternoon. I had no car, couldn't buy food.

As she had not been allowed to work while living with her husband, her economic circumstances remained extremely difficult. She was homeless for a long time.

Of the fourteen women who were in professional households, over half remained in this class when we spoke. But four women were now poor; two of them were homeless. Two other survivors were now working-class. One white woman spoke of the economic control she had experienced. She had lived in a professional community:

> At the time . . . I didn't realize that he was siphoning off money . . . because later on when he said he had no money, he got one of the best lawyers in [town] for the divorce. And has retained him through the years. . . . So is he a poor man? I don't think so. Yeah, I live in public housing. I'm happy to be alive to tell you this story.

She was poor when I interviewed her.

A different white woman spoke of her adjustment after leaving her abuser. She had gone from living in a professional household to being working-class:

> It's okay to be a single mother. It's okay to . . . not have financially what we used to. . . . I always say to myself now, "I might not get always what I want, but we seem to always get what we need." [The] importance of what society deems me as and how I live my life, they don't have as much bearing. . . . I'm very content living with roommates. They're great to be around my [child].

Most of the women who had lived in wealthy communities while in their relationships remained wealthy, owing to their education, investments, and access to new partners with stable jobs. But a number of wealthy women lost economic status. One white woman talked of the shift in her life:

> I had gone from being . . . in a marriage, in a family, in a social setting, you know, living according to certain standards and thoughts about the future and yeah a whole package. . . . [G]oing from a life that wasn't all hunky-dory [but] nevertheless felt stable, okay enough, and so on, to one that was completely out of control. . . . I was able to get a job. . . . I was able to financially support myself, if I couldn't support our children to the level that they had been accustomed.

She was living in a professional community when interviewed.

For many women, the shock of being alone with no resources was overwhelming. When they talked about why they felt trapped, one-third of the women emphasized their economic dependence on their partners, which for most was tied to concerns about supporting their children. For these reasons, leaving was a frightening move. For many women, when they did leave, their fears of what might happen to them came true. In order to free themselves from violence they took considerable risks.

WOMEN WHO HAD MORE MONEY
THAN THEIR PARTNERS

A quarter of the women either earned more, or had more money than their partners due to inherited assets. Given how important a lack of resources is to feelings of entrapment, how did the women who had more money describe their predicaments?

Some of these women had incomes that were only marginally higher than their partners'. For poor and working-class women, this was not enough of a difference to overcome the dominance of their partners. As I have argued, men's power in these relationships arose from many different forms of abuse. One Black survivor from a poor community spoke of feeling trapped. She worked part-time in food service. Her partner had just come out of a halfway house. He had done time in jail for drug crimes and firearm possession. He called her awful names. He hit her frequently and was sexually abusive. For her, having more economic resources made her feel obligated to help her partner:

> I felt trapped because . . . if I put him out, you know [he'd] have nowhere to go. . . . I felt like well I'm going to try to help him get on his feet. [So you felt trapped, you felt responsible for helping him?] Yeah.

For the working-class women, having more income seemed to cause their partners to seize control of their paychecks. One Asian American survivor did clerical work, and this was all they had for income for much of the time. This was difficult as they had a young child. Her husband insisted on deciding how the money was spent. He criticized everything about her, and did this on a daily basis. He would hit and kick her. She said he raped her. She became depressed and blamed herself for the abuse:

> I didn't feel like I was being a good wife. And I kept telling myself that I needed to be a good wife. [Would he talk to you in those ways? Would he use that kind of language with you?] Basically, yeah.

Fear, self-blame, and her inability to see a way out made her feel trapped. It wasn't until he started to abuse their child that she filed for divorce.

An African American woman had a steadier income than her husband. She was a full-time secretary; he worked on and off, either quitting or getting fired from his jobs. He frequently degraded her with hateful names. He was sexually and physically abusive; one time, he pointed a gun at her. Throughout the relationship she continued to believe he could change back into the man she fell in love with:

> I saw him before I knew that he was abusive and he was so nice. . . . I just saw this great potential and I couldn't get past that. I just feel like one day he'll go back to that person. Yeah I was holding out for that person but it never happened.

As with most women, it wasn't just one thing that made her feel trapped. She struggled to save enough money to leave. She didn't want to take her children to a shelter. But after he threatened her with a gun, she found a way to get out.

Several professional and wealthy women had substantially more money than their partners. This didn't prevent them from feeling trapped. There were many different elements to their predicaments. At one point in her long marriage, one white professional woman made three times what her husband did. She held an executive position while he worked on and off in construction. But she nonetheless felt trapped in her marriage with her children:

> He totally took control of my life. . . . And I was so trapped, there was nothing I could do. And he was a good-ol'-boy to the community. So, there was nothing I could do [*sounding upset*] . . . but succeed in my professional life. And that's what I did.

She was much younger than her husband. He was well-known and respected in the community. At times he was severely violent, and she suffered bruises and broken bones. He would tell her she provoked him, and for a long time she believed this. He resented her economic success and caused her to lose her job. She was many years into her marriage before she got the support she felt she needed to divorce.

Another white professional woman also suffered abuse for years in a long marriage. She made all the money in her household, while he devoted himself to his art. He called her vicious names and threatened to kill her. On a check sheet that asked how often she was slapped or hit or kicked, she wrote, "too many times to count." He told her it was all her fault, and she internalized this. She once called a suicide hotline. She became traumatized and severely depressed:

I was trapped because of what he was doing, how he was controlling me and keeping me in fear and crazy making. . . . Trapped would be a very good description.

A warning from a doctor was a turning point for her to leave her marriage.

Two white women who had inherited their own wealth reported feeling trapped. One woman said she was very much in love with her partner, who was ten years older. He had a working-class job. Her love persisted, although it came into conflict with his abusive behavior. He would frequently shout at her and call her vulgar names. He controlled what she wore and would be angry when she wouldn't do what he wanted. He was jealous of her friendships. He threatened to hit her and was forceful and hurtful when they had sex. He was angry "almost all the time . . . there was always something that I did." She became angry and sad and was always "walking on eggshells." Although she wasn't married and had millions in inherited wealth, she was with him for a number of years and had difficulty leaving him:

I . . . felt trapped by him, you know, because of the way he was, you know, all the restrictions he put on me, all of the limitations, all of the demands, all of the you know ridiculous whatevers. . . . You know, what I could and couldn't do, and all that kind of stuff. So I think it was all of that combined that felt, yeah, felt very, very stuck. You know. I mean, it almost felt more like prison sometimes than a relationship. You know, and he was the guard, and I was the prisoner.

Over time, his anger and their fighting escalated, and she finally ended it.

Another white woman brought inherited wealth into her marriage. Her husband did low-paid professional work. She said she was in love with him, but she quickly said she was afraid of him early on. It was a long marriage. It was confusing to her that she could feel both love and fear at the same time. He was good-natured when with friends and family members. But in private, he hit her many times and threatened to kill her. He envied her wealth. She became depressed and was diagnosed with PTSD. Interviewed many years after her divorce, she was still struggling to recover her identity and her sense of agency. When she was in this marriage, she was economically disempowered because her husband took charge of the money. He exerted a kind of psychological control over her. She was disoriented from the years of abuse:

I had a child in my belly from him and what was I going to do? It gets really disassociated and spacey and you don't believe it and what do you complain about and no one will believe me and he's so charming. . . . I was so

PTSD. I [had] like incredibly narrow vision, incredibly concrete. . . . It was like everything was backwards and it was part of how he entrapped me by keeping me so frightened and so confused about the world.

The physical violence increased, and she was finally able to leave the marriage.

THE TRAPPINGS OF PRIVILEGE

Economic dependency and economic abuse clearly affected women's abilities to resist or escape violence. Poor and working-class women, who were dependent on their partner's income, faced difficulty supporting themselves and their children if they left. Yet professional and wealthy women who had more money than their partners also felt trapped in abusive relationships. This raises a question: In a patriarchal society, does class privilege itself play a role in women's sense of entrapment?

There are three ways that class privilege affected women's abilities to resist and escape abuse. First, men used their economic status to disempower the women. The class status of most economically privileged women was dependent on their abusive partners. For as much status as many privileged women had, their abusive partners had more. Some of these men had prominent standing in their communities. This status could be used as a weapon against women. One man threatened his partner with his status. "He led me to believe that he was really powerful, that he had influence, and that he could make things happen. He just needed to pick up the phone," a white professional woman told me. This threat was one of the ways he made his wife follow his commands. When men with such privilege threatened to take custody of the children, this terrified the women. "I believed him that he could pull that off and that's why I stayed with him so long," one wealthy white woman said. When a wealthy white man told his wife that no one would believe her if she spoke about the violence, he was in many ways right. When she finally left her husband after two decades of marriage, some of her friends didn't believe what she said about the abuse and sided with her ex-husband.

The second point is that some women felt they were supposed to tolerate the abuse because of the men's economic status. One wealthy white woman, whose abuse was known among her family members, was told she should feel "lucky" to be married to such a wealthy man. She should put up with everything he did, no matter how violent, and she should keep the abuse hidden. Another wealthy white woman was married to a physician. She imagined how people around her would respond if she told them about the abuse:

> They believed that doctors, especially man doctors, were . . . to be respected and that I had a nice life, and "suck it up," that's what they would have said. And "maybe you caused it."

This is more evidence of the culture of affluence discussed in chapter 3. If violence and even divorce mark the distinction between the "haves" and the "have nots," then economically privileged women faced shame for violating these patriarchal rules.

The third and related point is that economically privileged women feared losing class status if they left their abusive partners. Fear of abuse collided with fear of economic loss for many women, especially those who were mothers. One wealthy white woman described how privilege and economic dependence created a difficult situation for her:

> I just felt that there was no way of—given the situation, given my financial status, that had I not had children I think it would have been very different, but I felt very trapped with . . . having three children and working but not making enough money to meet their needs in the way that they were accustomed. I felt really, really trapped. I felt I couldn't open up to the world, that this was my lot in life and I was gonna have to live it and it was not a good feeling, not a good feeling.

It was not just material losses that women feared; it was also the social losses. They feared the judgment, stigma, and marginalization that would affect them and their children. As shown in chapter 1, the abusive relationships in the professional and wealthy neighborhoods lasted much longer than those in poor and working-class communities.

In these three ways, economic privilege presented its own trappings, its own obstacles to freedom from violence and abuse.

SUMMARY

In criminology, there is a long tradition of linking crime to the class divisions in capitalist societies. As far back as 1916, the Dutch criminologist William Bonger wrote about how capitalism contributes to crime. According to Bonger, poverty "kills the social sentiments in man, destroys in fact all relations between men. He who is abandoned by all can no longer have any feeling for those who have left him to his fate."[17] Bonger also argued that capitalism affects the social instincts of wealthy people: "It develops, on the part of those with power, the spirit of domination, and of insensibility to the ills of others."[18]

Extending this line of thought, Elliott Currie has written that the United States has what he calls a "market society," by which he means one "in which the pursuit of personal economic gain becomes increasingly the dominant organizing principle of social life."[19] Market societies, Currie says, "are Darwinian societies. . . . They are 'sink or swim' societies, at least for those unable to corral enough private resources to stay afloat."[20] Currie talks about how this kind of society breeds a "culture of 'normal brutality'": "Market society promotes violent crime in part by creating something akin to a perpetual state of internal warfare in which the advancement of some is contingent on the fall of others."[21]

This ruthless individual competition for economic rewards is visible in women's accounts: the lack of social sentiments, the spirit of domination, and the "normal brutality" of economic competition. This ruthlessness is apparent in men from every social class.

But this economic struggle is not taking place only between labor and capital—it is taking place within marriages, within intimate heterosexual relationships. As indicated in the quote at the beginning of the chapter, Walby sees husbands and wives as competing social classes. I believe there is a perverse gendered class struggle going on here, with men seeking every chance to build themselves up financially by pushing women down. Gender inequality in the paid labor force causes many women to depend on men, setting the stage for exploitation in the household. Control, sabotage, and exploitation seemed the same for the men and women who were unmarried but were following the patriarchal script of women's household obligations. This is an important part of why women feel trapped in abusive relationships with men.

CHAPTER 7

The Emotional Dynamics
of Entrapment

Love, Fear, Anger, Guilt, and Shame

"Emotion work" refers . . . to the act of evoking or shaping,
as well as suppressing, feeling in oneself. . . . Emotion work
can be done by the self upon the self, by the self upon others,
and by others upon oneself.

—Arlie Russell Hochschild

Much of the power that men exert in abusive relationships is invisible.
There are forms of power that cannot be seen or touched in the same
way that we can see and touch a man's fist. The ever-present question of
"why women stay" in abusive relationships demonstrates how difficult
it is to make the relations of domination perceptible.

In the accounts of the women I interviewed, their husbands and boyfriends set down many rules that were enforced through violence and
abuse. As I have shown, these patriarchal rules concern sex; money;
housework; childcare; and women's relationships, jobs, and education.
Survivors described how their partners, out of delusional jealousy, monitored their appearance, activities, and phone calls. Similar edicts were
reported at every class level.

There is one other domain of rules: women's emotions. Like the other
rules, emotional obligations were imposed but not invented by the men;
such mandates, as I show in this chapter, are deeply rooted in our patriarchal culture. This chapter examines the dynamics of love, fear, anger,
guilt, and shame that affected the women's sense of entrapment.

Arlie Hochschild developed a perspective on emotions that guides
this exploration. Her work offers a way to map the emotional dimensions of power in abusive relationships. She is concerned with "how
social factors affect what people think and do about how they feel."[1]

In the quote at the beginning of the chapter, she says that "emotion work" involves "evoking or shaping, as well as suppressing, feeling."[2] She insists that emotions involve active intervention by individuals: "In my exploratory study respondents characterized their emotion work by a variety of active verb forms: 'I *psyched myself up.* . . . I *squashed* my anger down. . . . I *tried hard* not to feel disappointed. . . . I *made myself* have a good time. . . . I *tried* to feel grateful. . . . I *killed* the hope I had burning.'"[3]

In her analysis, emotions are rule governed; there are "shoulds" and "shouldn'ts" that guide feeling in social situations. Her term for this is "feeling rules." Individuals act upon their feelings in relation to these rules, either to bring feelings into conformity with the rules or to resist them. This is why people are generally happy at weddings and sad at funerals, as Hochschild sees it. We don't simply respond automatically with emotion in such situations, although unconscious processes in such situations can be powerful; we also act upon our feelings. In doing emotion work, Hochschild distinguishes between "surface acting" and "deep acting."[4] Surface acting is the management of external emotional expression, such as smiles or frowns. Deep acting involves changing internal emotional states, something that actors are trained to do. Emotion work is about more than just expression; it involves shaping actual feelings. This is not to suggest that evoking or suppressing feeling is easy or always successful, as I show in this chapter.

Emotion work highlights how one's feelings involve activity by both the self and other people. The experience of shame, for example, which can trap abused women in silence, is more than a personal feeling. It is guided by the rules of a patriarchal society, and others actively intervene to evoke such sentiments. "Emotion work can be done by the self upon the self, by the self upon others, and by others upon oneself," according to Hochschild.[5] By connecting personal feelings to interpersonal rules and the larger structures of gender inequality, Hochschild's work illuminates how power operates through feeling. Chapter 3, on psychological abuse, detailed how the men made the women feel guilty and ashamed; this can be understood as successful emotion work on the men's part. They were enforcing a set of patriarchal rules about feeling.

Emotion work also involves efforts to reject rules and resist feelings such as guilt and shame. For survivors, recovery from abuse requires much corrective emotion work, with the support of friends, family, advocates, and therapists.

LOVE

Most women in all classes said they were in love with their partners. Many said they fell in love easily, early, right away. "I was crazy in love with him," a white working-class woman said. It was a "great love," a white professional women declared. A white wealthy survivor told me, "I would have been with him forever." A Black woman spoke easily about feeling love. She lived in a poor community:

> [You were in love with him?] Yes. . . . Everything wasn't bad. We used to go the movies and go to barbecues, go swimming, go shopping—those are a lot of good things we did.

Because they were no longer with these men, survivors spoke of their feelings of love with self-doubt and even sarcasm. For many, it was painful to talk about. The women hedged, and added qualifications to distance themselves from their feelings. They were "probably" in love; they were "infatuated"; they "thought" they were in love. Survivors now questioned their feelings and were unsure if they really knew what love was at the time. Alluding to the different faces of masculinity her partner had presented, a white professional woman stated, "I did feel love for the person I thought I knew."

Women described the obligation to love their partners. They struggled with this rule because of the abuse. A working-class Asian American woman said, "I worked very hard to make myself believe" in love. She was describing emotion work; she had talked herself into feelings of love for her partner, something she thought she was supposed to have. A Black working-class woman spoke of the feeling rules she was trying to follow:

> I talked myself into or I tried to say, "Well you know he's sorry and he's acting really good today. And so you should—he said he loves you." So I would try to make myself be back in love with him.

Another woman shared a similar internal dialogue about loving her husband. She was a white woman from a working-class community:

> If it was a good day and he was in a good mood, we were having a good day, then I'm like, "That's why I love him." If it was a bad day—"but remember yesterday, I love him."

A white professional woman succeeded in following the rules and rekindled her feelings of love. Her husband called her horrible names. He hit her and was sexually violent:

I went at least two years where I had no feeling of love for him, but I committed myself to him. The feelings did come back. We had a good period for a year or two. I was all googly and gushy over him and warm and fuzzy. They came back for a while and then we'd cycle again. [How did you do that?] I just willed myself to want to enjoy being with him again, to have those warm, fuzzy feelings and get all tingly when we hold hands and that kind of stuff. I just really, really wanted that and eventually it did come back.

One Black woman from a poor community tried to suppress her feelings of love because of the abuse. But it didn't work. She went to the emergency room several times because of the violence. "The more I was trying, you know, I was more in love," she told me. For a Black professional woman, efforts to change her feelings of love were also a failure. She was physically assaulted and threatened by her partner:

I was trying to convince myself that I hated him, to make it easier on myself. . . . I really wanted to believe that I was disgusted by him, and, and I said, "If I believe that long enough, I will really be disgusted by him." And really worked hard. And, and, focused, at one point . . . just focused on everything that was negative about the relationship, more than ever before. And kept saying to myself, "See? It's horrible. He's a horrible person. . . ." You know, my head was doing the work, but my heart was doing something else. . . . It didn't work.

Some survivors discussed love in sharply critical ways. A white professional woman spoke of the obligation to love her husband:

I thought I loved him, and I think I sort of—it's called self-hypnosis. You love this man because you've got to justify living with him. That's the way I attribute it.

She is now rejecting this arrangement and is calling into question what she really felt about him.

A few women were involved in conservative religious communities that set out limited roles for women in family life. The mother of one white working-class survivor quoted the Bible to shame her for leaving her violent husband. Another white working-class woman described the beliefs of her church on rape in marriage: "You do this because you're a submissive wife. He's the head of the household. He gets to call all the shots."

A wealthy white women laid out the feeling rules that bound her to her husband:

From me being raised Catholic, there was no way I could ever leave him. There was no way I could leave this man who I had taken a vow to love, honor, cherish, in sickness and in health, good times and bad.

She did eventually divorce him. But she indicates the rules that had to be overcome to accomplish this, rules about love and obedience. Demonstrating the strength of the marital bond, the relationships of married women lasted three times longer than those of unmarried women. This was true even when comparing married and unmarried women within each social class.

Religious institutions have many rules about how women should feel toward their spouses. The current official website of the Southern Baptist Convention states: "A wife is to submit herself graciously to the servant leadership of her husband."[6] This doctrine denies women any righteous anger about gender inequality in the church. This rule is currently being challenged by Southern Baptist women.[7]

In 2004, a document released by the Catholic Church stated that feminism was "lethal" to families:

> Recent years have seen new approaches to women's issues. A first tendency is to emphasize strongly conditions of subordination in order to give rise to antagonism: women, in order to be themselves, must make themselves the adversaries of men. Faced with the abuse of power, the answer for women is to seek power. This process leads to opposition between men and women, in which the identity and role of one are emphasized to the disadvantage of the other, leading to harmful confusion regarding the human person, which has its most immediate and lethal effects in the structure of the family.[8]

These religious pronouncements are patriarchal reactions to feminism, attempts to reimpose conservative rules about love, anger, and obedience upon women.

Many survivors felt that their partners tried to control them by manipulating their feelings of love, which is another kind of emotion work. An African American woman from a poor community felt her partner somehow sensed that she was a survivor of child sexual abuse, and that this caused him to get close to her and abuse her sexually. He said he loved her. Then he raped her, and she fled the relationship out of fear.

A white working-class woman described how her boyfriend would try to get her to return to him after breaking up:

> He was always trying to find a way to lure me back into the relationship. Whether it was enlisting friends who would say "You just misunderstood him." "He really cares about you." "He does so much for you."

Her boyfriend tried to exert control over her by appealing to obligations about love.

A white woman from a wealthy community recalled how her husband would change his persona to maintain the marital bond. He threatened her and was psychologically abusive:

> He was very good at becoming—this is what I've learned today—becoming what you need in that moment to achieve his objective. So, when I had the doubt, and when I had the resolution to leave or to break it off, he would become that other person that I fell in love with, because he knew that's what I loved, and that was the hook.

There were some women who loved their partners until the end of the relationship. For most women, however, the abuse transformed their feelings. A Black working-class woman explained:

> I couldn't believe how rude he was and, "Why are you acting like this to me? I don't cheat on you, I'm a pretty lady." I was clean. I had a job. I came from a good family. "Why are you treating me like this?" I was a good girl. I wasn't a bad girl. I mean, "What is it? What's wrong?" . . . I was brokenhearted.

The men's betrayal of the women's love was so wounding that nearly half of the women said that by the end, they hated their partners. They said, "I couldn't stand being around him"; "He's disgusting to me"; "He can rot in hell for all I care." This presented its own dilemma, because hatred of one's partner or even ex-partner is not generally acceptable for women; it was also something the men would not tolerate. As a result, many women did emotion work to try to rein in these feelings:

> You can love someone and still not like them. So I would love him because he was my husband and that's what you're supposed to do. But utterly loathed him. (a white working-class woman)

> I hated him, but I was afraid that if I tried to leave, he would hurt me, would take [my child] and I would never see him again [*sounds upset*]. . . . I just walled him off, pretended I didn't have any feelings. I just survived. (a white professional woman)

Ten women went so far as to say they had imagined murdering their partners or seeing them die. This included women at every class level. A Black survivor from a poor community spoke of "wanting to kill him" after a beating that left her severely bruised. A white professional woman admitted that "at the end, I almost really wished he would die. If he would die, my troubles would be over." A wealthy white woman detailed her complex feelings about this:

> I [thought] sometimes that it would be so easy for me to kill him. . . . And then I thought to myself, how sick is this, that I'm having these thoughts?

And then I thought I was becoming just like him because I was having these horrible thoughts.

In her work on trauma and coercive control, Judith Herman writes of the "humiliated rage" of individuals who are trapped in abusive relationships and of the "revenge fantasy" that is commonly associated with trauma.[9] "The victim imagines that she can get rid of the terror, shame, and pain of the trauma by retaliating against the perpetrator. The desire for revenge also arises of the experience of complete helplessness. In her humiliated fury, the victim imagines that revenge is the only way to restore her own sense of power. She may also imagine that this is the only way to force the perpetrator to acknowledge the harm he has done her."[10] Herman notes that these fantasies, which are another kind of emotion work, don't really bring relief. Echoing the statement by the previously quoted woman, Herman finds that they "degrade her image of herself. They make her feel like a monster."[11]

FEAR

All of the women reported that men used either direct violence or the threat of violence in efforts to control them. Many women named fear as central to why they felt trapped in their relationships. Fear became its own bond between women and their partners. Recall that two-thirds of the men threatened to kill their partners. In many cases, men said they would kill the women, and the children, if they attempted to leave. Over half of the men used guns, knives, or other weapons to frighten their wives or girlfriends. Most women described acts of sexual abuse that meet the legal definition of rape.

Even after being divorced or separated, over half of the women remained afraid of their ex-partners for a long time. Many said they were still afraid when I interviewed them, even though this was often many years after they had separated. Even women who were no longer afraid of their ex-partners described a fear of men in general. This white survivor from a professional household was almost choked to death:

I'm very skeptical and reluctant to get involved in another relationship because I feel that, you know, the next one could be the end. You know?

I asked women how they coped with such levels of fear. Many left or called the police; these responses are addressed in chapter 8, on separation. Some women bought guns, took self-defense courses, or changed their locks and alarm systems to cope with their fears. These measures were particularly useful in protecting them immediately after divorce and separation, which is the period of time when women are at increased risk of abuse from their ex-partners.[12] Others dealt with fear through distraction or by trying to avoid conflict.

Many women sought ways to directly suppress their feelings of fear. Some survivors took antianxiety medication. One white working-class woman slept a lot and ate a lot after being abused:

> The funny thing is when I would feel afraid I would feel very tired. I would take a nap and not get out of bed until afternoon so I think my coping was sleeping. It eventually turned to eating and I became an eater. I would feel hungry all the time. I was eating so much and I still felt hungry and I think that was my way to block out the fear.

Refusing to eat was also seen as a way to suppress feeling:

> [How did you cope with these feelings of fear?] My anorexia. I would just not eat. I just wanted to die. (a white professional woman)

One woman meditated to calm down. Others sought relief through alcohol, although this created its own problems:

> I used to call it my mental vacation . . . because no matter what he said, I didn't care. . . . I mean, I was a blackout drinker. So, I drank to blackout, because I didn't want to remember. Not having a clue that that was actually putting me in more danger, because I was more vulnerable to attack. Um, but yeah, I would drink. I would numb out. (a white working-class survivor)

One woman lived in denial about the danger she was in. She was threatened with weapons many times. She described her interactions with an advocate at a domestic violence program. The advocate seemed to hold the fear that this woman could not bear:

> Over time I would feel so bad to witness her face [the advocate]. I'd go in there, she'd like—she'd be so upset and nervous, and I wouldn't be. And that made her even more nervous because I wasn't. And that was because I was in total denial about it. And I realized later that yeah, I lived with all these [weapons], but if I chose to think about how much danger I was in at the time I was living with them I could not survive the day. Period. So I just dealt with him hour by hour. (a wealthy white woman)

Denial is a kind of emotion work. Others in women's social circles would also use denial in response to women's disclosures of abuse. Their emotion work seemed to be about minimizing the threat of men's violence:

[So a lot of people denied this, huh? Who denied this? Your friends, your family?] People—the family, yeah. "He's such a nice guy." Oh my gosh. I thought, I would like to choke the next person that says, "He's such a nice guy." Because that's the façade he puts on. . . . They would say, "There's no way. Are you sure? What, you know, come on, it can't be all that bad." (a white professional woman)

As Hochschild makes clear, people around us help to enforce the rules about how we should and shouldn't feel.

In Hochschild's theory, emotion work represents conscious efforts to shape feeling. However, not all responses to fear are conscious actions. Some are unconscious, spontaneous defenses against violence. Some scholars have argued that the idea of emotion work could be expanded to include unconscious or involuntary processes. Tracey Burton, who draws upon Hochschild, seeks to identify unconscious elements affecting the emotional labor of schoolteachers.[13] Petya Fitzpatrick and Rebecca Olson, who are also seeking to extend Hochschild's work, investigate unconscious efforts to manage anxiety by researchers conducting emotionally difficult interviews.[14]

I think traumatic reactions can be seen as a kind of unconscious emotion work, as ways of managing overwhelming fear. Like conscious emotion work, traumatic reactions are efforts to suppress or evoke feeling as a form of psychological self-protection.

Herman identifies three types of traumatic responses that are all represented in the women's accounts: hyperarousal, constriction, and intrusion. She describes hyperarousal as a "persistent expectation of danger," a state of heightened anxiety that serves as a form of self-preservation.[15] This is a defense mechanism that evokes emotional arousal in order to manage fear. One white working-class woman described this in vivid terms:

Just the level of fear 24/7 and never being able to escape from it—I knew from the sound of the tires hitting the gravel in the driveway whether or not I'd be in for it for the night. By how he opened and closed the door. His footsteps on the treads of the stairway. I knew exactly what I would be in for on any given night. So hypervigilance doesn't even begin to describe it. Even now I have the ability to read people's emotions.

Over time, hyperarousal makes survivors lose sleep, which causes their physical health to deteriorate. Being in a prolonged state of "fight or flight" is also psychologically debilitating. Whatever it offers as self-protection in the short term, in the long term this psychic self-protection is harmful to survivors.

A second common traumatic response is what Herman calls intrusion, "the indelible imprint of the traumatic moment."[16] After experiencing violence, when some survivors recall the incident, they feel as if they are actually reliving it. This is an abnormal kind of memory, a way of bracketing off experiences so that they are not integrated into the rest of one's consciousness. As it is not easily controlled, traumatic memory haunts individuals in the form of flashbacks and nightmares. The slightest things can retrigger the original event in this intense form. A white professional woman described an ongoing struggle with fear of her ex-husband, years after divorcing him. She was repeatedly screamed at, threatened, and physically abused:

> [Was it a constant feeling of fear?] Yes. . . . [Did it change after you left, the feelings of fear?] I still get—I don't have someone who's threatening to kill me at any moment. So there's less fear. I get triggered very easily. . . . The other night . . . I thought he might be out there, going to . . . come in and kill me. . . . Part of me knows—highly unlikely. And the other part is just sure it's happening right now. So that PTSD thing, so that's still with me. It has gotten less very gradually but it's still much more a part of my life than I'd like it to be.

The effects of the violence and threats still remained, many years after divorce. She explained, "Even getting an email from him, I would be dysfunctional for hours. I would be shaking."

The third common traumatic response is constriction. This is seemingly the opposite of hyperarousal. Constriction is a suppression of feeling, a state of emotional detachment, numbness, or forgetting. Herman calls constriction "the numbing response of surrender."[17] "Surrender" in this sense needs to be seen as a means of surviving a terrifying event. Amnesia is an example of this:

> I would . . . blank it out and go places so I don't remember half of it. My friend . . . says [my husband] used to hit me because of how I looked the next day. People would ask me what happened; "Did you run into the door frame?" I honestly can't tell you, I have no memory of it. (a white working-class survivor)

Like other traumatic reactions, this means of survival is also maladaptive over time. Depression and suicidal feelings are examples of constriction. As I have shown, this state can also be brought on consciously through the use of alcohol and drugs.

There are reasons that it makes sense to see traumatic responses as related to emotion work. These are all ways of suppressing fear, or in the case of hyperarousal, of managing fear by evoking a fight-or-flight response. Traumatic responses are related to conscious ways of suppressing and evoking feeling, as in the case of the woman who became emotionally detached and pretended not to feel hatred, the woman who denied her feelings of fear, and the survivor who drank in order to black out and forget. Further, they are involuntary reactions that individuals nonetheless can become conscious of and talk about, which is part of Herman's therapeutic approach to healing from trauma.[18]

While these traumatic responses alter feelings of fear and desperation, none of them stop the abuse. When women continually experience them, they are signs of suffering, of a need to heal from the violence.

As fourteen of the sixty survivors are Black women, it is important to note that racism represents its own history of trauma. Inger Burnett-Zeigler states:

> Traumatic experiences among Black women are intergenerational and can date back to slavery. . . . The historical legacy of enslavement is now a part of collective trauma and cultural experience of mass suffering among Black women.[19]

Consistent with Hillary Potter's work on intimate violence against Black women, Burnett-Zeigler is saying that the legacy of racism intensifies the trauma of intimate violence.[20]

ANGER

In her writing on social inequalities, Audre Lorde says, "Anger is loaded with information and energy. . . . Its object is change."[21] Anger, as recognition of injustice, is apparently difficult for many women to express in a sexist society. There are feeling rules about this. Soraya Chemaly writes about race- and gender-based perceptions of anger: "In the United States, anger in white men is often portrayed as justifiable and patriotic, but in black men, as criminality; and in black women, as threat. In the Western world . . . anger in women has been widely associated with 'madness.'"[22]

Women's anger seemed especially hard for abusive men to bear. Some women raised their voices in anger and shouted or screamed at their partners. But this didn't make a difference in stopping the abuse. More than half of the women said their partners would not allow them to express anger. Prohibiting anger undermines the feeling that something is unjust. Women from all classes reported rules about anger:

> Whenever I would express even a level of frustration he would not allow me to get angry and would do what I call shove my anger back down my throat. If my voice got loud he would come at me physically and get in my space. He was like "You think you're gonna yell at me." He would get in my face. I always felt like I had to swallow my pride. He would do this all the time. (a white woman from a working-class community)

> I remember I was always getting so mad and I felt so out of control that I remember throwing things, breaking things. I remember throwing my phone. I remember throwing my glasses. I remember throwing anything I could find. . . . [Was he there?] No. He was never there. Because I could never do that in front of him. It was unacceptable. But if we were on the phone or something, and you know he just made me so mad I was just, I got off the phone. . . . It just all came out. (a white woman from a wealthy neighborhood)

In each of these statements, a fear of retaliation runs through the suppression of anger. Survivors had to manage their anger to appease their violent partners.

In addition to the fear of violence, women described other obstacles around their anger. For a number of women, their anger at themselves seemed to override anger at their partners:

> [Were you angry about the abuse?] Yes. [Right from the start?] Yes. And probably more at myself. Because how the hell did I get myself in this situation? You know, I consider myself an intelligent person. What the hell happened? How did I do this? (a white working-class woman)

Dana Crowley Jack explains how the suppression of women's anger leads to depression: "When women fear to express anger because they anticipate negative responses from others, they work hard to divert it, mute it, disguise it, and often learn to turn it against themselves, the safest target."[23] Beyond depression, Jack links the self-silencing of anger to a range of physical health issues including hypertension, cardiovascular disease, eating problems, and suicide.

Some survivors said that shame and guilt prevented them from feeling angry:

> [Did you feel angry about the abuse?] You know, not until way away from it. I was just ashamed, very ashamed that he would hurt me. But anger didn't come until I was clear and I had my head clear again and I wasn't being persecuted and then I was really angry. (a white working-class woman)

> [Were you angry right away when this abuse started happening?] The first time no. I thought maybe this was my fault the way I talk to him, maybe I shouldn't have said this or that. With time I saw that it was unfair, it was wrong. He would beat me. (a Black professional woman)

Sadness and depression displaced feelings of anger for some:

> [While the marriage was going on, did you feel angry about his abusiveness?] You know, not until the very end when I didn't care if he smashed me around. . . . No, I felt fear. I felt afraid. I felt controlled. I felt powerless. In hindsight [I] can't describe it as anger because I feel that if I was really angry then I would have done something. I was depressed. I internalized that anger and I was anxious. (a white woman from a wealthy community)

Friends and family members would at times challenge the women's lack of anger about the abuse. One friend of a wealthy white woman tried to evoke her anger. "How do you take this? How do you sit and take this? . . . I would feel so angry. How can you let him talk to you like that?"

Showing a relationship between surface acting and deep acting, not *expressing* anger led to difficulty in even *feeling* angry. Hochschild addresses anger and its expression: •

> Under certain social conditions, anger, insofar as it is deflected at all from its "rightful" target, tends to be deflected "down" into relative power vacuums. Thus anger is most likely to be aimed at people with less power, and least likely to be aimed at people with more power. . . . [A]nger runs in channels of least resistance. The pattern is clearest in the case of the *expression* of anger. But I think in a milder way it is there also for the very experience of anger.[24]

What this suggests is that women's anger will more likely be directed laterally toward other women or downward toward their children, and will less likely be directed toward men.

The suppression of women's anger had long-term effects. Some said they didn't really feel anger about the abuse until long after they separated. One woman who was sexually and physically assaulted by her husband said she felt mostly sadness, but not anger, until six months after leaving. Many years after her divorce, another woman who was repeatedly raped by her husband still does not feel angry, to the dismay of her friends. For another survivor, who was hospitalized for her injuries, anger didn't arise until fifteen years after the divorce.

According to Hochschild, feelings of anger are often a measure of entitlement. "I didn't have a right to be angry," one white working-class woman was told. Questions about what women should feel were raised by a white working-class survivor:

> I didn't know what I could be in trouble for or not. I didn't—basically, I felt—I—to this day, am very confused as a wife, as a girlfriend, what you are allowed to be mad at. And how you are allowed to express it.

In a sexist society, she is asking about women's rights to both raw feeling and its expression.

During the interviews, a third of the women stated that they were still angry with their ex-partners. But for many of them, now that the relationships were over, these feelings of anger had become a burden. Along with love, anger and hatred function as bonds that keep women connected to their abusers.[25] They spoke of being overwhelmed with anger and of being repeatedly upset when they talk about the abuse. They felt bound to their ex-partners by resentment and wanted to let go of it. Some sought therapy to learn how to manage these intense feelings. While anger is essential to a sense of injustice, Lorde sees anger as "an incomplete form of human knowledge." She names its limits: "Strength that is bred by anger alone is a blind force which cannot create the future. It can only demolish the past."[26] In Lorde's view, anger is a crude but essential feeling, a warning light about injustice that has to be acted upon, but a feeling that can become all-consuming.

GUILT

"In the aftermath of traumatic events," Herman writes, "as survivors review and judge their own conduct, feelings of guilt and inferiority are practically universal."[27] In cases of intimate violence, men play a key role in these feelings. Most men repeatedly blamed their partners for the violence, and this greatly affected the women. A Black professional woman explained:

> Somebody says to you, every day, the same thing, you gonna end up believing it. You buy into it. It becomes who you are. That's the scary part. You lose yourself. You completely lose yourself.

This was the feeling rule on guilt: women are always responsible for the abuse. According to the women, their partners said things like, "It was always my fault"; "You made me do this"; or "He was being forced to behave this way, because I was so inadequate." This made it hard to perceive their experiences as abusive. How does guilt undermine the sense that one was abused? A white woman from a working-class community put it this way:

> I wasn't a victim of violence. I just had a boyfriend who was angry a lot. And it was my fault because he kept telling me it was my fault. . . . I remember trying to figure out a way to change my behavior so that as it wouldn't cause

him to hit me, or rape me. . . . It was my fault that he was doing these things. He had every reason to treat me this way because I was a failure as a woman, as a girlfriend.

Most women did feel responsible. However, some resisted this rule:

There was always the "what did I do" . . . or "what did I do to set him off." . . . But I don't think I ever felt like it was actually my fault. (a white woman from a working-class community)

I always felt, "Something's wrong with him." . . . I never gave in[to] my thinking to some of the stuff that he was saying to me, trying to convince me I was wrong in this way or that way. So I would say anger saved me. (a white woman from a wealthy neighborhood)

For the second woman, righteous anger prevented feelings of guilt. For most women, however, the guilt seemed to prevent feelings of anger and the sense that what they were experiencing was unjust.

One white working-class woman saw guilt as a useful feeling, as something that could help her avoid violence:

If he was like verbally abusive, it was just like oh, you know, I deserved that. Um, you know, or that happened because I was behaving this way. . . . Like you want to almost feel guilty about it, and think that it was something you did wrong, because then you think, oh, then I can prevent it in the future.

However, women's efforts to prevent abuse by changing their own behavior were largely unsuccessful.

Beyond their partners, many other people created guilt feelings in the women. Family members were often unresponsive to the abuse. Women's mothers were at times a source of blame:

My mom said "It's your fault, I told you about him." . . . "You should have listened to me." (a white woman from a poor neighborhood)

Women were also blamed by other family members and by friends. They would remind women of the rules about love and men's authority:

[His friends] were for the behavior. . . . Sometimes they would say, "Oh you know you need to do something about her. She has a big mouth," things like that. . . . They were doing the same thing [to their partners] also. (a Black survivor from a poor neighborhood)

A lot of people see it too as my choice. I made the mistake. I married him. The blame—"You made a decision to marry him, so you deal with the consequences." (a wealthy white woman)

Long after leaving their abusive partners, a quarter of the women still wrestled with feelings of guilt. Nine years after her divorce, a white wealthy woman told me, "I wake up every day and still think, what could I have done differently to save that marriage?" Many felt guilty for exposing their children to the abuse. Some felt bad that they no longer had an intact family. Others regretted not leaving the relationships sooner. This guilt revealed they had not yet found peace with decisions they had made under the tyranny of their violent partners.

SHAME

Like guilt, shame is a powerful form of social control. Shame is best understood as a feeling distinct from guilt. Whereas guilt concerns a specific action, something one did or could have done, shame is a global feeling; it is a negative evaluation of the whole self.[28] Shame was an overwhelming feeling for many women. This is a highly gendered emotion, according to Melissa Harris-Perry: "Our internal moral guide may lead us to feel guilt, but shame comes when we fear exposure and evaluation by others. This may be especially true for girls and women, who draw a larger sense of self-identity from their friendly, familial, and romantic relationships."[29] Harris-Perry argues that shame is caused by stigmas that are imposed on groups of people, which reduce members of these groups to debased characteristics, like the examples of failed femininity discussed previously. "Shame is the psychological and physical effect of repeated acts of misrecognition," she argues.[30] Harris-Perry extends this understanding of shame to racism: "Though we seldom think of it this way, racism is the act of shaming others based on their identity. Blackness in America is marked by shame. . . . Shame makes us view our very selves as malignant. But societies also define entire groups as malignant. Historically the United States has done that with African Americans."[31]

Most women felt shame about being abused. The things women said about themselves were almost as harsh as the things their partners had called them. They felt "worthless," "hopeless," and "defective." They felt like a "reject," like a "loser," like a "failure." They were "ugly," "stupid," and "dumb." Some said they felt that they "deserved" the abuse. As in the case of guilt, shame represents the internalization of the abusers' views of the women. Viveka Enander and Carin Holmberg see this as its own kind of bond. Like love, anger, hatred, and fear, it ties women to their offenders.[32]

Harris-Perry notes that there is a physical dimension to shame; it is reflected in how we carry ourselves in public. This was observed in the accounts of survivors. One Black survivor from a poor neighborhood believed that her shame was actually visible:

> [How about shame? . . . Did you struggle with that?] I did struggle with that and even after the relationship I struggled with that. I thought wherever I was going, people would have seen it in me.

A white working-class survivor kept her head down, even when meeting people:

> I couldn't even look people in the eye when introductions were made. I would be head down and shaking hands. My dad would say, . . . "Lift your head up. It's okay, be proud of yourself." I just couldn't look people in the eye. At that point [my partner] had made very sure that I was aware that I was less than dirt. It took a long time for me to get any kind of sense of "I'm worthy."

Years after leaving her violent husband, a white wealthy woman was still ashamed about the abuse:

> I am grateful that I had the courage to finally leave, but I don't feel like a hero or anything. I stayed way too long and that's really embarrassing. Yeah, I survived abuse. I don't hold my head up high every day.

It was heartbreaking to witness this shame. These feelings were very much alive during the interviews. Nearly a third of the women reported that their struggles with shame were ongoing.

Many survivors called themselves "stupid" for remaining with their partners as long as they did. Their abusive partners used this word frequently against the women. According to Viveka Enander, allegations that women lack intelligence have such a long tradition in Western countries that this is best seen as a form of gendered shame. In the context of women's abusive relationships with men, Enander goes a step further and calls this "battered shame," a way that women are reminded of their inferior status in relation to men.[33] The abuse and degradation, in her view, directly produce these feelings. This kind of shame damages women's identities, as a white woman who was a sales clerk reports:

> He undermined my self-image so badly that I thought I was the scum of the earth, you know? I kind of dressed like that and acted like that. Apologized to everyone. . . . He really made me feel ashamed at who I was. . . . He made me feel stupid.

For some women, their family members evoked feelings of shame. One white working-class woman was verbally abused by her mother:

> She didn't agree with the divorce. She called me to her house and harangued me . . . and told me I was a morally bankrupt, disgusting and abhorrent person in society and [my ex-husband]'s so awesome. I should give him more sex and do all the work around the house myself.

These feelings changed over time for most of the women. The role of women's groups, organized by domestic violence programs, was pivotal in challenging this debilitating guilt and shame. "I didn't have to feel ashamed. That's what I got out of that. I didn't feel ashamed anymore," one white woman reflected. She lived in a professional suburb. "I said, that shame belongs to him, not to me. I'm not the one who's responsible for this horrible behavior, he is. He needs to feel the shame. That's what I got from the women's groups." Talking about their relationships with friends, sympathetic family members, and therapists was also helpful. Nearly half of the women in every class category sought help from domestic abuse programs. Unfortunately, in most cases this took place only after separation.

GUILT, SHAME, AND DISCLOSURE

Most women hid the abuse from their friends and family members; some didn't tell anyone about this until after they ended the relationships. There were many reasons for this. As has been previously shown, most women were isolated during their relationships, and in most cases this was a form of coercive control imposed upon them by their abusive partners. Some men threated to harm the women if they spoke to anyone about the violence and abuse.

Some survivors didn't immediately recognize their treatment as abuse; confusion about this was another reason for hiding it. Others saw it as abuse but were not yet prepared to act on this, causing them to remain silent. A few women feared they would not be believed; this came true for some who told their families and friends. In some cases, women feared that if they told family members, their relatives would attack or even kill their abusive partners. One woman from a poor community worried that if she told anyone she could lose her children to child protective authorities.

Guilt and shame played a central role in this self-silencing. Hiding the abuse was a type of emotion work, a way to prevent even worse feelings of guilt and embarrassment than women already felt. As a form of emotion work, however, this didn't really change these feelings. Instead, hiding the abuse served to disconnect women from their family and friends and keep them from seeking help.

CLASS STIGMAS, CLASS SHAME

"While we normally think of class relations as taking place between classes," Sherry Ortner argues, "in fact each class contains the other(s) within itself, though in distorted and ambivalent forms."[34] The "class myth" raised in chapter 1 represents this kind of distortion. This idea that only poor and working-class women are vulnerable to abuse turns on stigmas about class and race. Contempt for poor and working-class people is combined with racialized fears in this myth. This is about much more than just ignorance. In my opinion, one reason the class myth survives, despite decades of efforts to debunk it, is that it serves to mark and deepen both class and racial divisions.

In every class category, women sought to avoid the shame associated with abuse, poverty, and poor communities of color. In their efforts to escape this shame, the women revealed the emotional power of these stigmas. A white woman from a wealthy community who was physically and sexually abused described how her images of abuse did not match what she was going through:

> I'd never really read about the signs or knew the definition of domestic abuse because I always thought you had to be beaten up and have broken bones, be married to someone who's not educated. I really bought into the whole profile.

She did not name what happened to her as abuse until she attended a public meeting on intimate violence. Class privilege made it difficult to see what she was experiencing as abuse. The myth about class and intimate violence causes shame by association; if a woman is abused, this shame becomes attached to her regardless of her social standing.

A Black survivor from a professional household tried to avoid the stigma of the poor single mother of color. This trapped her in a physically and sexually abusive marriage:

> I told [a girlfriend] about the abuse I was going through. . . . You think these things happen to poor people so I told her. . . . I was kind of like blackmailed into staying. . . . Nobody wants to be called a divorcee or single mom. It all has connotations with society.

For economically privileged women, there are two aspects of shame operating here. One is a sense of being personally identified with problems that, supposedly, only poor people experience. In a racist society that demonstrates contempt for the poor, this is a powerful stigma. The other aspect is a fear of being rejected by the upper classes. A white woman from a wealthy community spoke of the how people responded when the abuse became known:

> I think a couple of people got angry because they thought we were . . . so perfect. . . . I think people were angry that we had misled them in a sense . . . and I think they felt betrayed.

Some standard about the proper behavior of the white upper class was apparently violated.

Survivors from working-class communities also felt shame by association with the class myth. They were less likely to feel rejection by upper-class friends and neighbors if they never had economic privilege. But they still sought to distance themselves from the stigma of poverty that is part of the class myth:

> I felt trapped because I didn't know that this happened to so many other women. I thought I was the only one, because it certainly didn't happen to people like me. It didn't happen to smart people, it didn't happen to people who—you know this was supposed to only happen to uneducated, poor, welfare women of color, [who] didn't speak English. . . . That's who this happened to. In my ignorance, that shame, my own shame . . . kept me trapped. (a white woman from a working-class community)

This woman's description of shame emphasizes the status of being educated; this was one way of distancing herself from the class myth. She is speaking self-critically about her belief in this stereotype. After leaving her abusive partner, she worked as an advocate for women who were abused.

And what about survivors who were impoverished, and who had to constantly face the humiliating images heaped upon them? The pain and anger this white woman from a poor community feels is evident in her remarks:

> It's not like I just went out and got pregnant for welfare or by choice or whatever. I'm a single mother because of domestic violence and that is extremely stigmatizing and that is shameful. People automatically assume, she's a single mom because she wants to get resources, but they don't consider the domestic violence.

At every class level, then, the power of the class myth can be seen. This myth affects women's ability to recognize their experiences as abusive. The dividing lines of class and race are marked by strong feelings.[35] Andrew Sayer writes, "Condescension, deference, shame, guilt, envy, resentment, arrogance, contempt, fear and mistrust . . . typify relations between people of different classes."[36] Such feelings both reflect and reproduce class and racial hierarchies.

SUMMARY

Emotions are often believed to be personal and unique aspects of the self. And yet there are fingerprints from many people on the feelings reported by the women. Hochschild's theory illuminates the activity of survivors, abusers, family members, and friends in the shaping of emotions. These emotional dynamics played an important role in women's sense of entrapment. In their own ways, love, hatred, fear, anger, guilt, and shame all bound women to their abusers.

Many women felt obligated to follow rules about love that they now reject—in hindsight, the rules seem unfair, unreciprocal, and damaging to their safety and well-being. In response to the violence, survivors did both conscious and unconscious emotion work to manage their fears. The suppression of women's anger by their partners prevented many survivors from expressing and even feeling anger about the abuse, something that is important to a perception of injustice. Some emotion work by survivors involved managing their partners' anger. Feelings of guilt and shame, which were created by men's psychological abuse, caused women to hide the violence. This ended up making women isolated, depressed, and unwilling to seek help. Following the insights of Enander and Holmberg, guilt and shame represent internalization, a way that women view men's motives and their own culpability through men's eyes. This is another important bond that requires disentanglement in order for healing to occur. But as I have shown, many people other than the perpetrators contributed to these damaging feelings of guilt and shame.

Stigmas of poverty and racism, along with stigmas about divorce, contributed to women's sense of entrapment. For wealthy, professional, and even working-class women, the association of violence with poor people and communities of color made it difficult to define their own experiences as abusive.

The emotion work of community activists, advocates, support groups, and counselors helped many women recover from the abuse and experience the full range of their feelings. This kind of emotion work seeks to validate women's fears and challenge patriarchal rules about love, hatred, anger, guilt, and shame. In this work, women are told they are entitled to anger, that they should not blame themselves for men's violence, and that no one deserves abuse.

Both gender and class inequalities operate, in part, through feeling; resistance to these inequalities requires attention to the rules that govern feeling. In her work on women and shame, Brené Brown argues: "Shame works only if we think we're alone in it. If we think there's someone else, a group of women, a city full of women, a country full of women, a world full of women, struggling with the same issue, the concept of shame becomes bankrupt."[37]

CHAPTER 8

Separation, Healing, and Justice

A complex traumatic bond binds an abused woman to her abuser. . . . We suggest that leaving entails three different, albeit overlapping processes: *Breaking Up* covers action, *Becoming Free* covers emotion, and *Understanding* covers cognition.

—Viveka Enander and Carin Holmberg

In their research with women in Sweden, Viveka Enander and Carin Holmberg found that leaving an abusive relationship takes place through three stages. "Breaking up" is the action of leaving and the turning points that are related to this. "Becoming free" is the emotional disengagement from the relationship. "Understanding" is the cognitive process of recognizing one's experience as abusive.[1] Each has different timelines. In particular, the burden of emotional bonds may last indefinitely. These three stages are used here to guide an examination of women's testimony on separation and healing. The last section explores the women's reflections on what justice would look like, given their experiences.

SEPARATION

Turning Points

Across the classes, there were several consistent turning points in women's movement toward separation. The first was a marked increase in physical and sexual violence. The second was fear for the well-being of others, especially their children. This is consistent with Enander and Holmberg's research.[2] In addition, survivors took action following other forms of abuse beyond violence.

For most of the women in poor communities, the turning points and endings of the relationships were identical; extreme violence caused women to separate. Four of the nine women were severely beaten. Police were called in several cases, which put abusers behind bars and enabled women to leave. One white woman was repeatedly punched and dragged by her hair. Frightened by this escalation in the violence, she managed to escape and have a neighbor call the police. He was arrested. An African American woman was stabbed and injured so badly that she was hospitalized for weeks. It took a long time to recover from her injuries. Her partner was convicted and served time.

Sexual violence was also a turning point, which was also seen in women from other classes. One African American woman was raped by her partner at gunpoint; she left town shortly afterward and never returned.

Most women in poor households were not taking care of children. But some did have turning points around this. A Black woman said, "We had a baby and I just didn't like the way things was going. There was just too much drugs involved and it just wasn't working. . . . I decided for us to break up."

An increase in violence and a concern for family members also appeared in the stories of working-class women. Many described how physical violence caused them to leave. For one white woman, it was a violent attack that took place at a party with close friends. For an African American survivor, "the black eyes and the bruises" caused a turning point. Others spoke of threats with guns and other weapons. Six of the twenty-six working-class women said that rape or attempted rape marked the end of the relationship.

Some women from working-class communities said the children were affected by the abuse they were witnessing. This altered those women's actions. A white working-class woman was clear about protecting her child:

> I mean it was one thing to abuse me, it was another to abuse my kid. You know, so that's kind of, I guess, where my invisible line was.

Other survivors thought about leaving when they were abused while pregnant, or when their children were abused.

Some women named turning points in relation to economic and psychological abuse. One white working-class man prevented his partner from going to work. She lost her job due to his interference. She left following this loss. Another woman became aware of how awful she felt about herself and decided her partner's relentless degradation was the cause.

An increase in violence was a turning point for most of the professional women. In some cases, the exposure of the violence to others shifted their thinking. A white woman explained:

> He grabbed me, shook me and screamed at me. It was that day, that moment that I said to myself, "You have to get out, you have to leave." I just didn't know when or how but I knew that I'd have to leave. My [child] did witness that event as well.

One white professional man choked his partner and almost killed her. He was arrested and convicted. Another white man beat and stabbed his partner; someone called the police and he was also prosecuted and incarcerated.

Sexual violence created a turning point for some professional women. Threats and physical abuse affected others. For one woman, it was the verbal degradation of her child that made a difference.

Women in wealthy communities reported the same pattern. For half of the women, the physical violence became worse and more frequent, causing them to end their relationships. A white woman spoke of the change in her thinking. Her husband was hitting her in the head:

> It was just getting worse and worse and worse . . . I said, "Is that blood?" So I looked at it. . . . And I said, "I can't do this anymore."

Like women in the other classes, wealthy women were hit, kicked, and threatened with weapons.

Some wealthy women were also worried about cruelty or indifference to their children. However, there was another pattern. The acknowledgment of men's affairs was a turning point for several women. Two survivors explained this:

> Well, there was so much that was abusive, but the big thing that jumps out in my mind. . . . He was telling me more and more stuff that was really crazy-making. . . . He kept telling me that he was not having a sexual affair with this woman. . . . What I discovered is that our entire marriage was a lie. I mean, he was having affairs from day one. . . . But at the end, he couldn't sustain the lie any more. (a white wealthy woman)

> My ticket out was [him] having an affair. . . . Oh my God. . . . I remember waking up in the middle of the night one night saying, "I don't have to do this anymore." . . . The next day I said you know, . . . "You gotta leave." (a white survivor from a wealthy neighborhood)

For these women the violation of their love was unbearable. Perhaps to their family and friends, affairs are also easier to understand than the larger pattern of abuse. When the affairs were exposed, the men were blamed for the end of the marriages, freeing the women from the shame and self-blame that had trapped them.

The Difficulties of Separating

If leaving is seen as a set of separate processes, this helps explain why it is so difficult. According to Enander and Holmberg, "breaking up" and emotionally "becoming free" are different stages. It is one thing to leave, and another thing to completely sever the bonds represented by love and for many, children and marriage. One woman from a poor neighborhood left three times before the final breakup. A working-class woman left and got back together at least ten times. One professional woman went through several separations and reunifications with her husband. A wealthy woman broke up many times with her partner.

A white working-class woman spoke of her mixed feelings following a violent assault:

> [After he was arrested and prosecuted, and you moved, were there things that were difficult about that separation for you?] . . . I missed him. I loved him. I visited him in jail. And then I took him back. And we broke up again, thank God. [And why did you break up the last time?] Because I guess I got a little bit of strength in me, and I had had enough. (a white woman from a working-class neighborhood)

She had previously left this man, but he found her and made her return.

A wealthy white woman revealed her own conflicting feelings about her violent husband:

> By the end I couldn't stand the sight of him. But at the same time, if he had changed, I could have like fallen back in love really fast. You know, I mean, because you—he was like . . . so different, that it was hard to believe that it was the same person. And it was horrible to feel that way. . . . I hated the fact that he turned me into that. . . . You don't want to feel hatred for somebody. (a white woman from a wealthy neighborhood)

Ambivalence reveals the power of these emotional bonds. But it is more than that. When women leave repeatedly, they are also learning about their options and often preparing for a future separation. They are testing the limits of the emotional bonds holding them in the relationships.[3]

The "breaking free" stage starts when these bonds begin to lose their hold on the women. Enander and Holmberg argue that bonds of love are the first to break. But as they see it, there are other bonds. After love weakens, "the other emotional ties still remain: hate, compassion, fear, guilt, and hope."[4] Ties around children complicate leaving:

> The girls . . . they still want their daddy. And they—they want the nuclear family, they want the picket fence. . . . They wanted that fairy tale that Disney sells. . . . The unattainable ideal. So it's really hard on them. When you have a baby, you want to give everything to them, you want to do everything right. You get brand new furniture, you want everything clean and pressed. You want it to be like that their whole life. And I tried everything. I tried dancing those steps to give them that fairy tale. I just couldn't keep it up any longer. (a white woman from a working-class neighborhood)

A Black professional woman describes her own mixed feelings about leaving:

> It was really hard for me. Really, really hard. . . . One part of me wanted this, but one part of me was also upset, because I'm like, you know what, I wasn't ready. I was ready, but I wasn't. . . . It's really one of those weird struggles that you have within yourself. . . . I kept going back and forth, back and forth.

Support from family members was critical in her ability to leave her violent partner, who was the father of her child.

Rather than leaving, some women were left by their abusive partners. One man left a Hispanic working-class survivor for someone else:

> I was mad. I was like, "How dare you leave me after everything you've done to me. I've been trying to get you out my life forever and you're leaving me." I was mad, I was devastated. I was hurt. . . . It was [the] worst thing that ever happened to me. It was like I was robbed of my life, the time that I wasted with him, all the years that I wasted with him . . . and he's gonna leave me? It was hell, but it was the best thing he could have done.

Even under these circumstances, her emotional involvement created deeply ambivalent feelings.

Economic Strain

As discussed in the chapter on economic abuse, the economic strain from leaving was overwhelming for most women. Only a third of the women had full-time jobs outside the home while in their relationships. Many left their jobs in order to escape the abuse. They were terrified of what the men would do next.

A Black woman from a poor neighborhood talked of her circumstances following extreme sexual violence:

I left my house, my car, everything. I left everything where it was. I came out here, stayed with [a relative] for a few months and then I checked into a shelter. . . . Now I'm in transitional housing trying to get my permanent housing. This was about two years ago at this point.

Economically privileged women had their own financial struggles. A white professional woman said, "I knew I was gonna lose. I had to look at my life like there was a fire and I lost everything. Because things, possessions, were not—I wasn't gonna get them." She knew she was heading into an abusive divorce process that would last for years.

Some survivors took their children and moved back in with their parents. Others became homeless and lived with friends. Some applied for food stamps and sought help from local charities. A white working-class woman talked about what it felt like to do this:

At the start I signed up for food stamps. We have a free store . . . people donate things, you go once a week. So I spent . . . three hours waiting to go in. . . . So that was humiliating.

Only a few women sought help from welfare offices. While those that were able to obtain economic support appreciated it, they were well aware of the negative images people have of welfare recipients. One white working-class woman met resistance because she apparently didn't match the cultural stereotype:

I went down to welfare, and it was just like, "You don't need to apply for our services." Because I had nice clothes on. And ah I was like, "Um, yeah, I do. I have a restraining order." "So?" And this woman gave me such a hard time.

The transformation of welfare described in chapter 3 led to many being denied economic assistance, including many women escaping abuse. The 1996 law that replaced welfare with Temporary Assistance for Needy Families (TANF) was passed with an amendment called the Family Violence Option. Recognizing that many women use welfare to escape violence, this option was designed to allow waivers regarding the strict new rules on lifetime limitations of receiving assistance, on mandatory work requirements, and on reporting who the abusive parent is. This last point is something that alone can effectively exclude women who are abused and are thus afraid of their abusive partners.[5] However, as TANF allowed each state to apply the 1996 law in its own fashion, the Family Violence Option has not even been offered in all states.[6] There are further different rules from state to state on which TANF rules the option affects. What's more, research shows that few individuals are screened for intimate violence and informed about this option. As a result, the number of people using the Family Violence Option is astonishingly low.[7] If the goal was to meet the economic needs of survivors of intimate violence, the Family Violence Option must be seen as a massive institutional failure.

More of the women sought disability assistance from Social Security than assistance from TANF. Eight of the sixty women were able to receive disability benefits. These were white and Black women from poor and working-class communities. They suffered with PTSD, physical injuries from their abusive partners, cancer, other chronic diseases, and mental health challenges. Susan Sered and Maureen Norton-Hawk observe that after the availability of welfare benefits declined, the number of people receiving disability benefits increased, making this "the de facto safety net" for Americans who are unable to work.[8] However, the amount women received in their disability checks was well below the poverty line for individuals set by the federal government, leaving these women in a long-term state of impoverishment.

This ongoing poverty was evident in the circumstances of two white women. One was attacked by her partner with a knife and suffered damage to her internal organs. She has PTSD from the violence. She was in a poor neighborhood when she was involved with her partner. Ten years after the relationship ended, she was on disability and living in a homeless shelter. Another white woman, who had a job in nursing while in her relationship, was hospitalized for the injuries she suffered. She still has flashbacks from the violence. She stated that the low self-esteem caused by the abuse continues to the present day. Nineteen years after leaving her abusive partner, she is on disability and is also staying in a homeless shelter. A total of six women, all of whom were white, were homeless at the time I met them. Two had lived in professional communities before they left their violent partners. Half of these women received disability benefits.

Depression

It is common for women to become depressed *after* leaving abusive partners. Research indicates that the more severe the violence, the higher the level of emotional and economic losses, and the fewer the coping resources, the more likely it is that women will feel depressed after separation. Previous childhood and adult victimization, along with economic difficulties, also influence this part of the leaving process.[9]

One study found that mothers experiencing intimate violence reported increasing rates of depression over time, regardless of whether the relationships ended.[10] In other words, leaving abusive partners does not solve all problems, and for mothers especially, it creates new issues around economic strain and childcare responsibilities.

An African American working-class woman detailed her feelings of loss:

> [You said that you went through a period of real depression. And that was after you left, right?] Yes. . . . [How long did that period last? That you felt depressed?] . . . I think that was probably about a month and a half, where you know, I was kind of reclusive. Then it probably took me another year or so before kind of the dark cloud went away. . . . He was my best friend for that period of time. . . . So, you know, to have lost that, that was definitely hard. To know I couldn't go back, that was hard. And then I didn't really have anyone to talk to, to really sort through my feelings at the time. So that was even harder.

The suppression of emotion during the relationship could also lead to overwhelming feelings afterward. One wealthy white woman reflected on this:

> It was massive depression. . . . I was starting to feel all this stuff, really, all the pain, all the fear, all the stuff I couldn't feel before, because I was just— I couldn't do it. And I—and I understand now that's true for a lot of people. While they're in it, they can't process it, they can't feel it, they can't afford to. And then when they get out, it all comes flooding at you. Because it doesn't go away. You gotta process it eventually. And it was so bad, so they put me on medication.

Some survivors remained depressed for a long time after leaving. One white working-class woman attempted suicide several years after separating from her husband. A number of women were on antidepressants at the time of the interview.

A Sense of Freedom

Amid all this strain and loss, it is important to observe that many survivors found a sense of peace after separation:

> It was relief, it was a real relief off my shoulders. It was a real relief. And then he moved on. He found—moved on with somebody else. (a Black survivor from a poor neighborhood)

> While I was married to him I will tell you I didn't sleep one night in ten years, through the night. He would always have me up until like 2 or 3 in the

morning talking about the way I act, and for the first time I was able to sleep after a couple of years and have a nice sound sleep. (a Hispanic survivor from a working-class community)

You know what, when he left I was just relieved. I was so tired of dealing with it that I was just glad he was gone. It was like having a 250-pound toddler in the house. (a white professional woman)

When I left the relationship I can't tell you how free I felt. . . . The feeling was inexplicable. I felt like I was walking on air. It was just—there was a sense of freedom of being able to breathe . . . even though I was scared. . . . I still felt this sense of relief and freedom; it was just wonderful. (a white woman from a wealthy community)

Even under the tremendous strain caused by separation, women from all classes found some degree of freedom and safety by leaving.

The Responses of Family and Friends

Most women hid the abuse when they were in the relationships. When they finally did disclose the abuse, the first people they told were generally family members and friends. In terms of whether people were supportive or unsupportive, it was more or less evenly split at every class level. It is important to examine how people responded in order to understand women's sense of entrapment.

The women from poor neighborhoods described parents who were supportive, who would visit them in the hospital, and who would talk to and even confront their abusers. Some parents encouraged women to leave their partners. One aunt read the situation clearly and helped her niece escape a violent relationship. But survivors also reported disappointment in how family members responded, especially their mothers. Poverty seemed to weaken the bonds in women's families of origin. The father of one white woman, who may have been alcoholic, died when she was young; her mother struggled with mental illness. Her mother blamed her for being abused. An African American woman was abandoned by her mother: "She gave me up at three . . . she was really heavy into drugs and prostitution and things like that." One white woman had a mother who was in a controlling relationship herself. She couldn't really offer any help. She had a boyfriend who wouldn't let her daughter live with them. Histories of family abuse weighed upon the lives of many survivors.

In some families from poor communities, there was open support for violence against women. An African American woman said her mother, who had been physically abusive to her, had given her previous husband explicit permission to beat her. Another Black survivor said that her partner's mother knew about the violence and "just let it happen. She should be locked up too."

Due to isolation by their partners, many women in poor neighborhoods said they had no real friends. Some women withdrew from friends and family because of their own drug use or their depression, something that was found at every class level. Those who did have friends reported that they were supportive after the relationships were over.

Working-class women indicated that many family members responded well once they knew about the abuse. Some actively sought to stop the violence. One woman's father would call regularly and check in to see if she was okay. He would argue with her abuser on the phone. The father of one abusive man physically intervened to stop his son from choking his wife. Another abusive man was threatened by his partner's sister, a move that appeared to be effective.

Half the women from working-class communities felt unsupported by their families. Some parents refused to let the women stay with them. Some parents didn't believe the accounts of violence and abuse. The husband of a white working-class woman physically abused her and threatened her with a gun. Her mother did not support her, but instead blamed her. One African American survivor from a working-class neighborhood described her mother's response:

> My mom, she kind of took his side when it was all over. I told her about him wanting to set me on fire. And she was like, "I mean he's not really going to do that. He's just upset that you want to leave. I think you should give him another chance for the kid's sake."

Like the women from poor neighborhoods, some working-class women didn't have friends. For those who did, their friends were generally helpful when they were told about the abuse. Like family members, however, some friends didn't believe the women. There were friends who urged women to forgive their partners and return to them.

The professional women gave similar accounts of the responses of family and friends. Brothers and sisters were particularly concerned for their safety:

> My mom was aware. . . . She knew and most of my younger siblings knew. They always wanted me to leave the relationship but I was always hoping the guy would change. (an African American professional woman)

Siblings took women to the hospital and assisted them when they left their relationships.

Professional women's relatives were as likely to be unsupportive as supportive. One white woman said her parents witnessed a violent attack by her husband that knocked her to the ground; they didn't say or do anything. After another white woman left her husband, she was told, "I cannot believe that a daughter of mine would do such a cruel thing."

In contrast, the friends of the professional women were overall concerned and helpful.

Wealthy women shared the same pattern of mixed responses by friends and family to the abuse. In some cases, the interventions of family members were essential supports in the process of leaving. A wealthy white woman explained:

> [My parents] were helping me try to figure out ways to get out of it. . . . When it got really, really scary, and they would say, "What are you gonna do?" And, "Do you want us to come up?" . . . They were just there, and supportive, and, you know, they'd never get angry and mad and say, "If you don't get out, you're gonna die!"

But not all parents were so helpful. A woman who was with a wealthy man felt that her parents were basically intimidated and bought off by gifts they received from him. They appeared to defend him and were unresponsive to her needs.

Friends were overall more supportive. One white wealthy woman described how neighbors took her for coffee regularly and supported her after she moved out. But some judged the women and withdrew their friendships:

> A couple of people were really mad. They couldn't—they just didn't understand like why I didn't get out . . . why I couldn't leave. They were really angry and frustrated, and just. . . . "Well, just leave." . . . . They just couldn't get it, and got mad, and frustrated, and just walked away. (a white woman from a wealthy neighborhood)

One white survivor viewed people's responses to her story as voyeuristic:

> I thought I could talk to the right people and it would bring about a change but what I discovered was I was talking to this passive, enabling, observer audience. People who called themselves friends, policemen, judges, professionals . . . nobody felt any responsibility to confront the cause; they just wanted to hear the story.

The material and emotional support from friends and family was critical in helping women to leave. It is important to see that the lack of support was also pivotal; being abandoned, shamed, and blamed caused some women to stay with or return to violent partners.

Interventions by the Criminal Legal System

No institution was called upon by women more often than the criminal legal system. Two-thirds of survivors either called the police or had them called by friends, relatives, or neighbors. This included most women at every class level, although poor and working-class women were more likely to call. Some women called the police a number of times. In many cases, the police did just what women wanted them to do. Survivors wanted support and recognition of the danger they were in; they wanted the police to remove their violent partners from the household; they wanted help getting their belongings so that they could safely leave; and they wanted to interrupt the rule, imposed by their partners, that it is women's fate to tolerate men's abuse. As has been shown, some of the police interventions became turning points and marked the end of relationships.

One white working-class woman described the support she received from a police officer after her partner sexually assaulted her:

> [My friends] ended up calling the cops for me and the cops came and found me on the road. I was walking towards the hospital and the cops brought me to the hospital for the rape kit. . . . He said "I'm going to bring you to the hospital." He made sure he didn't do anything upsetting because he knew I was terrified. He brought me to the hospital and he sat with me while waiting for the doctor to come in. He was a very, very nice gentleman. Once the doctor came in to start examining he stepped out in the hallway. He stayed there for moral support so that was a really good experience.

In some cases, the police saved women's lives. One Black professional woman said that she was stabbed with a sharp object by her partner and gravely injured. A neighbor called the police, but at first they couldn't find the address. One of the officers apparently found her by following the trail of blood. They got her to the hospital; she could have died.

The police arrested twenty of the abusive men for crimes against the women. Eighteen men were charged; seven were convicted. However, when women were asked whether calling the police reduced the abuse, most women said it didn't help. Despite answering the calls, going to women's homes, and arresting the men, in most cases the efforts of the police didn't seem to matter. One abusive man boasted that the police wouldn't do anything to him.

Sometimes the police were not just ineffective but openly patriarchal in their responses to women. Some officers expressed frustration and hostility. A Black woman from a poor neighborhood was badly beaten by her partner, and a relative called the police:

> The police came and I was still afraid so I denied what happened. . . . [So the police came. Did they see your face was swelled?] Yeah they did. And I denied. They said, "Well next time when he kills you don't call us."

Women reported that some police officers bonded with their abusive partners against them. One white working-class husband had friends at the police department. The officers there tried to prevent his wife from filing criminal charges:

> I went to the police department because I was going to press charges and get a restraining order. The police officer just finished taking pictures of all my injuries and said to me, "Are you sure you want to press charges against [him]? He's such a nice guy."

Many police officers refused to take women's reports seriously. A Black professional woman reported her difficulty with the police. Her husband had a prominent position in the community:

> The criminal justice system is not fair. Even when I went to the police they did nothing. They couldn't even put him behind bars for one day. . . . It's a man's world in domestic violence. . . . They were like you are the woman and so I should try and make it work. Whatever I'm doing that's making him do this to me I should stop.

These officers empathized with her violent husband.

Some officers laughed at or made fun of women seeking help. One police officer advised that an abusive man should contact the police first and accuse his partner of being abusive. Pretending to be the victim would then sabotage his partner if she called the police. One Black woman said the police roughed up her partner, shoving and hitting him. He was a Black man. These kinds of actions cause women to see the police as unpredictable and dangerous themselves, as both sexist and racist.

Nearly half of the women obtained restraining or protection orders against their partners. Many had good experiences seeking these orders from the courts, especially when advocates were present to assist them and explain the legal process. Some women were denied orders, as they were unable to convince judges of the abusiveness of their partners.

When asked if the restraining orders actually reduced the abuse, most women who obtained them said they didn't.

There were other ways that women sought help through the courts. Several women sought charges, unsuccessfully, for child sexual abuse. There were fights in family court over child custody, child support, and visitation issues, some lasting many years. Many women expressed great anger and bitterness over these battles with the law, which cost them so much time, money, and energy.

Some men, especially white, married, economically privileged men, used the courts as a way to continue abusing women after the relationships were over. With their economic power, they attempted to take custody of the children, rework child support settlements, and turn children against their mothers. Among advocates, this is called "domestic abuse by proxy," meaning that disputes over children become a means to continue the pattern of abuse. One advocate shared what she learned from working with economically privileged women:

> I cannot stress enough how realistic women's assessments are . . . when they think that leaving will cause them to 1) experience deep financial hardship and 2) possibly lose their children, in whole or in part, in a custody fight or through psychological manipulation of the children. . . . We routinely tell women that they will be trading every asset they have for a greater measure of some alternative kinds of safety. . . . Abusive ex-partners also drag survivors back into court once every six months to contest . . . well, anything they can think of. Sometimes it is an effort to bankrupt the survivor. . . . Sometimes it is just to continue to psychologically torture the survivor.

With the ability to hire attorneys, professional and wealthy white men had yet another weapon to use against their partners.

The Helping Professions

The responses of domestic abuse programs, counselors, doctors, and religious leaders were important in the leaving process. Almost half of the survivors contacted domestic violence programs. Women from all classes found them to be extremely helpful. Shelters were mostly used by poor and working-class women. A Black woman from a poor neighborhood talked of how important it was to find a shelter:

> I would advise anyone who is going through it . . . to go to [a] place, to a shelter, to transitional housing where you have all those resources available to you. And they're to guide you and not to judge you. . . . I'm a mother and I should have an emergency plan. . . . They showed me ways to have a plan

or where to keep all personal things in case anything like this happens again, in case I need to get up and leave the household in an emergency situation and things like that. So I feel more control and more empowered.

A white woman from a working-class community questioned whether she had been abused enough to qualify for services at a domestic abuse agency:

> I never thought that [the abuse program] was for me. Because I thought that was for the women who had a black eye, broken bones—and I never saw myself as being abused until after I am talking with my friend who is in [the program] . . . and she goes, you know, "that's abuse. What he did was abuse."

Domestic violence programs helped women leave and helped them disentangle the bonds that tied them to their abusers, especially guilt and shame. They also helped with understanding the context of the abuse that would afford more self-forgiveness about their experiences. A Hispanic working-class woman shared her observations:

> I joined [the abuse program] after my divorce because I told you I still have a lot of issues. Going there, I don't know, they just had this motherly feeling when you go in there. They're just such good people. . . . They gave me a mentor who was incredible. They brought us into this group of other battered women and we all just like let loose, and we'd just talk. I'm just like, wow, I thought I was in this by myself and I wasn't. . . . After you leave that man your life just changes dramatically.

Many women sought therapy or counseling during the relationships. This was common for survivors from all classes, except those from poor neighborhoods. Most women felt their individual work with therapists was beneficial. Much therapy took place after separation; some men refused to allow their partners to seek therapy. While not all of the therapists understood the dynamics of intimate violence, women said they felt supported, were told about resources available to them, and improved their overall feelings of self-esteem. However, some therapists minimized the abuse and blamed the women for the problems in the relationship. In a session with church-based counselors, one white working-class woman spoke of being beaten and raped by her husband. This is what she was told:

> I needed to submit myself to God and become a better wife. . . . The last session that I went to [I was told] that I needed to write a list of all the sins I had committed against [my husband] and I needed to go back to ask for forgiveness.

This is more evidence of patriarchy within religious organizations. Such a response makes women the cause of all the problems in a relationship, including their own victimization.

Some tried couples counseling with their abusive partners, something that is not recommended by advocates or by therapists who work with survivors. Sara Elinoff Acker, who has worked with abusive men, believes that counselors without a background in intimate violence may cause women to feel that they have responsibility for their abusers' violence. Acker warns women: "Couples' counseling allows him to criticize your behavior rather than focusing on his own."[11] Women's descriptions of couples counseling illuminated the coercive control that the men exercised. The counseling failed because the men either became enraged by the process, didn't tell the truth, disrespected the therapists, or unilaterally decided to end the sessions.

Because of the violence, almost half of the women were seen by doctors, mostly in the emergency room. The less economic privilege the women had, the more likely they were to see doctors for the violence. These were mostly supportive experiences, even though many women did not disclose the cause of their injuries. They felt genuine concern from the hospital staff, many of whom seemed to know the real reasons for their suffering. Survivors gave positive accounts of these encounters:

> I went to [the hospital] and their domestic violence unit talked to me. They knew that I was homeless so they kept me overnight. (a white woman from a poor neighborhood)

> The doctor who treated me that day was very upset when he saw me because of the bruising. . . . I had no broken bones, but every part of my body was bruised. (a Black professional woman)

In one case, the words of a doctor were a turning point. An African American woman was struck so hard that she lost consciousness and was taken to the hospital. This is her account:

> At first I lied to the doctor because of the shame. But there's something inside me saying just tell him the truth. So eventually I told the doctor. And he told me the next time he's [the partner] going to kill me, based on my injuries. So the next time he's going to kill me. I have to leave. So I went back home. . . . My nose was bleeding, I was coughing up blood. I was thinking about killing him. . . . That was the end. (a Black survivor from a poor community)

She left the next day.

More than a quarter of the sixty women spoke to priests, ministers, or rabbis about the abuse. Women from all classes sought help from religious leaders. Some were compassionate and offered the survivors resources. A white woman who was desperately poor was supported by one church:

> It was the graciousness of the church that they noticed I was malnourished and they would come in and bring me groceries or whatever I needed so that was helpful. . . . They gave me a computer. I eventually spilled my guts and I said this is what happened, I'm really, really sorry and they really, really helped me. A couple of months later, after the assault, someone gave me a car. (a white woman from a poor community)

For some survivors, getting support around divorce helped them break out of entrapment:

> I want to know if I'm going to be excommunicated from the church because . . . divorce wasn't big and, I just—church is important to me. And pastor told me, he pointed me . . . to Second Corinthians, and he said, . . . "You've just been unequally yoked." And so, I took that as my okay to get out of the abuse. (a white professional woman)

However, most women who spoke to religious officials regretted it. These leaders appeared to lack concern for survivors and any real knowledge of intimate violence. One minister said that the survivor had made her bed and "should lie in it." Another told the woman that since she was not married, she was living in sin, and he was unwilling to help a sinner. Some religious leaders didn't believe the survivors were telling the truth. This is more evidence of misogyny and the patriarchal rules about love and marriage that are imposed on women.

HEALING

Many women felt stronger and more confident after leaving. With some distance from the relationships, they began to move past feelings of guilt and arrived at new perspectives on their experiences. Enander and Holmberg found that the third leaving process of understanding generally occurs after leaving: "Women do not leave because they realise they are abused; rather, they realise they are abused because they have left."[12] In their work, the beginning of the understanding stage is when "a woman defines the relationship as abusive and herself as a battered woman."[13] The majority of women said that the term "abuse" described their experiences. But few liked the term "battering." For some, it was too graphic, too focused on physical abuse. The term that was most popular was "survivor." And just as Enander and Holmberg indicate, this term was embraced generally after women separated from their abusers. So for this study, the term "survivor" marked the beginning of the understanding phase. To say that they were survivors involved a shift in their thinking and in their identities:

> [How about the term "survivor"?] Yes. . . . [When did you first relate to that term about yourself?] You know . . . I started relating to that when I—as I started going to the women's group and I heard other women's stories. . . . It just started making me feel, oh my God, that I'm not alone. (an African American woman from a poor community)

> [How about the term survivor, does that term work for you?] Yeah, I've learned to kind of adapt to that term. You know, more recently. I mean, I—I kind of thought of myself as that. But it seems like—it seems so strong, but yet I realize, you know, the more I think about it, what a horrible situation I was in. (a white woman from a working-class neighborhood)

When asked about the extent of their healing, roughly a third of the women talked of being substantially healed. One white woman from a poor community spoke of her journey. She had left her abuser seven years before the interview. She had benefited from healing groups at a domestic violence program:

> I was able to go to school and just sort all these experiences that I have been through. I'm a high achiever. I'm rockin' it. . . . I didn't just fall down. When he pushed me down I got right back up and I was like "fuck you." I'm still struggling but I continue.

A white woman from a professional community spoke of changes she went through since leaving. Her feelings of guilt and shame appeared to shift. She had been separated for nine years:

> I went through a whole period of thinking, God if I ever got into another relationship, who would want me? . . . Who would want a woman that was stupid enough to stay in a relationship that long? I never looked at it that that woman was loyal. That woman cared about someone. That woman tried to get him all the help. No. I looked at it—why would they want me, I was so stupid.

Her thoughts reflect compassion for herself and some distance from feelings of guilt and shame.

One woman said that since she left she was a "completely different person. I know now that it wasn't my fault." Another reported, "I'm the way I used to be in high school. I mean, I'm bubbly, I'm back to normal." Women said they were happier, more relaxed, more peaceful, and had regained their self-esteem and their sense of humor. They felt they had found their voices again and were more self-accepting.

Still, for most women there was a mix of feelings about healing; there was progress, and yet there was so much more that needed to change. Many survivors still experienced the symptoms of PTSD. Despite their efforts to manage their feelings, some remained burdened by intense anger, guilt, shame, and depression. Women identified difficulties in trusting anyone, but particularly men. There was pain from chronic injuries. Their children blamed them for the divorce. The was strain from seemingly endless court cases. Some were homeless, which made it extremely difficult to heal.

One white working-class woman expressed her sense of healing. She was physically and sexually abused, and lost a pregnancy due to violence. It was sixteen years since she had left her partner:

> What I experienced, it's going to have a lifetime impact. One of my favorite phrases is, "You can take the girl out of domestic violence, but you can't take domestic violence out of the girl." It's always going to impact. . . . I'm still dealing with long-term physical issues. There will always be consequences, but I guess at the end of the day it's how I choose to deal with this. I'm not a victim.

A complicated sense of healing was shared by a white survivor from a professional neighborhood. She had broken bones from her husband's violence. He threatened to kill her. She had left her husband five years before the interview and felt both relieved and much stronger since doing so. But she still had to manage strong feelings:

> I have to be able to let it go. . . . If I can't let it go, then the moments that I'm angry or incredibly sad, I have to give myself permission to feel like that, because I am angry, and there are times that I am really sad, and there are times when I feel the guilt and the shame but I have to let myself feel it and know it's okay. I just can't stay there.

For a small group of survivors, it was hard to see much movement at all toward healing. One Black woman had been unable to restore her spirits since leaving her abusive partner. She was from a poor community. It had been twenty-two years since she left town to escape the violence. Her partner beat her severely, threatened her with a gun, and sexually assaulted her. She went to the emergency room many times:

> [To what extent have you healed or recovered from the abuse you experienced with this man?] . . . I will never be healed from all of his abuse, never

ever. I think I always, until the day I die, I'll always be depressed from that abuse to the day I die. I'm still depressed.

Coming from a wealthy community, a white woman detailed the aftermath of her abuse. She suffered sexual abuse and "endless" verbal degradation. Her husband injured her and threatened to kill her. She had PTSD from the abuse. She had left him ten years before:

> I'm still an absence in a way. . . . I'm still destroyed and I don't think that's possible to heal from. And I don't think there's any part of the world where I could be safe and held in a way that would make it possible. I've tried and tried and tried.

These two women remain affected by the violence and abuse and are still searching for a healing path. Bonds of fear, anger, guilt, and shame remained for many of the survivors at the time of the interviews.

JUSTICE

What Would Justice Look Like?

Women need many things after leaving their violent partners. Surveying recent research with survivors, Mary Koss makes a distinction between two kinds of needs: "In the aftermath of sexual assault and other crimes of intimate violence, SVs [survivor-victims] have two major categories of needs—*survival needs* and *justice needs*. Survival needs include safety; physical health; economic issues such as housing and employment, education, or retraining; and immigration problems. Justice needs involve an innate motivation to right wrongs. After rape, SVs frequently do not experience the criminal justice system as meeting these needs."[14] Survival needs are obvious, and many of them need immediate attention. Justice needs address the moral aspects of victimization. This concerns vindication, the need of abused individuals to make things right and absolve unjust blame. For the survivors in this study, healing required attention to both kinds of needs.

When talking about what justice would look like to them, many survivors said their partners were never held accountable by anyone for their abuse. A quarter of the sixty women wanted greater punishment by the criminal legal system. Arrest and incarceration were emphasized especially by poor and working-class survivors. Her boyfriend's getting probation for his violent attack was just a "slap on the wrist" for one poor white woman. According to a Black woman from a poor community, prison time did good things for her partner; he got help for drug addiction there. "He should have done time for that type of crime," a working-class African American woman said, referring to her having been hit in the head repeatedly with a heavy object. She could have died from the violence. Some women wanted changes in the criminal legal system so that it would do a better job of meeting survivors' needs.

Greater punishment was seen as a way of addressing both survival needs and justice needs. It addressed the women's own safety and the well-being of other women as well. It also represented moral accountability for their partners' crimes.

At the same time, many women doubted what the criminal legal system could accomplish. "I don't know what kind of justice could be done in the form of incarceration or anything like that," a Black woman from a poor neighborhood reflected. She was threatened and sexually assaulted by her partner. He had done prison time; he seemed to come out even more violent than he had been.

When asked about justice, some women spoke of vengeance. Their rage was caused by the lack of any real accountability for the abuse:

> I'd like to see somebody do to him what he's done to me. I'd like to see him—I'd like him to feel the feelings that I felt, the fear that I felt. The feeling of hopelessness, of like, having absolutely nobody and nowhere to go in the whole world—it's like, I want to see him like sit . . . and have nothing, and have just nothing. Sit there, it's like, what can I do, where can I go? And have nowhere and nothing to rely on. . . . That would feel like justice. (a white working-class woman)

She was repeatedly choked and sexually abused by her partner. A white woman from a professional neighborhood shared a similar feeling about justice:

> I would like to see his present wife beat the living daylights out of him. I would like him to become afraid of her in a way that I have been afraid of him. I would like to see him suffer. . . . I want to see him experience a little bit of his own medicine.

She was physically abused and used the word "rape" to describe what she experienced. Such rage is understandable given what these women suffered.

For a number of survivors, justice meant something else, something relational: they wanted the men to fully admit to what they did. One Black woman from a poor community had the chance to see this in court. Her abuser admitted what he did as part of a plea deal:

[So how is it important to you that he admitted this?] It made [me] feel great. It just made me feel good that he—I just was shocked, you know what I mean. . . . Do you really know anybody that does that? That really shocked me. . . . No fight, no nothing, no denying.

To have the men acknowledge that the abuse was real and take responsibility for it: this was a deep wish for many survivors. A white woman from a working-class neighborhood stated that for her, "justice would look like him having to be really honest." A Black professional woman said, "I need an apology from the bottom of his heart." Such an admission would dissolve the shame and guilt survivors felt. It would expose the lies and reverse the crazy-making denials. While women wanted this kind of justice, they felt it was a hopeless dream:

> Justice to me would be his acknowledgment of this problem . . . both to his children . . . and myself. I really feel that would be justice for me. I mean, I don't think he deserves to be in prison. I think he needs therapy . . . but an acknowledgment, I think that would be very healing. But it's not gonna happen ever. (a white woman from a wealthy neighborhood)

Another hope of women regarding justice was that their partners would get either counseling on intimate violence or some kind of intervention that would make them understand the harm they were doing. One white working-class woman had her own idea about this: "I would like for him to sit in a chair and listen to what he put me through, to be honest."

A few women saw justice in yet another way; they felt that surviving and healing were their own realization of justice:

> I get to live a quiet and peaceful life and I get to have a really interesting and productive career and I have beautiful friends. . . . And I get to be part of . . . a community of scholars that is creating a better world. . . . That is powerful justice to me. (a white woman from a working-class community)

> [What would justice look like from your perspective?] . . . Just getting the support I need to recover from the incident. And you know, finally being able to be in like a healthy, functional relationship. (a white working-class woman)

Apologies and Forgiveness

In theory, apologies represent one way to address the justice needs of women. Most men made some kind of apologies for the violence; this was true of most men from every social class. Some did this rarely, or only when it was clear the relationship was ending. Ten of the sixty men never apologized, not even once. Hardly any of these apologies were viewed as sincere or meaningful, especially when they were repeatedly followed by more violence and abuse. They were largely "lip service" apologies, or manipulative apologies. One survivor said, "He had to apologize or else he couldn't get sex." A Black working-class woman saw her husband's apologies as an empty gesture:

> I remember him one time saying to me that he didn't know why he did this, and he was so sorry. And so on and so forth. And I just felt absolutely no sympathy for—I felt absolutely nothing for him when he started talking to me like that.

A white wealthy woman in a relationship with a wealthy man saw a pattern to the apologies she received:

> I got "sorrys" 500 times. And then, the first three made sense, and I accepted it. After that, it is completely hollow, I'm sorry. He continues to do the same thing over and over and over.

The apologies often had a strategic aspect: they were meant to suppress women's anger, to keep them from leaving, or to prevent them from filing criminal charges:

> [What would his apology sound like?] It'd be like, "I'm sorry, okay? What else do you want me to say? What else do you want from me? I apologize." (a white woman from a working-class neighborhood)

Some men blamed their partners at the same time that they were apologizing. A white professional woman said her husband would say, "'Oh, I'm so sorry,' but there was always a 'but.'" There was always a justification for his abuse.

One woman revealed the power of a meaningful apology. She had a conversation with her partner some years after leaving him. She asked him why he had been so cruel to her. He offered a full apology:

> And I thought, "Okay, I can accept that." That was, like, that [lifted] some level of the burden off of my shoulders when he said that to me. And I was appreciative of that. So I think that has affected my feelings about him now.

Insincere apologies did not earn much forgiveness for the men. Perhaps as a result, some men went so far as to demand forgiveness. Like empty apologies, this is another strategy to silence women's anger about the abuse.

None of the women suggested that apologies are sufficient to "remedy" the long-lasting harms of abuse. However, it is clear that there was a need for justice, a yearning for moral accountability along with the needs for safety and survival. But despite the crisis caused by separation and divorce, despite the intervention of friends, relatives, the police, courts, therapists, and religious officials, most men were unwilling to begin this conversation. The testimony on apologies demonstrates that the majority of the men refused to recognize, in any meaningful sense, their responsibility for the abuse.

Survivor Missions

Judith Herman wrote about the work that many individuals take up in the wake of violence: "Most survivors seek the resolution of their traumatic experience within the confines of their personal lives. But a significant minority, as a result of the trauma, feel called upon to engage in a wider world. These survivors recognize a political or religious dimension in their misfortune and discover that they can transform the meaning of their personal tragedy by making it the basis for social action."[15] Among the women who participated in this study, many have developed what Herman calls a "survivor mission." Fully half have either worked in domestic violence programs, have shared their experiences publicly, or plan to do so in the future. Most of these women have done direct work with survivors, seeking to support them on a path toward safety and healing. The women shared their experiences doing this kind of work. One Black woman from a poor community has worked as an advocate for ten years and hopes to do more in the future as an attorney. She believes her healing has made this possible:

> I saw a lot of people who are in an abusive relationship, especially people who are not from this country. . . . They're victimized by the system, the lawyers. So I want to become an immigration lawyer and address domestic violence. . . . If I wasn't healed, I wouldn't be able to do what I'm doing right now. If I wasn't healed I wouldn't be able to go places and talk about what happened to me.

An Asian American woman from a working-class community also linked her advocacy to her personal experience:

I'm . . . a domestic violence advocate. I . . . talk to victims of abuse to help get them resources, and try to help them get out of the relationships as well. And that is healing, too. . . . I have this savior complex now. And I want to help people now—because I was never helped.

For one Black professional woman, working with abused women was part of her healing process:

I think I've recovered almost fully. . . . I think the reason it happened, it's because of the work that I do. . . . I had done some work with young women, and I knew that there was something, there was something pushing me to do something more about that. My first one was at a battered women's program. . . . Through the counseling and the support groups, they were getting something out of it, but I was getting something out of it. So that was when my healing process started. By doing the work.

The experience of speaking about her experience changed a white woman from a wealthy community. She began doing work with domestic violence shelters:

I publicly acknowledged that I had been abused. . . . I started to heal on a very deep level, in a way that I never got to with counseling. And I'm not sure, if I hadn't done that, that I would be who I am right now, and where I am right now. . . . Because I thought, if you can give back . . . that would be a healing mechanism.

Herman sees a "survivor mission" as both giving to others and pursuing healing at the same time. These women gained tremendous strength from their ongoing work on behalf of survivors.

SUMMARY

From the perspective of Enander and Holmberg, separation is only one of three stages in the leaving process. There is also an emotional stage and a cognitive stage. Many survivors demonstrated substantial healing and a renewed sense of confidence, with the help of sympathetic friends, family, and domestic violence programs. But most women had difficulties with healing. The emotional bonds of love, fear, anger, guilt, and shame continued to affect survivors in a way that showed the extensiveness of the harm and the limits of their healing. For some, little healing of any kind has taken place, even many years later.

In her theory of patriarchy, Sylvia Walby describes the state as an important site of gender inequality.[16] She notes that the state is directly involved in violence against women in its laws and court practices, as well as in its overall failure in stopping such violence. In their interactions with police and judges, women revealed both supportive and distinctly unsupportive encounters. Many abusive men seemed to understand the limits of what the state is willing to do for women, and they used this knowledge to their advantage.

After separation, many women sought a survivor mission as a way to heal and a way to do justice in the wider world.

Conclusion

Intimate Violence as Social Entrapment

Intimate partner violence does not emanate from one identifiable source that, if eliminated, would prevent future violence.
—Kathleen J. Ferraro

Kathleen Ferraro sees intimate violence as arising from multiple social inequalities and believes that we will not stop it without addressing these broader issues. As she puts it, intimate violence does not have a single, easily identifiable cause. In this conclusion, I address the many social factors raised in this study that contribute to men's violence against women.

FEELING TRAPPED

Toward the end of the interviews, I asked the women whether they had seen themselves as trapped in their relationships. Most women in every class said this described their experience. Most women named a number of reasons for feeling trapped. Fear of violence was stressed. Especially in relation to their children, economic dependency was important at every class level. Women talked about the bonds of love and their longing for a family as part of their predicament. They spoke of isolation, of psychological abuse, and of guilt and shame. They feared judgment if they left and felt they were somehow failing their responsibilities as women.

There were class differences in what women emphasized. Most women in poor neighborhoods stressed the fear of violence as making them feel trapped. Many were afraid their abuser would track them down and harm them if they left. Psychological abuse was also important to women in poor communities. They spoke of how coerced isolation and verbal abuse created low self-esteem and depression.

The women in working-class neighborhoods also named a fear of violence, but in speaking about feeling trapped most raised economic dependency. The needs of their children, along with their unsteady and often part-time employment, undermined their ability to break free of their abusive partners. The men's economic abuse further contributed to their entrapment.

The professional and wealthy women had many issues in common. Economic dependency involving young children was important. There was a fear of losing class status if they left their abusive partners. They named fear of violence as part of what made them feel trapped. Constant verbal abuse and isolation caused further problems for them. A number of professional and wealthy women had difficulty recognizing that they were being abused.

SOCIAL CLASS AND INTIMATE VIOLENCE

There are three broad ways that class divisions are evident in the abuse that women detailed. First, there were class-based differences in the kinds of abuse and the contexts of abuse. Second, economic inequalities were part of the conflict within these relationships. And third, at the individual level, social class affected women's perceptions about being abused, along with feelings of guilt and shame.

Class-Based Group Differences

There were both similarities and differences in intimate abuse across social classes. It is the argument of this book that while intimate violence can be found in virtually all communities, social inequalities greatly affect women's abilities to resist or escape violence. Survivors were asked about their experiences of abuse growing up, about abuse among their friends and relatives, and about any other kinds of victimization they had suffered. Previous occurrences of abuse and victimization were reported at every class level. But women who were poor or working-class were more likely to have been sexually abused as children, more likely to have witnessed abuse in their families, and more likely to have had abused mothers, compared to professional and wealthy women. They were more likely to know relatives and friends who were in abusive relationships. They were also more likely to have previously been in an abusive relationship themselves. Survivors who were poor and working-class further reported more frequent and more severe violence, as well as more injuries, than economically privileged women. Consistent with other research findings on this topic, this indicates that economic disadvantage places women at a greater risk of violence.[1]

There were both class and racial differences in fighting back against the violence. While overall most women fought back verbally and physically, more than half of the poor and working-class women fought back physically, while fewer than half of the economically privileged women did. Black women were more likely to physically fight back than white women.

There were class-based differences in the masculinities of abusive men. How they presented themselves as men was connected to both economic disadvantage and economic entitlement. The stigmas of poverty, unemployment, racism, incarceration, and drug addiction presented challenges to masculine status for many poor and working-class men, and violence offered a resource to compensate for this. Not all of the men's violence was hidden; being known as a violent man was for some a measure of status. For economically privileged abusers, hiding their abusiveness was important to maintaining masculine status. If prison masculinities shaped the lives of poor men, ruthless corporate masculinities may have influenced professional and wealthy men.

There were class-specific challenges to the expectations of being a "good wife" and a "good mother" that are dominant in our patriarchal culture. None of the women living in poor communities were married. Many had problems with drug and alcohol addiction, which was also a problem for working-class women. This created difficulties in caring for their children; some women served time for drug crimes. For economically privileged women, divorce could cause a loss of social status within their communities; the fear of this happening caused some women to feel trapped. Some were shunned by friends and relatives after separating from abusive partners.

While patterns in sexual abuse appeared largely similar across class categories, poor and working-class women were more likely to report incidents consistent with the legal definition of rape. Wealthy women were the least likely to name occurrences of forced sex as rape.

Concerning efforts to stop the violence and abuse, two-thirds of the women either called the police or had the police called by neighbors or relatives. This was most common among poor and working-class women. Women in poor communities were least likely to see counselors or therapists as a way to obtain support.

Social Class and Conflict within the Relationships

There are class aspects to the verbal degradation that was part of the psychological abuse. Women of all classes were called names that reflect the harsh edges of a winner/loser capitalist society, such as "worthless," "useless," "trash," a "reject," "pathetic," "stupid," and "ignorant." This kind of language harmed the women and at the same time served as justification for the men's violence and abuse.

Class inequalities lived within these relationships. Most men seemed to be engaged in a kind of class conflict with their partners. Women's unpaid labor of housework and childcare was often enforced by violence. Men controlled the household money, even the women's wages. They sabotaged women's jobs and undermined their schooling. Among women living in poor communities, many men seemed to be economically predatory, seeking to obtain the women's money more than anything else. Many women were kept in the dark about the amount of money in the checking accounts. Putting women on allowances was common, especially for women in the privileged classes. There was a "bait-and-switch" pattern of exploitation among wealthy couples in which men invited women to stop working or to work less in exchange for promises that were never fulfilled. This left women without any of their own money and without any control over the household resources.

Professional and wealthy men, who were mostly white, used their economic power to threaten their partners. Because of the unequal economic status in many of these relationships, women felt they were obligated to put up with the abuse. After separation, many professional and wealthy men used the courts as another weapon against their ex-partners.

Class at the Individual Level:
Perceptions of the Abuse and Class Shame

The shame of poverty and racism is evident in the class myth. The power of this myth made it difficult for professional and wealthy women to conceive of their experiences as abusive. Even working-class women sought to distance themselves from this racialized stigma and its connections to poverty. Many women expressed a class-based shame about disclosing the abuse to their friends and families.

Class shame also affected the abusers. I have argued that the verbal degradation tells us much more about the men than the women. The class-inflected examples previously cited may be projections that reflect men's insecurities in a winner/loser society. Many men blamed their partners for their own economic failings. According to the women, for some men the abuse was an expression of this strain.

PATRIARCHY AND SOCIAL CLASS

Sylvia Walby's theory of patriarchy forms a theoretical background to this study.[2] She delineates six sites where patriarchy is concentrated in contemporary Western industrial societies: paid employment, unpaid domestic labor, culture, sexuality, the state, and violence against women. All of the first five institutional sites are related to violence. I have argued that each of these is best examined through an intersectional lens.

Women's participation in the paid labor force is a major element of gender inequality. Racism and patriarchy structure the labor market, creating profound inequality for women of color. The failure to design jobs with parents in mind, along with the lack of affordable childcare, causes mothers to make economic sacrifices to meet the needs of their children. The survivors in this study had more education than their partners but most earned less money, owing to their obligations as mothers. This created a power imbalance in most relationships. The men took advantage of this unequal economic status and exploited it further through economic abuse.

Women's unpaid household labor is related to paid work, but it is its own institutional site of inequality. Men of all classes refused to do childcare and housework, and most women resented this. This was another way of limiting women's economic opportunities.

According to Walby, the mass media, religious organizations, and educational institutions shape our understandings of gender. Culture is therefore another key site of gender inequality. There are competing cultural representations of masculinities and femininities. Hierarchies within masculinities and femininities involve class, race, and sexuality. This was examined in terms of the hidden dramas of masculinity described by survivors and how this conflicted with the presentations of masculinity men made in public. Failed femininity is a central theme in the verbal degradation reported by women. Culture was further addressed in terms of the gendered feeling rules governing intimate relationships.

In stating that sexuality is important to patriarchy, Walby focuses on the institution of heterosexuality. Drawing on the work of radical feminists, she argues that compulsory heterosexuality and the sexual double standard are core elements of gender inequality. She sees both of these as pressuring women to see unions with men as the only choice available to them. Relating to the double standard of men's and women's sexuality, the verbal abuse covered in chapter 3 contained highly sexualized slurs meant to debase women as a group. As has been shown, these insults are racialized; there are specific controlling images that are applied to Black women and other women of color. In chapter 5, Liz Kelly's concept of a continuum was used to expand this analysis and identify a range of sexually abusive behaviors beyond rape.

Government institutions such as courts and legislatures play an important part in women's lives in terms of marriage, divorce, child custody, reproductive justice, sexuality, and violence against women. In this study, the action and inaction of the police was addressed in chapter 8, along with men's use of economic privilege in the courts. The sexual abuse to prison pipeline was discussed in chapter 1 as a source of harm done to families by the state, especially families of color. The long-term impact of incarceration upon men and their communities was addressed in chapter 2.

It may sound odd to say this, but the male partners of these women appeared to have an intuitive understanding of patriarchy. The tactics they used paralleled Walby's focus on paid work, unpaid work, femininity, sexuality, and the state. The men appeared to know all about the sources of women's strength and how best to undermine them.

INTIMATE VIOLENCE AS SOCIAL ENTRAPMENT

I previously introduced the concept of social entrapment in a book on women's experiences seeking restraining orders in cases of intimate violence.[3] The goal was to connect intimate violence with the social elements that contribute either to women's entrapment or to women's empowerment. The diagram in figure 1 is an expansion of this model and serves as a summary of this book. This way of examining abuse highlights the influence of the social world on the violent relationship.

This model begins with the things that men do to harm and constrain women. This includes psychological, physical, sexual, and economic

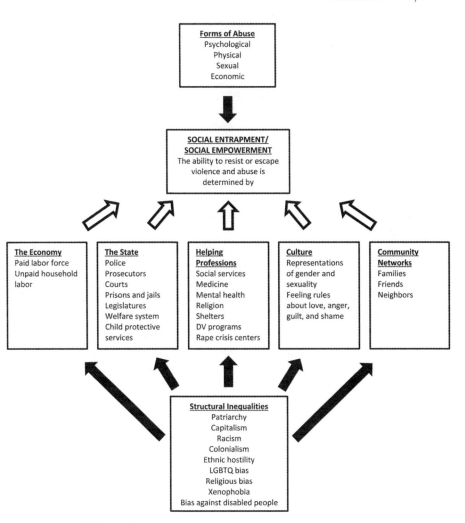

FIGURE 1. Intimate violence as social entrapment

abuse. The second box in the diagram is labeled "social entrapment/ social empowerment." Whether women feel trapped in their relationships is determined by a range of social factors, as indicated by the white arrows. Incorporating aspects of Walby's theory of patriarchy, five major factors are identified. The first is the economy, including both paid labor and unpaid household labor. Gendered discrimination in paid and unpaid work makes women economically dependent on abusive men. This is especially a problem for women in poor and working-class communities. The patriarchal and racist segmentation of the workforce, along with the lack of paid parental leave and afford- able childcare, limits women's choices. The second factor is the state. As shown in chapter 8, police and court responses can either further women's entrapment or help to empower women. The larger prison industrial complex, which ties all of the elements in this box together, is a major source of oppression for Black, Indigenous, Latinx, and queer communities. This rightly causes many survivors to see the police as more of a cause of violence than a solution to it.

The third factor, the responses of the helping professions, were also detailed in chapter 8. Most women praised shelters, domestic vio- lence organizations, and individual therapists for the support that they provided.

Culture is the fourth important social factor. Cultural representations of gender in the mass media have tremendous effects on how we view ourselves. These images shape men's motivations to commit violence and the treatment of survivors in the wake of this violence. In chapters 2 and 3, I outlined how there are competing images of gender and a hi- erarchy within the range of masculinities and femininities presented in the dominant culture. Patriarchal versions of masculinity and femininity continue to dominate US society, although they are being challenged by multiracial feminists and lesbian, gay, bisexual, and transgender activ- ists. Religious institutions of many kinds have views on the obligations of married women, and a number of survivors struggled with their vows and with the counsel of religious leaders.

The fifth factor, community networks, has been shown to be critical for women seeking to escape violence.

The last box on the diagram addresses structural inequalities. This study has focused on patriarchy and class divisions, but there are many inequalities that shape the social factors listed in the diagram. These struc- tural inequalities include racism, colonialism, ethnic hostility, bias against LGBTQ individuals, religious bias, xenophobia, and bias against dis- abled people. This diagram could be used to conduct studies of intimate violence in relation to these and other structural inequalities. These in- equalities shape the economy, the state, and the broader culture. They live in the responses of friends, family, and relatives to abuse. Struc- tural inequalities corrupt the responses of the helping professions to survivors. Meaningful support from the helping professions requires knowledge of these inequalities and skills designed to meet the needs of individuals affected by them.[4]

MOVING FORWARD

Many feminist scholars and activists share the perspective of Ferraro that began this conclusion. They argue that intimate violence against women is rooted in multiple social inequalities. As this investigation of social entrapment and social empowerment focuses on the role of structural inequalities, what are some approaches to stopping violence that show an awareness of these larger forces?

Economic Resources

Susan Sered and Maureen Norton-Hawk studied women in Massachusetts who spent time moving between homeless shelters, rehabilitation programs, prisons and jails, emergency rooms, and welfare offices. Almost all of the women experienced either sexual assault, intimate violence from partners, or both. In this important study of social class, they argue against individual explanations for poverty and instead reframe it as a human rights issue: "We believe that by shifting the public conversation from the 'problems of the needy' to the 'rights of all human beings,' we can encourage the development of long-term, cohesive, adequately funded public institutions. What we are calling for is a change from the Medicaid model of providing assistance to individuals who can prove to the satisfaction of the state that they are truly needy, to the Medicare model of acknowledging that all human beings are vulnerable to illness and old age and deserve the support of their fellow human beings."[5]

Donna Coker focuses on the importance of economic resources as pivotal to violence against poor women of color.[6] She states, "Every domestic violence intervention strategy should be subjected to a *'material resources test.'*" "This means that in every area of anti-domestic law and policy, whether it be determining funding priorities, analyzing criminal law or arrest policies, developing city ordinances or drafting administrative rules, priority should be given to those laws and policies which improve women's access to material resources."[7] The material resources Coker identifies include immediate survival needs such as housing, food, and clothing, as well as services such as transportation, job training, and childcare. Without a focus on material resources, laws and policies will not meet the needs of the most vulnerable women, and therefore will further their entrapment.

Deborah Weissman highlights anti-violence programs that address class and patriarchy at the same time.[8] One is the Center for Survivor

Agency and Justice (CSAJ), which works to empower survivors by addressing consumer rights, racism, and poverty. The organization advocates for survivors by engaging in civil litigation to stop predatory lending and debt collection practices and by fighting housing discrimination. She quotes the CSAJ as wanting to develop "a *partnership* between the DV [domestic violence], anti-poverty, and anti-racist fields that attends to the ways in which physical and economic risks facing survivors fundamentally shape their opportunities for securing safety."[9] The CSAJ is a model of advocacy that seeks to change the institutional dimensions of women's entrapment.

Another model raised by Weissman is the Alma Center in Milwaukee, Wisconsin. This organization focuses on the economic needs of men who have abused their partners. The Alma Center has as its mission "the transformation of oppression in all its forms," including "misogyny, sexism, racism [and] homophobia." According to its website, "The Alma Center's community-based programming helps adult males with violent histories become caring fathers, partners, husbands, and community advocates."[10] Seeing economic strain as one of the common characteristics of violence, the Alma Center helps these men find jobs. Weissman believes that economic hardship is not sufficiently addressed in many counseling programs for abusive individuals.

The Criminal Legal System and Abolition Feminism

Women of color, especially Black feminists, have long criticized what has been called the "over-reliance" of the anti-violence movement on the criminal legal system.[11] The very term, "criminal justice system," is an oxymoron to many feminist activists, and many use the term "criminal legal system" as a substitute.[12] This usage has been followed throughout this book.

Beth Richie delineates the ways that the state, rather than helping women, harms Black women: "Grassroots mobilizing to end violence [should] focus squarely on dismantling America's prison nation. . . . It would require a deep analysis of the impact of community divestment and subsequent concentration of disadvantages, with particular attention to the impact that conservative state policies have had on Black women's experience of male violence."[13] Richie sees the state as directly involved in creating concentrated poverty in communities of color.

Donna Coker and Ahjané Macquoid review the literature on the effects of incarceration on individuals, families, and communities.[14] Their analysis is worth reviewing in some detail. Coker and Macquoid find that there is a host of "collateral consequences" of incarceration for individuals, families, and communities. Men and women who have been convicted of crimes are ineligible for many kinds of public support, including financial aid for education, food stamps, public housing, and licenses needed for employment. Incarceration creates job discrimination and educational discrimination. For men, prisons are places of hypermasculinity and violence. This causes problems with physical and mental health, including sleep disorders, depression, PTSD, and suicidality. Substance abuse is generally untreated behind bars. For families, incarceration produces economic strain and places the children of inmates at risk for homelessness. Mothers who are inmates lose custody of their children. The children themselves experience high rates of depression, anxiety, and problems in school. Communities are also heavily affected by incarceration. Where there are large numbers of community members in prison, the social bonds that prevent crime are weakened.

Coker and Macquoid ask, Which of these consequences of incarceration serve to reduce violence against women? Their answer is: none of them. Poor women experience high rates of intimate violence. Unstable employment increases the likelihood of intimate violence. Low levels of education increase the risks of violence. Substance abuse also increases the risks. Given these facts, Coker and Macquoid argue that opposing mass incarceration must become a central goal of the anti-violence movement.

Women in this study reported positive, ineffectual, and negative experiences with police officers. The widespread demonstrations in support of Black Lives Matter have created new demands to transform policing. It is important to point out that a number of killings of Black men have involved police responses to intimate violence. One study of police shootings in seventeen states found that 13 percent were related to intimate violence.[15]

Adding more evidence of the need for structural change, Andrea Ritchie has documented extensive cases of police violence against Black women, women of color, LGBTQ, and gender-nonconforming individuals in her book *Invisible No More*.[16] Leigh Goodmark has compiled evidence of intimate partner violence committed by police officers. Policing is yet another site of hypermasculinity, in her view.[17] This all points to the need to hold police officers accountable for their actions and to rethink the meaning of public safety.[18]

"Abolition feminism" seeks to completely transform how we address crime and social problems. In the words of Angela Davis, Gina Dent,

Erica Meiners, and Beth Richie: "Abolition is a political vision with the goal of eliminating imprisonment, policing, and surveillance and creating lasting alternatives to punishment and imprisonment."[19] Davis emphasizes that "abolition is about rebuilding, reenvisioning, reimagining, reconceptualizing."[20]

According to Davis and her coauthors, abolition is about more than prisons and policing. It means "challenging the migration of carcerality from brick-and-mortar jails and prisons to the places in everyday life where surveillance and punitive control dominate other aspects of the state's enterprise."[21] The removal of children from their parents and placement in foster care is an important issue in abolition feminism. As illustrated by the sexual abuse to prison pipeline, this places many children on a path to incarceration. The racially discriminatory implementation of the child protective system is so profound that Dorothy Roberts and Angela Burton have called for its abolition.[22] As I reported in chapter 3, Roberts sees the welfare system as a form of surveillance and control over the reproductive decisions of Black women.[23] This too is on the agenda of abolition feminism. The education system is another site where prisons have extended an influence. The school to prison pipeline identifies the way that children are harshly punished for actions that don't even amount to crimes, leading to expulsions and subsequent involvement in the juvenile detention system. This criminalization is applied disproportionately to Black and Latinx students.[24]

In 2020, a group of abolition feminists sent a letter to anti-violence activists challenging their overreliance on a deeply flawed criminal legal system. The letter charged that as a result, they had "repeatedly failed Black, Indigenous, and people of color (BIPOC) survivors, leaders, organizations, and movements." Some forty-seven anti-violence coalitions from twenty states signed the letter, and by doing so, expressed solidarity with the goals of abolition.[25]

Given the scope of the activism addressed by abolition feminism, Davis, Dent, Meiners, and Richie argue that this is "the most inclusive and persuasive feminism for these times."[26]

Restorative Justice and Transformative Justice

"Restorative justice" is the label for a range of informal, dialogue-based practices that can be used to address the harms of crime. These practices directly address the justice needs of survivors that are unmet by the criminal legal system. They seek to limit the role of the state in responding to crime while expanding the involvement of families and community members in creating justice. A number of the models of restorative justice used around the world originated in Maori communities in New Zealand, Indigenous nations in Canada, and Native American traditions.[27] While much restorative justice in the United States concerns youth crime and school misconduct, these practices have been applied to severe harms, including murder, vehicular homicide, child sexual abuse, wrongful conviction, and violence against women.[28]

The use of restorative justice in cases of violence against women and children is rightfully controversial. These practices were not originally designed with these crimes in mind, and restorative practitioners have not always prioritized the needs of survivors. However, feminist activists and scholars have sought to transform existing restorative practices to address the unique circumstances of intimate violence and sexual assault.[29] A restorative justice process has been created in connection with the Duluth Domestic Violence Intervention Programs in Minnesota.[30] A restorative justice conference held in Boston in 2020 was sponsored by sexual assault and intimate violence programs and by a counseling agency for domestic violence offenders.[31]

The women interviewed in this study expressed a desire for a relational kind of justice, an acknowledgment of the wrongs by their ex-partners. They also saw this as unrealistic, given the lack of remorse they witnessed. Without some kind of group involvement, such as through an extended-family intervention or actions taken by religious leaders or their employers, it is difficult to see how these particular men could be encouraged to change. They don't appear to be good candidates for a restorative dialogue with the women or for group counseling programs on intimate violence. Recall that nearly a third of the men had been abusive in previous relationships.

There are surely many men who are willing to change their violent behavior. However, we must create a crisis for abusive individuals to motivate change. Men who attend counseling programs are generally referred by the courts, threatened with divorce, or otherwise pressured by their partners. I have certainly seen many motivated men in my own work as a group counselor. Evaluation research on counseling for abusive men is promising, and there are published accounts of men who have stopped abusing their partners and children.[32] We can't give up on abusive individuals who are remorseful and who want to change their behavior. It must be acknowledged that this process takes time. The current standard for certified intimate partner abuse educational programs in Massachusetts is a minimum of forty weeks (eighty hours). Even after this point, many men are required to reenroll in the program if they fail to make sufficient progress.[33]

Restorative justice can be done with many different people besides survivors and offenders. There were serious harms done to the women's relationships with their children, families, friends, and communities. These too could be addressed through restorative dialogues.[34] There is evidence to support the use of restorative practices with violent men who are incarcerated.[35]

Many feminists see restorative justice as a means of displacing the racism and oppressiveness of the current criminal legal system.[36] Fania Davis sees restorative justice programs offering ways of keeping youth of color out of the system entirely. Drawing upon a restorative practice used in South Africa, Davis recommends the truth and reconciliation process as a way to address police violence against Black men and women.[37]

In a related proposal, seeking justice for violence against African American women could involve local tribunals, modeled on international tribunals for war crimes, according to Traci West: "It would place on trial those public and private sector leaders (perhaps some of them in absentia) who have made pivotal political and economic decisions that help to foster the violence and to marginalize those who survive it. The tribunal could be organized by local advocates and activists already working on this issue, together with sympathetic community leaders. . . . Testimony would be offered about the harm endured by women and some form of restitution decided upon."[38]

There is a difference between restorative justice and "transformative justice." This is explained by Soniya Munshi, Bhavana Nancherla, and Tiloma Jayasinghe: "Restorative justice approaches to domestic violence generally work within criminal legal responses. Transformative justice, on the other hand, seeks safety and accountability without relying on punishment-based strategies or systemic violence, including incarceration, policing, and other criminal legal responses. In other words, restorative justice models usually work as alternatives within criminal legal processes whereas transformative justice approaches work outside these systems."[39] Transformative justice seeks to address the multiple social inequalities that shape societies. One program following this approach is Creative Interventions in Oakland, California. This organization states, "Our vision is based upon liberation—the positive, life-affirming, transformative potential within our most oppressed communities."[40]

Mimi Kim, the founder of Creative Interventions, sees informal community networks as the best focus for stopping sexual violence, domestic violence, and family violence. Her program "begins with the assumption that those closest to and most impacted by violence have the greatest motivation to end that violence."[41] Kim is concerned about police mistreatment of women and men of color, immigrant communities, and LGBTQ individuals. Her project gathers stories of successful ways of stopping violence that don't rely on the state. Creative Interventions offers an extensive toolkit of community-based strategies for mobilizing safety and support for survivors.[42] There are related community-based projects in Germany, the United Kingdom, India, and New Zealand.[43]

Justice-Making

Given the many failures of the criminal legal system to right wrongs, it must be understood that there are many things that people can do to help create justice. Marie Fortune identifies the process of justice as involving seven different elements: "truth-telling, acknowledgment of the violation, compassion, protection of the vulnerable, accountability, restitution, and vindication."[44] The survivor missions pursued by many of the women in this study are forms of "justice-making," in Fortune's words.[45] They are ways of doing truth-telling, of showing compassion, of seeking accountability, and of offering vindication to survivors.

Fortune is clear that justice requires broad social change. She says, "Justice will only be made in a context that challenges the fundamental arrangements of our social and familial order."[46] Following her analysis, abolition feminism is engaged in justice-making. Challenging racist institutions that harm survivors is justice-making. Protesting social inequalities is a form of truth-telling. Mobilizing communities against violence is a way of showing compassion and seeking accountability. Exposing misogyny at all class levels is a way of doing truth-telling and seeking accountability. Expanding the rights of lesbian, gay, bisexual, and transgender individuals is a form of compassion and protection.

In the age of the #MeToo and Black Lives Matter movements, which have inspired campaigns for social change across the country and around the world, this is the time to be alive for anti-violence activism. More of us need to get involved in these kinds of justice-making.

Notes

CHAPTER I. CONVERSATIONS WITH WOMEN ABOUT ABUSE

Epigraph: Kimberlé Crenshaw, "Mapping the Margins: Intersectionality, Identity Politics, and Violence against Women of Color," *Stanford Law Review* 43, no. 6 (July 1991): 1245.

1. All names have been changed to protect confidentiality.

2. Suzanne K. Steinmetz and Murray A. Straus, *Violence and the Family* (New York: Harper and Row, 1974), 7.

3. Martin D. Schwartz, "Ain't Got No Class: Universal Risk Theories of Battering," *Contemporary Crises* 12 (1988): 373 ("universal risk"); and Angela Moore, "Intimate Violence: Does Socioeconomic Status Matter?," in *Violence between Intimate Partners: Patterns, Causes, and Effects*, ed. Albert P. Cardarelli (Boston: Allyn and Bacon, 1997), 93 ("classless intimate violence").

4. Amy E. Bonami et al., "Intimate Partner Violence and Neighborhood Income: A Longitudinal Analysis," *Violence Against Women* 20, no. 1 (January 2014): 42–58; Claire M. Renzetti, "Economic Issues and Intimate Partner Violence," in *Sourcebook on Violence against Women*, 2nd ed., ed. Claire M. Renzetti, Jeffrey L. Edleson, and Raquel Kennedy Bergen (Los Angeles, CA: Sage, 2011), 171–87; and Stella M. Resko, *Intimate Partner Violence and Women's Insecurity* (El Paso, TX: LFB Scholarly Publishing, 2010).

5. Beth Ritchie, *Arrested Justice: Black Women, Violence, and American's Prison Nation* (New York: NYU Press, 2012); and Andrea Ritchie, *Invisible No More: Police Violence against Black Women and Women of Color* (Boston: Beacon Press, 2017).

6. Anannya Bhattacharjee, *Whose Safety? Women of Color and the Violence of Law Enforcement* (Philadelphia: American Friends Service Committee and the Committee on Women, Population, and the Environment, 2001); Richie, *Arrested Justice*; and Ritchie, *Invisible No More*.

7. Patricia Hill Collins, *Black Feminist Thought: Knowledge, Consciousness, and the Politics of Empowerment* (Boston: Unwin Hyman, 1990), 228 (framing social inequalities); and James Ptacek, *Battered Women in the Courtroom: The Power of Judicial Responses* (Boston: Northeastern University Press, 1999), 28–29 (resist or escape violence).

8. Ptacek, *Battered Women in the Courtroom*.

9. Erik Olin Wright and Joel Rogers, *American Society: How it Really Works* (New York: W. W. Norton, 2010).

10. Barbara Ehrenreich, *Fear of Falling: The Inner Life of the Middle Class* (New York: Harper Perennial, 1989); Wright and Rogers, *American Society*; Earl Wysong, Robert Perrucci, and David Wright, *The New Class Society*, 4th ed. (Lanham, MD: Rowman and Littlefield, 2014); Michael Zweig, *The Working Class Majority: America's Best Kept Secret* (Ithaca, NY: Cornell University Press, 2012).

11. David Leonhardt and Kevin Quealy, "The American Middle Class Is No Longer the World's Richest," *New York Times*, April 22, 2014; Peter Temin, *The Vanishing Middle Class* (Cambridge, MA: MIT Press, 2017); and US Department of Commerce, *Middle Class in America* (Washington, DC: US Department of Commerce, 2010).

12. Wysong, Perrucci, and Wright, *New Class Society*; and Zweig, *Working-Class Majority*.

13. U.S. Bureau of the Census, "Income and Poverty in the United States: 2020," last modified September 14, 2021, www.census.gov/library/publications /2021/demo/p60-273.html.

14. How Much Does a Lawyer Make?" and "How Much Does a Physician Make?," *US News & World Report*, accessed August 9, 2021, https:// money.usnews.com/careers/best-jobs/lawyer/salary, https://money.usnews.com /careers/ best-jobs/physician/salary.

15. Anne Case and Angus Deaton, *Deaths of Despair and the Future of Capitalism* (Princeton, NJ: Princeton University Press, 2020.

16. Robert B. Hawkins, Eric J. Charles, and J. Hunter Mehaffey, "Socio-Economic Status and COVID-19-Related Cases and Fatalities," *Public Health* 189 (December 2020): 129–34.

17. National Institutes of Health, "NCI Study Highlights Pandemic's Disproportionate Impact on Black, American Indian/Alaska Native, and Latino Adults," news release, October 4, 2021, www.nih.gov/news-events/news-releases/nci -study-highlights-pandemics-disproportionate-impact-black-american-indian -alaska-native-latino-adults.

18. Diane Boesch and Shipla Phadke, "When Women Lost All the Jobs: Essential Actions for a Gender-Equitable Recovery," Center for American Progress, February 1, 2021, www.americanprogress.org/article/women-lose-jobs-essential -actions-gender-equitable-recovery.

19. Misty L. Heggeness et al., "Tracking Job Losses for Mothers of School-Age Children during a Health Crisis," *Moms, Work, and the Pandemic* (blog), US

Census Bureau, March 3, 2021, www.census.gov/library/stories/2021/03/moms
-work-and-the-pandemic.html.

20. National Women's Law Center, *A Year of Strength & Loss: The Pandemic, the Economy, and the Value of Women's Work* (Washington, DC: National Women's Law Center, March 2021), https://nwlc.org/wp-content/uploads/2021/03/Final_NWLC_Press_CovidStats.pdf.

21. Boesch and Phadke, "When Women Lost All the Jobs."

22. Katie Benner, "Domestic Violence Has Increased during the Pandemic, Studies Show," *New York Times*, February 24, 2021.

23. Chuck Collins, "U.S. Billionaire Wealth Surged by 70 Percent, or $2.1 Trillion, during Pandemic," Institute for Policy Studies, October 18, 2021, https://ips-dc.org/u-s-billionaire-wealth-surged-by-70-percent-or-2-1-trillion-during-pandemic-theyre-now-worth-a-combined-5-trillion.

24. Wysong, Perrucci, and Wright, *New Class Society*, 32.

25. Diana B. Elliott and Tavia Simmons, *Marital Events of Americans: 2009* (Washington, DC: US Census Bureau, August 2011).

26. Annette Kuhn, *Family Secrets: Acts of Memory and Imagination* (London: Verso, 1995), 98.

27. Patricia Hill Collins and Sirma Bilge, *Intersectionality* (Cambridge, UK: Polity Press, 2016); and Crenshaw, "Mapping the Margins," 1241–99.

28. Collins and Bilge, *Intersectionality*, 7, 27.

29. Charles C. Ragin, Joane Nagel, and Patricia White, *Workshop on Scientific Foundations of Qualitative Research* (Arlington, VA: National Science Foundation, 2004), 14.

30. James Ptacek, "Why Do Men Batter Their Wives?," in *Feminist Perspectives on Wife Abuse*, ed. Kersti Yllö and Michele Bograd (Newbury Park, CA: Sage, 1988), 133–57 (abuse their partners); Todd W. Crosset et al., "Male Student-Athletes and Violence against Women: A Survey of Campus Judicial Affairs Offices," *Violence Against Women* 2, no. 2 (June 1996): 163–79 (assault on college campuses); and Ptacek, *Battered Women in the Courtroom* (restraining orders).

31. James Ptacek, ed., "Feminism, Restorative Justice, and Violence against Women," special issue, *Violence Against Women* 11, no. 5 (May 2005); and James Ptacek, *Restorative Justice and Violence against Women* (Oxford: Oxford University Press, 2010).

32. Metropolitan Milwaukee Fair Housing Council, *City of Milwaukee Impediments to Fair Housing* (Milwaukee, WI: Metropolitan Milwaukee Fair Housing Council, 2005); and Olivia Richardson, "The Story of the First Black-Owned Home in Wauwatosa," WUWM Radio, February 4, 2020, www.wuwm.com/podcast/lake-effect-segments/2020-02-24/the-story-of-the-first-black-owned-home-in-wauwatosa.

33. Matthew Desmond, *Evicted: Poverty and Profit in the American City* (New York: Crown, 2016); and Douglas S. Massey and Nancy A. Denton, *American Apartheid: Segregation and the Making of the Underclass* (Cambridge, MA: Harvard University Press, 1993).

34. Rebecca Campbell et al., "Training Interviewers for Research on Sexual Violence: A Qualitative Study of Rape Survivors' Recommendations for Interview Practice," *Violence Against Women* 15, no. 5 (2009): 595–617.

35. Susan T. Fiske, *Envy Up, Scorn Down: How Status Divides Us* (New York: Russell Sage Foundation, 2011); Melissa V. Harris-Perry, *Sister Citizen: Shame, Stereotypes, and Black Women in America* (New Haven, CT: Yale University Press, 2011); and Arlie Russell Hochschild, *The Managed Heart: Commercialization of Human Feeling* (Berkeley: University of California Press, 1983).

36. Rebecca Campbell et al., "What Has It Been Like for You to Talk With Me Today? The Impact of Participating in Interview Research on Rape Survivors," *Violence Against Women* 16, no. 1 (2010): 60–83.

37. Gwen Hunnicut, "Varieties of Patriarchy and Violence against Women," *Violence Against Women* 15, no. 5 (May 2009): 553–73; and Bob Pease, *Facing Patriarchy* (London: Zed Books, 2019).

38. "Search the New York Times," *New York Times*, accessed August 4, 2021, www.nytimes.com/search.

39. Walter S. DeKeseredy and Martin D. Schwartz, *Male Peer Support and Violence against Women* (Boston: Northeastern University Press, 2013); R. Emerson Dobash and Russell P. Dobash, *Violence against Wives* (New York: Free Press, 1979); and Hillary Potter, *Battle Cries: Black Women and Intimate Partner Abuse* (New York: NYU Press, 2008).

40. bell hooks, *Feminism Is for Everybody*, 2nd ed. (New York: Routledge, 2014); Collins and Bilge, *Intersectionality*; Angela P. Harris, "Heteropatriarchy Kills: Challenging Gender Violence in a Prison Nation," *Washington University Journal of Law & Policy* 37 (2011): 13–65; and Richie, *Arrested Justice*.

41. Sylvia Walby, "Theorising Patriarchy," *Sociology* 23, no. 2 (May 1989): 213–34; and Sylvia Walby, *Theorizing Patriarchy* (Oxford, UK: Basil Blackwell, 1990).

42. Walby, *Theorizing Patriarchy*, 200.

43. Sylvia Walby, *The Future of Feminism* (Cambridge, UK: Polity Press, 2011), 104.

44. Pease, *Facing Patriarchy*.

45. Walby, *Theorizing Patriarchy*, 20.

46. Malika Saada Saar et al., *The Sexual Abuse to Prison Pipeline: The Girls' Story* (Washington, DC: Human Rights Project for Girls, Georgetown Law Project on Poverty and Inequality, and the Ms. Foundation for Women, 2015).

47. Saar et al., *Sexual Abuse to Prison Pipeline*, 7.

48. Anita Raj et al., "Prevalence and Patters of Sexual Assault across the Life Span among Incarcerated Women," *Violence Against Women* 14, no. 5 (2008): 528–41; Ashley G. Blackburn, Janet L. Mullings, and James W. Marquart, "Sexual Assault in Prison and Beyond: Toward an Understanding of Lifetime Sexual Assault among Incarcerated Women," *Prison Journal* 88, no. 3 (September 2008): 351–77; Shannon M. Lynch et al., "A Multisite Study of the Prevalence of Serious Mental Illness, PTSD, and Substance Use Disorders of Women in Jail," *Psychiatric Services* 65, no. 5 (May 2014): 670–74; and Cathy MacDaniels-Wilson and Joanne Belknap, "The Extensive Sexual Violation and Sexual Abuse Histories of Incarcerated Women," *Violence Against Women* 14, no. 10 (2008): 1090–1127.

49. Bonnie L. Green et al., "Trauma Experiences and Mental Health Among Incarcerated Women," *Psychological Trauma: Theory, Research, Practice, and Policy* 8, no. 4 (2016): 455–63; Raj et al., "Prevalence and Patterns of Sexual Assault"; US Commission on Civil Rights, *Women in Prison: Seeking Justice behind Bars* (Washington, DC: United States Commission on Civil Rights,

2020); and Nancy Wolff, Jing Shi, and Jane A. Siegel, "Patterns of Victimization among Male and Female Inmates: Evidence of an Enduring Legacy," *Violence and Victims* 24, no. 4 (2009): 469–84.

50. Gabriel Arkles, "Regulating Prison Sexual Violence," *Northeastern University Law Journal* 7, no. 1 (2015): 69–124.

51. The Sentencing Project, *Fact Sheet: Incarcerated Women and Girls* (Washington, DC: The Sentencing Project, 2020), 1–2.

52. Leah Wang, "The U.S. Criminal Justice System Disproportionately Hurts Native People: The Data, Visualized," Prison Policy Initiative, October 8, 2021, www.prisonpolicy.org/blog/ 2021/10/08/indigenouspeoplesday.

53. Sentencing Project, *Fact Sheet*, 4.

54. ACLU, "ACLU National Prison Project," accessed February 23, 2022, www .aclu.org/other/aclu-national-prison-project; Amnesty International, "USA: Prisoners Held in Extreme Solitary Confinement in Breach of International Law," July 16, 2014, https://www.amnesty.org/en/latest/news/2014/07/usa-prisoners-held-extreme -solitary-confinement-breach-international-law; Human Rights Watch, "US: Look Critically at Widespread Use of Solitary Confinement," June 18, 2012, www.hrw .org/news/2012/06/18/us-look-critically-widespread-use-solitary-confinement; and Richie, *Arrested Justice*.

55. Sentencing Project, *Fact Sheet*, 1.

56. Critical Resistance, "The Prison Industrial Complex," accessed February 23, 2022, http://criticalresistance.org/about/not-so-common-language.

57. Gregg Barak, Paul Leighton, and Allison Cotton, *Class, Race, Gender and Crime*, 5th ed. (Lanham, MD: Rowman and Littlefield, 2018), 13–14.

58. Walby, *Theorizing Patriarchy*, 171.

59. Ptacek, *Battered Women in the Courtroom*.

60. Linda Gordon, *Heroes of Their Own Lives: The Politics and History of Family Violence* (New York: Viking, 1988), 285.

61. Liz Kelly, *Surviving Sexual Violence* (Minneapolis: University of Minnesota Press, 1988); Liz Kelly, "Standing the Test of Time? Reflections on the Concept of the Continuum of Sexual Violence," in *Handbook on Sexual Violence*, ed. Jennifer M. Brown and Sandra L. Walklate (London: Routledge, 2012), xviii–xxxvi.

CHAPTER 2. THE HIDDEN DRAMAS OF MASCULINITY

Epigraph: Simone de Beauvoir, *The Second Sex*, trans. Constance Borde and Sheila Malovany-Chevallier (New York: Alfred A. Knopf, 2010), 652.

1. Beauvoir, *Second Sex*, 500.

2. Viveka Enander, "Leaving Jekyll and Hyde: Emotion Work in the Context of Intimate Partner Violence," *Feminism & Psychology* 21, no. 1 (2011): 29–48; and Erin Street Mateer, "Compelling Jekyll to Ditch Hyde: How the Law Ought to Address Batterer Duplicity," *Howard Law Journal* 48, no. 1 (2004): 525–70.

3. Sylvia Walby, *Theorizing Patriarchy* (Oxford, UK: Basil Blackwell, 1990).

4. Raewyn Connell and Rebecca Pearse, *Gender: In World Perspective*, 3rd ed. (Cambridge, UK: Polity Press, 2014), 101; and James W. Messerschmidt, *Crime as Structured Action: Doing Masculinities, Race, Class, Sexuality, and Crime* (Lanham, MD: Rowman and Littlefield, 2014), 24.

5. James W. Messerschmidt, *Masculinities and Crime: Critique and Reconceptualization of Theory* (Lanham, MD: Rowman and Littlefield, 1993), 81.

6. Raewyn Connell and James W. Messerschmidt, "Hegemonic Masculinity: Rethinking the Concept," *Gender and Society* 19, no. 6 (2005): 848.

7. Messerschmidt, *Masculinities and Crime*, 82.

8. Sylvia Walby, "Theorising Patriarchy," *Sociology* 23, no. 2 (1989): 225; and Raeywyn Connell, *Masculinities*, 2nd ed. (Berkeley: University of California Press, 2005), 104.

9. Joey L. Mogul, Andrea J. Ritchie, and Kay Whitlock, *Queer (In)Justice: The Criminalization of LGBT People in the United States* (Boston: Beacon Press, 2012).

10. Messerschmidt, *Masculinities and Crime*, 80.

11. Messerschmidt, *Masculinities and Crime*, 84.

12. Raewyn Connell, "Masculinity Research and Global Change," *Masculinities and Social Change* 1, no. 1 (2012): 4–18.

13. Angela J. Hattery and Earl Smith, *Gender, Power, and Violence: Responding to Sexual and Intimate Partner Violence in Society Today* (Lanham, MD: Rowman and Littlefield, 2019).

14. Swanee Hunt, "#MeToo Women Punished in Ways They Feared," *Boston Globe*, October 12, 2019; and Rebecca Traister, "The Toll of #MeToo: Assessing the Costs for Those Who Came Forward," *New York Magazine*, October 25, 2019.

15. Messerschmidt, *Masculinities and Crime*, 85.

16. R. Emerson Dobash and Russell P. Dobash, *Violence against Wives* (New York: Free Press, 1979); Ellen Pence and Michael Paymar, *Education Groups for Men Who Batter: The Duluth Model* (New York: Springer, 1983); Hillary Potter, *Battle Cries: Black Women and Intimate Partner Abuse* (New York: NYU Press, 2008); and Evan Stark, *Coercive Control: How Men Entrap Women in Personal Life* (New York: Oxford University Press, 2007).

17. Connell and Messerschmidt, "Hegemonic Masculinity," 848.

18. James Messerschmidt, *Gender, Heterosexuality, and Youth Violence: The Struggle for Recognition* (Lanham, MD: Rowman and Littlefield, 2012), 151.

19. Connell and Messerschmidt, "Hegemonic Masculinity," 848.

20. Raewyn Connell, *Gender and Power: Society, the Person and Sexual Politics* (Stanford, CA: Stanford University Press, 1987), 186–87.

21. Connell, *Gender and Power*, 187.

22. Charles Taylor, "The Politics of Recognition," in *Multiculturalism: Examining the Politics of Recognition*, ed. Amy Gutman (Princeton, NJ: Princeton University Press, 1994), 25.

23. Taylor, "Politics of Recognition," 25.

24. Taylor, "Politics of Recognition," 36.

25. Taylor, " Politics of Recognition," 26.

26. Walby, *Theorizing Patriarchy*.

27. Taylor, "Politics of Recognition," 25.

28. Melissa V. Harris-Perry, *Sister Citizen: Shame, Stereotypes, and Black Women in America* (New Haven, CT: Yale University Press, 2011), 104.

29. Michelle Alexander, *The New Jim Crow,* 10th anniversary ed. (New York: New Press, 2020); and Michael Tonry, *Punishing Race: A Continuing American Dilemma* (New York: Oxford University Press, 2011).

30. Douglas S. Massey and Nancy A. Denton, *American Apartheid: Segregation and the Making of the Underclass* (Cambridge, MA: Harvard University Press, 1993); and William Julius Wilson, *The Truly Disadvantaged: The Inner City, the Underclass, and Public Policy,* 2nd. ed. (Chicago: University of Chicago Press, 2012).

31. Alexander, New Jim Crow; Todd R. Clear, *Imprisoning Communities: How Mass Incarceration Makes Disadvantaged Neighborhoods Worse* (New York: Oxford University Press, 2009); Marc Mauer and Meda Chesney-Lind, eds., In*visible Punishment: The Collateral Consequences of Mass Imprisonment* (New York: The New Press, 2002); and Keramet A. Reiter, *Mass Incarceration* (New York: Oxford University Press, 2017).

32. Ujunwa Anakwenze and Daniyal Zuberi, "Mental Health and Poverty in the Inner City," *Health & Social Work* 38, no. 3 (2013): 147–57; Christopher G. Hudson, "Socioeconomic Status and Mental Illness: Tests of the Social Causation and Selection Hypotheses," *American Journal of Orthopsychiatry* 75, no. 1 (2005): 3–18; and Branndon Vick, Khristine Jones, and Sophie Mitra, "Poverty and Severe Psychiatric Disorder in the U.S.: Evidence from the Medical Expenditure Panel Survey," *Journal of Mental Health and Economics* 15, no. 2 (2012): 83–96.

33. Angela P. Harris, "Heteropatriarchy Kills: Challenging Gender Violence in a Prison Nation," *Washington University Journal of Law & Policy* 37 (2011): 13–65; Don Sabo, Terry A. Kupers, and Willie London, eds., *Prison Masculinities* (Philadelphia: Temple University Press, 2001; and SpearIt, "Gender Violence in Prison & Hyper-Masculinities in the 'Hood': Cycles of Destructive Masculinity," *Washington University Journal of Law & Policy* 37 (2011): 89–147.

34. Robert Louis Stevenson, *Strange Case of Dr. Jekyll and Mr. Hyde* (London: Longman, Greens, 1886).

35. Todd Venezia, "The Terrifying 'Psychopath' Who Inspired 'Dr. Jekyll and Mr. Hyde,'" *New York Post,* November 6, 2016.

36. Steven Padnick, "What Everyone Gets Wrong about Jekyll and Hyde," Tor.com, June 22, 2012, www.tor.com/2012/06/22/what-everybody-gets-wrong -about-jekyll-and-hyde.

37. Walter S. DeKeseredy and Martin D. Schwartz, *Male Peer Support and Violence against Women* (Boston: Northeastern University Press, 2013).

38. Walter S. DeKeseredy and Marilyn Corsianos, *Violence against Women in Pornography* (New York: Routledge, 2016).

39. Messerschmidt, *Masculinities and Crime,* 85.

40. Messerschmidt, *Masculinities and Crime,* 147.

41. Messerschmidt, *Crime as Structured Action,* 13–36.

42. Messerschmidt, *Crime as Structured Action,* 85.

43. Steven F. Messner and Richard Rosenfeld, *Crime and the American Dream,* 4th ed. (Belmont, CA: Wadsworth, 2007), 8.

20

44. Robin Cox, "The Ruthless Overlords of Silicon Valley," *Newsweek*, March 12, 2012, https://www.newsweek.com/ruthless-overlords-silicon-valley -63639; and Will Oremus, "The Ruthless Tactics Keeping Amazon on Top," *OneZero*, July 25, 2020, https://onezero.medium.com/the-ruthless-tactics-keeping -amazon-on-top-fa6bd2e91117.

45. Katy Cook, *The Psychology of Silicon Valley: Ethical Threats and Emotional Unintelligence in the Tech Industry* (Cham, Switzerland: Palgrave Macmillan, 2020).

46. Allison Scott, Freada Kapor Klein, and Uriridiakoghene Onovakpuri, "Tech Leavers Study," Kapor Center, April 27, 2017, www.kaporcenter.org/wp -content/uploads/2017/08/TechLeavers2017.pdf.

47. Sky Ariella, "Diversity in High Tech Statistics," Zippia: The Career Expert, December 9, 2021, www.zippia.com/advice/diversity-in-high-tech-statistics.

48. Alexander, *New Jim Crow*; Clear, *Imprisoning Communities*; Donna Coker and Ahjané D. Macquoid, "Why Opposing Hyper-Incarceration Should Be Central to the Work of the Anti-Domestic Violence Movement," *University of Miami Race & Social Justice Law Review* 5 (2015): 585–618; and SpearIt, "Gender Violence in Prison."

49. Connell, *Masculinities*, 68.

CHAPTER 3. FAILED FEMININITY AND PSYCHOLOGICAL CRUELTY

Epigraph: Stephanie McCarter, "The Bad Wives: Misogyny's Age-Old Roots in the Home," *Eidolon*, April 9, 2018.

1. Kathleen Ferraro, *Neither Angels nor Demons: Women, Crime, and Victimization* (Boston: Northeastern University Press, 2006); Katherine Kirkwood, *Leaving Abusive Partners* (London: Sage, 1993); and Hillary Potter, *Battle Cries: Black Women and Intimate Partner Abuse* (New York: NYU Press, 2008).

2. Simone de Beauvoir, *The Second Sex*, trans. by Constance Borde and Sheila Malovany-Chevallier (New York: Alfred A. Knopf, 2010), 156, 162.

3. Patricia Hill Collins, *Black Feminist Thought: Knowledge, Consciousness, and the Politics of Empowerment* (Boston: Unwin Hyman, 1990), 69.

4. Luana Ross, *Inventing the Savage: The Social Construction of Native American Criminality* (Austin: University of Texas Press, 1998); Rosiland S. Chou, *Asian American Sexual Politics: The Construction of Race, Gender, and Ethnicity* (Lanham, MD: Rowman and Littlefield, 2005); and Natalie Delia Deckard et al., "Controlling Images of Immigrants in the Mainstream and Black Press: The Discursive Power of the 'Illegal Latino,'" *Latino Studies* 18 (2020): 581–602.

5. Martin Gilens, *Why Americans Hate Welfare* (Chicago: University of Chicago Press, 1999); Wahneema Lubiano, "Black Ladies, Welfare Queens, and State Minstrels: Ideological Wars by Narrative Means," in *Race-ing Justice, Engendering Power: Essays on Anita Hill, Clarence Thomas and the Construction of Social Reality*, ed. Toni Morrison (New York: Pantheon Books, 1992), 323–63; and Jill Quadagno, *The Color of Welfare: How Racism Undermined the War on Poverty* (New York: Oxford University Press, 1994).

6. Alana Semuels, "The End of Welfare as We Know It," *Atlantic*, April 1, 2016, www.theatlantic.com/business/archive/2016/04/the-end-of-welfare-as-we -know-it/476322.

7. Dorothy E. Roberts, "Critical Race Feminism," in *Research Handbook on Feminist Jurisprudence*, ed. Robin West and Cynthia G. Bowman (Cheltenham, UK: Edward Elgar Publishing, 2019), 112–26.

8. Roberts, "Critical Race Feminism," 118.

9. Roberts, "Critical Race Feminism," 120.

10. Luis Ayala, Elena Barcela-Martin, and Jorge Martinez-Vasquez, "Devolu-tion in the U.S. Welfare Reform: Divergence and Degradation in State Benefits," ECINEQ Working Papers 587, Society for the Study of Economic Inequality, 2021, www.ecineq.org/milano/WP/ECINEQ2021-587.pdf; and Leah Hamil-ton, *Welfare Doesn't Work: Promises of Basic Income for a Failed American Safety Net* (Cham, Switzerland: Palgrave Macmillan, 2020).

11. Rachel J. Gallagher, "Welfare Reform's Inadequate Implementation of the Family Violence Option: Exploring Dual Oppression of Poor Domestic Violence Victims," *Journal of Gender, Social Policy, and the Law* 19, no. 3 (2011): 987–1007; and Deborah M. Weissman, "In Pursuit of Economic Justice: The Political Economy of Domestic Violence Laws and Policies," *Utah Law Review* 1, no. 1 (2020): 1–67.

12. Andrea L. Lewis and Sara L. Sommervold, "Death, But Is It Murder? The Role of Stereotypes and Cultural Perceptions in the Wrongful Convictions of Women," *Albany Law Review* 78, no. 3 (2014–2015): 1035–58; and Elizabeth Webster, "Gendering and Racing Wrongful Conviction: Intersectionality, Nor-mal Crimes and Women's Experience of Miscarriage of Justice," *Albany Law Review* 78, no. 3 (2014–2015): 973–1033.

13. Joey L. Mogul, Andrea J. Ritchie, and Kay Whitlock, *Queer (In)Justice: The Criminalization of LGBT People in the United States* (Boston: Beacon Press, 2011).

14. Andrea J. Ritchie, *Invisible No More: Police Violence Against Black Women and Women of Color* (Boston: Beacon Press, 2017).

15. Melissa V. Harris-Perry, *Sister Citizen: Shame, Stereotypes, and Black Women in America* (New Haven, CT: Yale University Press, 2011), 87.

16. Bitch Media, "About Us," accessed August 11, 2021, www.bitchmedia .org/about-us.

17. Nikki Graf, "Key Findings on Marriage and Cohabitation in the U.S.," Pew Research Center, November 6, 2019, www.pewresearch.org/fact-tank/2019 /11/06/key-findings-on-marriage-and-cohabitation-in-the-u-s.

18. Kim Parker and Renee Stepler, "As U.S. Marriage Rate Hovers at 50%, Edu-cation Gap in Marital Status Widens," Pew Research Center, September 14, 2017, www.pewresearch.org/fact-tank/2017/09/14/as-u-s-marriage-rate-hovers-at-50 -education-gap-in-marital-status-widens; and Wendy Wang, "The Link Between a College Education and a Lasting Marriage," Pew Research Center, December 4, 2015, www.pewresearch.org/fact-tank/2015/12/04/education-and-marriage.

19. Megan L. Haselschwerdt and Jennifer L. Hardesty, "Managing Secrecy and Disclosure of Domestic Violence in Affluent Communities," *Journal of Mar-riage and Family* 79 (April 2017): 562.

20. Karen M. Devries et al., "Intimate Partner Violence and Incident Depressive Symptoms and Suicide Attempts: A Systematic Review of Longitudinal Studies," *PLoS Medicine* 10, no. 5 (May 2013), https://doi.org/10.1371/journal.pmed.1001439.

CHAPTER 4. TERROR, FEAR, AND CAUTION: PHYSICAL VIOLENCE AND THREATS

Epigraph: Lakshmi Puri, "Fear of Violence affects the Everyday Lives of Women and Girls," UN Women, March 16, 2016,www.unwomen.org/en/news/stories/2016/3/lakshmi-puri-at-habitat-iii-agenda-and-gender-equality.

1. United Nations, "Gender Statistics," United Nations Department of Economic and Social Affairs, accessed August 11, 2021, https://unstats.un.org/unsd/gender/vaw.

2. Shannan Catalano et al., *Female Victims of Violence* (Washington, DC: Bureau of Justice Statistics, US Department of Justice, Office of Justice Programs, September 2009).

3. Emiko Petrosky et al., "Racial and Ethnic Differences in Homicides of Adult Women and the Role of Intimate Partner Violence—United States, 2003–2014," *Morbidity and Mortality Weekly Report* 66, no. 28 (July 21, 2017): 741.

4. Amy E. Bonami et al., "Intimate Partner Violence and Neighborhood Income: A Longitudinal Analysis," *Violence Against Women* 20, no. 1 (January 2014): 42–58; Claire M. Renzetti, "Economic Issues and Intimate Partner Violence," in *Sourcebook on Violence against Women*, 2nd ed. (Los Angeles, CA: Sage, 2011), 171–87; and Stella M. Resko, *Intimate Partner Violence and Women's Insecurity* (El Paso, TX: LFB Scholarly Publishing, 2010).

5. Max Horkheimer, "Authority and the Family," in Horkheimer, *Critical Theory: Selected Essays*, trans. Matthew J. O'Connell (1936; New York: Continuum, 1972), 57.

6. Brian Ogawa, *Walking on Eggshells: Practical Counsel for Women in or Leaving an Abusive Relationship* (Dubuque, IA: Kendall Hunt, 2009).

7. Nancy Glass et al., "Non-Fatal Strangulation is an Important Risk Factor for Homicide of Women," *Journal of Emergency Medicine* 35, no. 3 (2008): 329–35.

8. Kenneth R. Conner, Catherine Cerulli, and Eric D. Caine, "Threatened and Attempted Suicide by Partner-Violent Male Respondents Petitioned to Family Violence Court," *Violence and Victims* 17, no. 2 (2002): 115–25.

9. Hillary Potter, *Battle Cries: Black Women and Intimate Partner Abuse* (New York: NYU Press, 2008), 136–37.

10. Lisa Goodman et al., "The Intimate Partner Violence Strategies Index: Development and Application," *Violence Against Women* 9, no. 2 (2003): 163–86.

11. Dana Crowley Jack and Alisha Ali, eds., *Silencing the Self Across Cultures: Depression and Gender in the Social World* (Oxford: Oxford University Press, 2010); Michelle N. Lafrance, *Women and Depression: Recovery and Resistance* (London: Routledge, 2009); and Michelle N. Lafrance and Janet M. Stoppard, "Constructing a Non-Depressed Self: Women's Accounts of Recovery from Depression," *Feminism & Psychology* 16, no. 3 (2006): 307–25.

12. Monica A. Lutgendorf, "Intimate Partner Violence and Women's Health," *Obstetrics & Gynecology* 134, no. 3 (2019): 470–80.

CHAPTER 5. THE CONTINUUM OF SEXUAL ABUSE

Epigraph: Liz Kelly, *Surviving Sexual Violence* (Minneapolis: University of Minnesota Press, 1988), 42.

1. Sharon G. Smith et al., *The National Intimate Partner and Sexual Violence Survey (NISVS): 2015 Data Brief—Updated Release* (Atlanta, GA: National Center for Injury Prevention and Control, Centers for Disease Control and Prevention, 2018).

2. Michele C. Black et al., *The National Intimate Partner and Sexual Violence Survey (NISVS): 2010 Summary Report* (Atlanta, GA: National Center for Injury Prevention and Control, Centers for Disease Control and Prevention, 2011).

3. Sylvia Walby, *Theorizing Patriarchy* (Oxford, UK: Basil Blackwell, 1990).

4. Kelly, *Surviving Sexual Violence*; and Liz Kelly, "Standing the Test of Time? Reflections on the Concept of the Continuum of Sexual Violence," in *Handbook on Sexual Violence*, ed. Jennifer M. Brown and Sandra. L. Walklate (London: Routledge, 2012), xvii–xxvi.

5. Kelly, *Surviving Sexual Violence*, 41.

6. Kelly, *Surviving Sexual Violence*, 76.

7. Kelly, *Surviving Sexual Violence*, 97.

8. Kelly, *Surviving Sexual Violence*, 95.

9. Kathleen Ferraro, *Neither Angels nor Demons: Women, Crime, and Victimization* (Boston: Northeastern University Press, 2006); and Evan Stark, *Coercive Control: How Men Entrap Women in Personal Life* (Oxford Oxford University Press, 2007).

10. Charles Taylor, "The Politics of Recognition," in *Multiculturalism: Examining the Politics of Recognition*, ed. Amy Gutman (Princeton, NJ: Princeton University Press, 1994), 25.

11. American College of Obstetricians and Gynecologists (ACOG), "Committee Opinion no. 554: Reproductive and Sexual Coercion," *Obstetrics and Gynecology* 121 (2013): 411–15; and Elizabeth Miller et al. "Reproductive Coercion: Connecting the Dots between Partner Violence and Unintended Pregnancy," *Contraception* 81, no. 6 (2010): 457–59.

12. Jana Jasinski, "Pregnancy and Domestic Violence: A Review of the Literature," *Trauma, Violence, & Abuse* 5, no. 1 (2004): 47–64; and Sandra L. Martin et al., *Domestic Violence during Pregnancy and the Postpartum Period* (Harrisburg, PA: VAWnet, a Project of the National Resource Center on Domestic Violence, 2012).

13. Walter S. DeKeseredy and Marilyn Corsianos, *Violence against Women in Pornography* (New York: Routledge, 2016).

14. Massachusetts General Laws, Chapter 265, Section 22 (n.d.); 10 U.S. Code § 920, Art. 120 (2012).

15. Raquel Kennedy Bergen, *Wife Rape: Understanding the Response of Survivors and Service Providers* (Thousand Oaks, CA: Sage, 1996); Raquel Kennedy Bergen, *Marital Rape: New Research and Directions* (Harrisburg, PA: VAWnet,

a Project of the National Resource Center on Domestic Violence, 2006); David Finkelhor and Kersti Yllö, *License to Rape: Sexual Abuse of Wives* (New York: Henry Holt, 1985); Louise McOrmond-Plummer, ed., *Intimate Partner Sexual Violence* (London: Jessica Kingsley, 2014); and Diana E. H. Russell, *Rape in Marriage* (Bloomington: Indiana University Press, 1990).

16. Bergen, *Wife Rape.*

17. Kelly, *Surviving Sexual Violence*, 75.

18. Raquel Kennedy Bergen, "An Overview of Marital Rape Research in the United States: Limitations and Implications for Cross-Cultural Research," in *Marital Rape: Consent, Marriage, and Social Change in a Global Context*, ed. Kersti Yllö and M. Gabriela Torres (New York: Oxford University Press, 2016), 19–28.

19. UN Women, *Progress of the World's Women 2019–2020: Families in a Changing World* (New York: UN Women, 2019).

20. Madison Pauly, "It's 2019, and States Are Still Making Exceptions for Spousal Rape," *Mother Jones*, November 21, 2019.

21. Kersti Yllö, "Rape, Marital," in *Encyclopedia of Victimology and Crime Prevention*, ed. Bonnie S. Fisher and Steven P. Lab (Thousand Oaks, CA: Sage, 2010), 721.

22. Yllö, "Rape, Marital."

23. Sarah E. Ullman, *Talking about Sexual Assault: Society's Response to Survivors* (Washington, DC: American Psychological Association Press, 2010), 7.

24. Ullman, *Talking about Sexual Assault*; and Yllö, "Rape, Marital."

25. Ipsos/NPR, *Sexual Assault: A New and Divided Era of Understanding* (Washington, DC: Ipsos, October 31, 2018).

26. Ullman, *Talking about Sexual Assault*, 17.

27. Joanne Belknap, "Rape: Too Hard to Report and Too Easy to Discredit Victims," *Violence Against Women* 16, no. 12 (2010): 1335–44; Liz Kelly, "The (In)credible Words of Women: False Allegations in European Rape Research," *Violence Against Women* 16, no. 12 (2010): 1345–55; David Lisak et al., "False Allegations of Sexual Assault: An Analysis of Ten Years of Reported Cases," *Violence Against Women* 16, no. 12 (2010): 1318–34; and Kimberly A. Lonsway, "Trying to Move the Elephant in the Living Room: Responding to the Challenge of False Reports," *Violence Against Women* 16 no. 12 (2010): 1356–71.

28. Jennifer L. Dunn, *Judging Victims: Why We Stigmatize Survivors, and How They Reclaim Respect* (Boulder, CO: Lynne Rienner, 2010); and Nicola Henry and Anastasia Powell, eds., *Preventing Sexual Violence: Approaches to Overcoming a Rape Culture* (London: Palgrave Macmillan, 2014).

29. Charisse Jones and Kumea Shorter-Gooden, *Shifting: The Double Lives of Black Women in America* (New York: Harper Perennial, 2004), 60.

30. Ullman, *Talking about Sexual Assault*, 99.

31. Patricia Hill Collins, *Black Feminist Thought: Knowledge, Consciousness, and the Politics of Empowerment* (Boston: Unwin Hyman, 1990), 77.

32. Andrea Ritchie, *Invisible No More: Police Violence against Black Women and Women of Color* (Boston: Beacon Press, 2017); and Ullman, Talking about Sexual Assault.

33. Prachi H. Bhuptani and Terri L. Messman-Moore, "Blame and Shame in Sexual Assault," in *Handbook of Sexual Assault and Sexual Assault Prevention*, ed. William T. O'Donohue and Paul A. Schewe, 309–35 (Cham, Switzerland: Springer, 2019), 309.

34. Melanie F. Shepard and James A. Campbell, "The Abusive Behavior Inventory: A Measure of Psychological and Physical Abuse," *Journal of Interpersonal Violence* 7, no. 3 (1992): 291–305.

35. Lesia M. Ruglass and Kathleen Kendall-Tackett, *Psychology of Trauma 101* (New York: Springer, 2015.

36. Andrew P. Levin, Stuart B. Kleinman, and John S. Adler, "DSM-5 and Posttraumatic Stress Disorder," *Journal of the American Academy of Psychiatry and the Law* 42, no. 2 (2014): 146–58.

37. Levin, Kleinman, and Adler, "DSM-5 and Posttraumatic Stress Disorder," 149.

38. Rebecca Campbell, Emily Dworkin, and Giannina Cabral, "An Ecological Model of the Impact of Sexual Assault on Women's Mental Health," *Trauma, Violence, & Abuse* 10, no. 3 (2009): 225–46; and Nicole P. Yuan, Mary P. Koss, and Mirto Stone, *The Psychological Consequences of Sexual Trauma* (Harrisburg, PA: VAWnet, a Project of the National Resource Center on Domestic Violence, 2006).

39. Rebecca Campbell, "The Psychological Impact of Rape Victims' Experiences with the Legal, Medical, and Mental Health Systems," *American Psychologist* 63, no. 8 (2008): 702–17.

40. Jennifer M. Gómez and Robyn L. Gobin, "Black Women and Girls & #MeToo: Rape, Cultural Betrayal, & Healing," *Sex Roles* 82, nos.1–2 (2020): 1–12; Ruglass and Kendall-Tackett, *Psychology of Trauma 101*; and Carolyn M. West and Kalimah Johnson, *Sexual Violence in the Lives of African American Women* (Harrisburg, PA: VAWnet, a Project of the National Resource Center on Domestic Violence, 2013).

41. Jennifer A. Bennice et al., "The Relative Effects of Intimate Partner Physical and Sexual Violence on Post-Traumatic Stress Disorder Symptomatology," *Violence and Victims* 18, no. 1 (2003): 87–94; Bergen, "Overview of Marital Rape Research in the United States"; Shannon B. Harper, "Exploring the Relationship between Intimate Partner Sexual Assault, Severe Abuse, and Coercive Control," in *Handbook of Sexual Assault and Sexual Assault Prevention*, ed. William T. O'Donohue and Paul A. Schewe (Cham, Switzerland: Springer, 2019), 813–31; and Jessie L. Krienert and Jeffrey A. Walsh, "An Examination of Intimate Partner Sexual Violence: Comparing Marital and Nonmarital Incidents Employing NIBRS Data, 2008–2012," *Partner Abuse* 9, no. 1 (2018): 41–57.

42. Bergen, "Overview of Marital Rape Research in the United States"; and Krienert and Walsh, "Examination of Intimate Partner Sexual Violence."

43. Krienert and Walsh, "Examination of Intimate Partner Sexual Violence."

44. Walby, *Theorizing Patriarchy*.

45. Kersti Yllö, "Wife Rape: A Social Problem for the 21st Century," *Violence Against Women* 5, no. 9 (1999): 1059–63; and Kersti Yllö, "Prologue: Understanding Marital Rape in Global Context," in *Marital Rape: Consent, Marriage,*

and Social Change in a Global Context, ed. Kersti Yllö and M. Gabriela Torres (New York: Oxford University Press, 2016), 1–6.

46. Yllö, "Wife Rape," 1062.

47. Yllö, "Wife Rape," 1062.

48. Krienert and Walsh, "Examination of Intimate Partner Sexual Violence"; Kersti Yllö and M. Gabriela Torres, eds., *Marital Rape: Consent, Marriage, and Social Change in a Global Context* (New York: Oxford University Press, 2016).

49. Andrea Dworkin, *Pornography: Men Possessing Women* (New York: Penguin, 1981), 10.

CHAPTER 6. ECONOMIC ABUSE:
CONTROL, SABOTAGE, AND EXPLOITATION

Epigraph: Sylvia Walby, "Gender, Class and Stratification," in *Gender and Stratification*, ed. Rosemary Crompton and Michael Mann (Cambridge, UK: Polity Press, 1986), 42.

1. Adrienne E. Adams et al., "Development of the Scale of Economic Abuse," *Violence Against Women* 14, no. 5 (2008): 563–88.

2. National Institute of Justice, "Overview of Intimate Partner Violence," October 23, 2007, https://nij.ojp.gov/topics/articles/overview-intimate-partner -violence.

3. US Department of Justice, "What Is Domestic Violence?" accessed August 11, 2021, www. justice.gov/ovw/domestic-violence.

4. Cynthia Hess and Alona Del Rosario, *Dreams Deferred: A Survey on the Impact of Intimate Partner Violence on Survivors' Education, Careers, and Economic Security* (Washington, DC: Institute for Women's Policy Research, 2018), 8–9.

5. Rosemary Crompton and Michael Mann, eds., *Gender and Stratification* (Cambridge, UK: Polity Press, 1986); Caroline Ramazanoglu, *Feminism and the Contradictions of Oppression* (London: Routledge, 1986); and Sylvia Walby, *Theorizing Patriarchy* (Oxford, UK: Basil Blackwell, 1990).

6. Erik Olin Wright and Joel Rogers, *American Society: How It Really Works* (New York: W. W. Norton, 2010) (produce social classes); and Joan Acker, *Class Questions, Feminist Answers* (Lanham, MD: Rowman & Littlefield, 2006); and Patricia Hill Collins, "Shifting the Center: Race, Class, and Feminist Theorizing about Motherhood," in *Mothering: Ideology, Experience, and Agency*, ed. Evelyn Nakano Glenn, Grace Chang, and Linda Rennie Forcey (New York: Routledge, 1994), 371–89 (gendered and racialized processes).

7. David Morgan, "Class and Masculinity," in *Handbook of Studies on Men & Masculinities*, ed. Michael S. Kimmel, Jeff Hearn, and R. W. Connell (Newbury Park, CA: Sage, 2005), 165–77.

8. Walby, *Theorizing Patriarchy*.

9. Judy L. Postmus, Sarah-Beth Plummer, and Amanda Sytlianou, "Measuring Economic Abuse in the Lives of Survivors: Revising the Scale of Economic Abuse," *Violence Against Women* 22, no. 6 (2016): 692–703.

10. Robin Bleiweis, "Quick Facts about the Gender Wage Gap," Center for American Progress, March 24, 2020, www.americanprogress.org/article/quick-facts-gender-wage-gap.

11. Leila Schochet, "The Child Care Crisis Is Keeping Women Out of the Workforce," Center for American Progress, March 28, 2019, www.american progress.org/article/child-care-crisis-keeping-women-workforce (daycare); and Sarah Jane Glynn and Jane Farrell, "The United States Needs to Guarantee Paid Maternity Leave," Center for American Progress, March 8, 2013, www.american progress.org/article/the-united-states-needs-to-guarantee-paid-maternity-leave (maternity or paternity leave).

12. Yekateria Chzhen, Annan Gromada, and Gwyther Rees, *Are the World's Richest Countries Family Friendly? Policy in the OECD and EU* (Florence, Italy: United Nations Children's Fund [UNICEF] Office of Research, 2019).

13. Arlene Daniels, "Invisible Work," *Social Problems* 34, no. 5 (1987): 403–15.

14. Arlie Russell Hochschild (with Anne Machung), *The Second Shift: Working Parents and the Revolution at Home* (New York: Viking, 1989).

15. Organisation for Economic Co-Operation and Development (OECD), "Employment: Time Spent in Paid and Unpaid Work, by Sex," accessed August 11, 2021, https://stats.oecd.org/index.aspx? queryid=54757.

16. Postmus, Plummer, and Sytlianou, "Measuring Economic Abuse in the Lives of Survivors."

17. William Adrian Bonger, *Criminality and Economic Conditions*, trans. Henry P. Horton (Boston: Little, Brown, 1916), 486.

18. Bonger, *Criminality and Economic Conditions*, 667.

19. Elliott Currie, "Market, Crime and Community: Toward a Mid-Range Theory of Post-Industrial Violence," *Theoretical Criminology* 1, no. 2 (1997): 151–52.

20. Currie, "Market, Crime and Community," 152.

21. Currie, "Market, Crime and Community," 163.

CHAPTER 7. THE EMOTIONAL DYNAMICS OF ENTRAPMENT: LOVE, FEAR, ANGER, GUILT, AND SHAME

Epigraph: Arlie Russell Hochschild, "Emotion Work, Feeling Rules, and Social Structure," *American Journal of Sociology* 85, no. 3 (1979): 561, 562.

1. Hochschild, "Emotion Work," 552.

2. Hochschild, "Emotion Work," 551.

3. Hochschild, "Emotion Work," 561.

4. Hochschild, "Emotion Work," 558.

5. Hochschild, "Emotion Work," 562.

6. Southern Baptist Convention, "The Baptist Faith and Message 2000," accessed May 27, 2021, https://bfm.sbc.net/ bfm2000/#sviii-the-family.

7. David Crary, "Growing Number of Southern Baptist Women Question Roles," *ABC News*, March 24, 2021, https://abcnews.go.com/US/wireStory /doubts-southern-baptists-limits-womens-roles-76651536.

8. Holy See, "Letter to the Bishops of the Catholic Church on the Collaboration of Men and Women in the Church and in the World," *Daily Bulletin of the Holy See Press Office*, accessed June 9, 2021, www.vatican.va/roman_curia /congregations/cfaith/documents/rc_con_cfaith_doc_20040731_collaboration _en.html.

9. Judith Herman, *Trauma and Recovery* (New York: Basic Books, 1992), 94, 189.

10. Herman, *Trauma and Recovery*, 189.

11. Herman, *Trauma and Recovery*, 189.

12. Douglas Brownridge, "Violence against Women Post-Separation," *Aggression and Violent Behavior* 11, no. 5 (2006): 514–30; and Walter S. DeKeseredy, Molly Dragiewicz, and Martin D. Schwartz, *Abusive Endings: Separation and Divorce Violence Against Women* (Berkeley: University of California Press, 2017).

13. Tracey Burton, "'He's Always in My Head, Always in My Mind': A Psycho-Social Study into the Emotional Experience of Teaching a Child at Risk of Exclusion (doctoral thesis, University of Essex, May 2019).

14. Petya Fitzpatrick and Rebecca E. Olson, "A Rough Road Map to Reflexivity in Qualitative Research into Emotions," *Emotion Review* 7, no. 1 (2014): 49–54.

15. Herman, *Trauma and Recovery*, 35.

16. Herman, *Trauma and Recovery*, 35.

17. Herman, *Trauma and Recovery*, 35.

18. Herman, *Trauma and Recovery*.

19. Inger Burnett-Zeigler, *Nobody Knows the Trouble I've Seen: The Emotional Lives of Black Women* (New York: Amistad, 2021), 46.

20. Hillary Potter, *Battle Cries: Black Women and Intimate Partner Abuse* (New York: NYU Press, 2008).

21. Audre Lorde, *Sister Outsider: Essays & Speeches by Audre Lorde* (Trumansburg, NY: Crossing Press, 1984), 127, 129.

22. Soraya Chemaly, *Rage Becomes Her: The Power of Women's Anger* (New York: Atria Books, 2018), xiv.

23. Dana Crowley Jack, "The Anger of Hope and the Anger of Despair: How Anger Relates to Women's Depression," in *Situating Sadness: Women and Depression in Social Context*, ed. Janet M. Stoppard and Linda M. McMullen (New York: NYU Press, 2003), 83.

24. Arlie Russell Hochschild, "The Sociology of Feeling and Emotion: Selected Possibilities," in *Another Voice: Feminist Perspectives on Social Life and Social Science*, ed. Marcia Millman and Rosebeth Moss Kanter (Garden City, NY: Anchor, 1975), 295.

25. Viveka Enander and Carin Holmberg, "Why Does She Leave? The Leaving Process(es) of Battered Women," *Health Care for Women International* 29, no. 3 (2008): 200–226.

26. Lorde, *Sister Outsider*, 152.

27. Herman, *Trauma and Recovery*, 53.

28. June Price Tangney and Ronda L. Daring, *Shame and Guilt* (New York: Guilford Press, 2003).

29. Melissa V. Harris-Perry, *Sister Citizen: Shame, Stereotypes, and Black Women in America* (New Haven, CT: Yale University Press, 2011), 104.

30. Harris-Perry, *Sister Citizen*, 107.

31. Harris-Perry, *Sister Citizen*, 109.

32. Enander and Holmberg, "Why Does She Leave?"

33. Viveka Enander, "'A Fool to Keep Staying': Battered Women Labeling Themselves Stupid as an Expression of Gendered Shame," *Violence Against Women* 16, no. 5 (2010): 5–31.

34. Sherry B. Ortner, *Anthropology and Social Theory* (Durham, NC: Duke University Press, 2006).

35. Susan T. Fiske, *Envy Up, Scorn Down: How Status Divides Us* (New York: Russell Sage Foundation, 2011); Andrew Hacker, *Two Nations: Black and White, Separate, Hostile, Unequal* (New York: Scribner, 2003); Harris-Perry, *Sister Citizen*; Diane Reay, "Beyond Consciousness? The Psychic Landscape of Social Class," *Sociology* 39, no. 5 (2005): 911–28; and Andrew Sayer, *The Moral Significance of Class* (Cambridge: Cambridge University Press, 2005).

36. Sayer, *Moral Significance of Class*, 1.

37. Brené Brown, *I Thought It Was Just Me: Women Reclaiming Power and Courage in a Culture of Shame* (New York: Gotham Books, 2007), 107.

CHAPTER 8. SEPARATION, HEALING, AND JUSTICE

Epigraph: Viveka Enander and Carin Holmberg, "Why Does She Leave? The Leaving Process(es) of Battered Women," *Health Care for Women International* 29, no. 3 (2008): 211–12.

1. Enander and Holmberg, "Why Does She Leave?," 200–226.

2. Enander and Holmberg, "Why Does She Leave?," 200–226.

3. Deborah K. Anderson and Daniel G. Saunders, "Leaving an Abusive Partner: An Empirical Review of Predictors, the Process of Leaving, and Psychological Well-Being," *Trauma, Violence, & Abuse* 4, no. 2 (April 2003): 163–91.

4. Enander and Holmberg, "Why Does She Leave?," 218.

5. Rachel J. Gallagher, "Welfare Reform's Inadequate Implementation of the Family Violence Option: Exploring Dual Oppression of Poor Domestic Violence Victims," *American University Journal of Gender, Social Policy, and the Law* 19, no. 3 (2011): 987–1007; and Pranava Upadrashta, "Recent Developments: Child Exclusion Provisions: The Harmful Impacts on Domestic Violence Survivors," *Berkeley Journal of Gender, Law & Justice* 27, no. 1 (2012):113–41.

6. Stephanie Holcomb et al., "Implementation of the Family Violence Option 20 Years Later: A Review of State Welfare Rules for Domestic Violence Survivors," *Journal of Policy Practice* 16, no. 4 (2017): 415–31.

7. Gallagher, "Welfare Reform's Inadequate Implementation of the Family Violence Option," 1002.

8. Susan Sered and Maureen Norton-Hawk, *Can't Catch a Break: Gender, Jail, Drugs, and the Limits of Personal Responsibility* (Oakland: University of California Press, 2014), 46.

9. Anderson and Saunders, "Leaving an Abusive Partner"; and Deborah K. Anderson et al., "Long-Term Trends in Depression Among Women Separated from Abusive Partners," *Violence Against Women* 9, no. 7 (July 2003): 807–38.

10. Kate S. Adkins and Claire M. Kamp Dush, "The Mental Health of Mothers in and after Violent and Controlling Unions," *Social Science Research* 39, no. 6 (November 2010): 925–37.

11. Sara Elinoff Acker, *Unclenching Our Fists: Abusive Men on the Journey to Nonviolence* (Nashville, TN: Vanderbilt University Press, 2013), 168.

12. Enander and Holmberg, "Why Does She Leave?," 218.

13. Enander and Holmberg, "Why Does She Leave?," 218.

14. Mary P. Koss, "Restorative Justice for Acquaintance Rape and Misdemeanor Sex Crimes," in *Restorative Justice and Violence Against Women*, ed. James Ptacek (Oxford: Oxford University Press, 2010), 221.

15. Judith Lewis Herman, *Trauma and Recovery* (New York: Basic Books, 1992), 207.

16. Sylvia Walby, *Theorizing Patriarchy* (Oxford, UK: Basil Blackwell, 1990).

CONCLUSION

Epigraph: Kathleen J. Ferraro, *Neither Angels nor Demons: Women, Crime, and Victimization* (Boston: Northeastern University Press, 2006), 111.

1. Amy E. Bonami et al., "Intimate Partner Violence and Neighborhood Income: A Longitudinal Analysis," *Violence Against Women* 20, no. 1 (2014): 42–58; Claire M. Renzetti, "Economic Issues and Intimate Partner Violence," in *Sourcebook on Violence Against Women*, ed. Claire M. Renzetti, Jeffrey L. Edleson, and Raquel Kennedy Bergen (Los Angeles: Sage, 2011), 171–187; and Stella M. Resko, *Intimate Partner Violence and Women's Economic Insecurity* (El Paso, TX: LFB Scholarly Publishing, 2010).

2. Sylvia Walby, *Theorizing Patriarchy* (Oxford: Basil Blackwell, 1990).

3. James Ptacek, *Battered Women in the Courtroom: The Power of Judicial Responses* (Boston: Northeastern University Press, 1999).

4. Etiony Aldarondo, ed., *Advancing Social Justice through Clinical Practice* (New York: Routledge, 2007); Thema Bryant-Davis, *Thriving in the Wake of Trauma: A Multicultural Guide* (Lanham, MD: AltaMira Press, 2005); Inger Burnett-Zeigler, *Nobody Knows the Trouble I've Seen: The Emotional Lives of Black Women* (New York: Amistad, 2021); Xavier L. Guadalupe-Diaz, *Transgressed: Intimate Partner Violence in Transgender Lives* (New York: NYU Press, 2019); Michelle Lafrance, *Women and Depression: Recovery and Resistance* (London: Routledge, 2009); Adam M. Messinger, *LGBTQ Intimate Partner Violence* (Oakland: University of California Press, 2020); Shavonne J. Moore-Lobban and Robyn J. Gobin, *The Black Woman's Guide to Overcoming Domestic Violence* (Oakland, CA: New Harbinger Publications, 2022); and Brenda Russell, ed., *Intimate Partner Violence and the LGBT+ Community* (Cham, Switzerland: Springer, 2020).

5. Susan Sered and Maureen Norton-Hawk, *Can't Catch a Break: Gender, Jail, Drugs, and the Limits of Personal Responsibility* (Oakland: University of California Press, 2014), 163.

6. Donna Coker, "Shifting Power for Battered Women: Law, Material Resources, and Poor Women of Color," *U.C. Davis Law Review* 33, no. 4 (Summer 2000): 1009–1055.

7. Coker, "Shifting Power for Battered Women," 1009.

8. Deborah M. Weissman, "In Pursuit of Economic Justice: The Political Economy of Domestic Violence Laws and Policies," *Utah Law Review* 2020, no. 1 (2020): 1–67.

9. Weissman, "In Pursuit of Economic Justice," 64.

10. Alma Center, "About: Our Core Values," accessed March 1, 2022, https://almacenter.org/about.

11. Anannya Bhattacharjee, *Whose Safety? Women of Color and the Violence of Law Enforcement* (Philadelphia: American Friends Service Committee, Committee on Women, Population, and the Environment, 2001), 26.

12. Bhattacharjee, "Whose Safety?"; and Beth E. Richie, *Arrested Justice: Black Women, Violence, and America's Prison Nation* (New York: NYU Press, 2012.

13. Richie, *Arrested Justice*, 164.

14. Donna Coker and Ahjané D. Macquoid, "Why Opposing Hyper-Incarceration Should Be Central to the Work of the Anti-Domestic Violence Movement," *University of Miami Race & Social Justice Law Review* 5 (2015): 585–618.

15. Sarah DeGue, Katherine A. Fowler, and Cynthia Calkins, "Deaths Due to Use of Lethal Force by Law Enforcement," *American Journal of Preventive Medicine* 51, no. 5, supp. 3 (2016): S173–87.

16. Andrea Ritchie, *Invisible No More: Police Violence against Black Women and Women of Color* (Boston: Beacon Press, 2017).

17. Leigh Goodmark, "Politics, Safety, and Officer-Involved Intimate Partner Violence," in *The Politicization of Safety: Critical Perspectives on Domestic Violence Responses*, ed. Jane K. Stoever (New York: NYU Press, 2019), 227–45.

18. Leigh Goodmark, *Decriminalizing Domestic Violence: A Balanced Policy Approach to Intimate Partner Violence* (Berkeley: University of California Press, 2018); and Jane K. Stoever, ed., *The Politicization of Safety: Critical Perspectives on Domestic Violence Responses* (New York: NYU Press, 2019.

19. Angela Y. Davis et al., *Abolition. Feminism. Now.* (Chicago: Haymarket Books, 2022), 50.

20. Angela Davis, cited in Hanna Phifer, "For Angela Davis and Gina Dent, Abolition Is the Only Way," *Harper's Bazaar*, January 14, 2022, www.harpersbazaar.com/culture/art-books-music/a38746835/angela-davis-gina-dent-abolition-feminism-now-interview.

21. Davis et al., *Abolition*, 50.

22. Angela Olivia Burton, "Toward Community Control of Child Welfare Funding: Repeal the Child Abuse Prevention and Treatment Act and De-Link Child Protection from Family Well Being," *Columbia Journal of Race and Law* 11, no. 3 (2021): 639–80; Dorothy E. Roberts, "Prison, Foster Care, and the Systemic Punishment of Black Mothers," *UCLA Law Review* 59, no. 6 (2012): 1474–1500; and Dorothy E. Roberts, *Torn Apart: How the Child Welfare System Destroys Black Families—and How Abolition Can Build a Safer World* (New York: Basic Books, 2022).

23. Dorothy E. Roberts, "Critical Race Feminism," in *Research Handbook on Feminist Jurisprudence*, ed. Robin West and Cynthia G. Bowman (Cheltenham, UK: Edward Elgar Publishing, 2019), 112–26.

24. Andrew Bacher-Hicks, Stephen B. Billings, and David J. Deming, "Proving the School-to-Prison Pipeline," *Education Next* 21, no. 4 (2021): 52–57.

25. Davis et al., *Abolition*, 77.

26. Davis et al., *Abolition*, 2.

27. James Ptacek, "Resisting Co-Optation: Three Feminist Challenges to Antiviolence Work," in *Restorative Justice and Violence against Women*, ed. James Ptacek (Oxford: Oxford University Press, 2010), 5–36.

28. Lara Bazelon, *Rectify: The Power of Restorative Justice after Wrongful Conviction* (Boston: Beacon Press, 2018); Susan L. Miller, *After the Crime: The Power of Restorative Justice Dialogues between Victims and Offenders* (New York: NYU Press, 2011); Danielle Sered, *Until We Reckon: Violence, Mass Incarceration, and a Road to Repair* (New York: NYU Press, 2019; Ptacek, *Restorative Justice and Violence against Women*; and Estelle Zinsstag and Marie Keenan, *Restorative Responses to Sexual Violence* (London: Routledge, 2017).

29. Mary P. Koss, "The RESTORE Program of Restorative Justice for Sex Crimes: Vision, Process, and Outcomes," *Journal of Interpersonal Violence* 29, no. 9 (2014): 1623–60; Joan Pennell et al., "Family and Community Approaches to Intimate Partner Violence: Restorative Programs in the United States," *Violence Against Women* 27, no. 10 (2021): 1608–29; Ptacek, *Restorative Justice and Violence against Women*; and Zinsstag and Keenan, *Restorative Responses to Sexual Violence*.

30. Emily Gaarder, "Lessons from a Restorative Circles Initiative for Intimate Partner Violence," *Restorative Justice: An International Journal* 3, no. 3 (2017): 342–367.

31. Jane Doe, Inc.: The Massachusetts Coalition Against Sexual Assault and Domestic Violence, "Transformative and Restorative Justice for Survivors of Sexual and Domestic Violence in Massachusetts" (conference sponsored by Jane Doe, Inc., Boston, December 20, 2020), https://janedoeinc.wildapricot.org/event-396846.

32. Sara Elinoff Acker, *Unclenching Our Fists: Abusive Men on the Journey to Nonviolence* (Nashville, TN: Vanderbildt University Press, 2013); and Edward Gondolf, *The Future of Batterer Programs: Reassessing the Future of Evidence-Based Practice* (Boston: Northeastern University Press, 2012).

33. Massachusetts Department of Public Health, *Guidelines and Standards for the Certification of Intimate Partner Abuse Education Programs* (Boston: Massachusetts Department of Public Health, 2015).

34. Judith Herman, "Justice from the Victim's Perspective," *Violence Against Women* 11, no. 5 (2005): 571–602.

35. James Gilligan and Bandy Lee, "The Resolve to Stop the Violence Project: Reducing Violence in the Community through a Jail-Based Initiative," *Journal of Public Health* 27, no. 2 (2005): 143–48; and Bandy Lee and James Gilligan, "The Resolve to Stop the Violence Project: Transforming an In-House Culture of Violence through a Jail-Based Programme," *Journal of Public Health* 27, no. 2 (2005): 149–55.

36. Fania E. Davis, *The Little Book of Race and Restorative Justice: Black Lives, Healing, and US Social Transformation* (New York: Good Books, 2019); and Angela P. Harris, "Heteropatriarchy Kills: Challenging Gender Violence in a Prison Nation," *Washington University Journal of Law & Policy* 37, no. 13 (2011): 13–65.

37. Davis, *Little Book of Race and Restorative Justice.*

38. Traci C. West, *Wounds of the Spirit: Black Women, Violence, and Resistance Ethics* (New York: NYU Press, 1999), 197–98.

39. Soniya Munshi, Bhavana Nancherla, and Tiloma Jayasinghe, "Building Towards Transformative Justice at Sakhi for South Asian Women," *University of Miami Race & Social Justice Law Review* 5, no. 2 (2015): 425.

40. Creative Interventions, home page, accessed March 9, 2022, www.creative-interventions.org.

41. Mimi M. Kim, "Alternative Interventions to Violence: Creative Interventions," *International Journal of Narrative Therapy and Community Work* 4 (2006): 45–52.

42. Creative Interventions, home page.

43. Davis et al., *Abolition*, 6–7.

44. Marie Fortune, *Is Nothing Sacred?* (Eugene, OR: Wipf & Stock, 1999), 114.

45. Marie Fortune, "Justice-Making in the Aftermath of Woman-Battering," in *Domestic Violence on Trial*, ed. Daniel Jay Sonkin (New York: Springer, 1987), 237–48; and Fortune, *Is Nothing Sacred?*

46. Fortune, "Justice-Making in the Aftermath of Woman-Battering," 247.

Bibliography

Acker, Joan. *Class Questions, Feminist Answers*. Lanham, MD: Rowman and Littlefield, 2006.

Acker, Sara Elinoff. *Unclenching Our Fists: Abusive Men on the Journey to Nonviolence*. Nashville, TN: Vanderbilt University Press, 2013.

Adams, Adrienne E., Chris M. Sullivan, Deborah Bybee, and Megan R. Greeson. "Development of the Scale of Economic Abuse." *Violence Against Women* 14, no. 5 (2008): 563–88.

Adkins, Kate S., and Claire M. Kamp Dush. "The Mental Health of Mothers in and after Violent and Controlling Unions." *Social Science Research* 39, no. 6 (November 2010): 925–37.

Aldarondo, Etiony, ed. *Advancing Social Justice through Clinical Practice*. New York: Routledge, 2007.

Alexander, Michelle. *The New Jim Crow*. 10th anniversary ed. New York: The New Press, 2020.

Alma Center. "About: Our Core Values." Accessed March 1, 2022. https://alma center.org/about.

American Civil Liberties Union (ACLU). "ACLU National Prison Project." Accessed February 23, 2022. www.aclu.org/other/aclu-national-prison -project.

American College of Obstetricians and Gynecologists (ACOG). "Committee Opinion No. 554: Reproductive and Sexual Coercion." *Obstetrics and Gynecology* 121 (2013): 411–15.

Amnesty International. "USA: Prisoners Held in Extreme Solitary Confinement in Breach of International Law." July 16, 2014. www.amnesty.org/en/latest

/news/2014/07/usa-prisoners-held-extreme-solitary-confinement-breach
-international-law.

Anakwenze, Ujunwa, and Daniyal Zuberi. "Mental Health and Poverty in the Inner City." *Health & Social Work* 38, no. 3 (2013): 147–57.

Anderson, Deborah K., and Daniel G. Saunders. "Leaving an Abusive Partner: An Empirical Review of Predictors, the Process of Leaving, and Psychological Well-Being." *Trauma, Violence, & Abuse* 4, no. 2 (April 2003): 163–91.

Anderson, Deborah K., Daniel G. Saunders, Meiko Yoshihama, Deborah I. Bybee, and Chris M. Sullivan. "Long-Term Trends in Depression Among Women Separated from Abusive Partners." *Violence Against Women* 9, no. 7 (July 2003): 807–38.

Ariella, Sky. "Diversity in High Tech Statistics." Zippia: The Career Expert, December 9, 2021. www.zippia.com/advice/diversity-in-high-tech-statistics.

Arkles, Gabriel. "Regulating Prison Sexual Violence." *Northeastern University Law Journal* 7, no. (2015): 69–124.

Ayala, Luis, Elena Barcela-Martin, and Jorge Martinez-Vasquez. "Devolution in the U.S. Welfare Reform: Divergence and Degradation in State Benefits." ECINEQ Working Papers 587. Society for the Study of Economic Inequality, 2021. www.ecineq.org/milano/WP/ECINEQ2021-587.pdf.

Bacher-Hicks, Andrew, Stephen B. Billings, and David J. Deming. "Proving the School-to-Prison Pipeline." *Education Next* 21, no. 4 (2021): 52–57.

Barak, Gregg, Paul Leighton, and Allison Cotton. *Class, Race, Gender and Crime.* 5th ed. Lanham, MD: Rowman and Littlefield, 2018.

Bazelon, Lara. *Rectify: The Power of Restorative Justice after Wrongful Conviction.* Boston: Beacon Press, 2018.

Beauvoir, Simone de. *The Second Sex.* Translated by Constance Borde and Sheila Malovany-Chevallier. New York: Alfred A. Knopf, 2010.

Belknap, Joanne. "Rape: Too Hard to Report and Too Easy to Discredit Victims." *Violence Against Women* 16, no. 12 (2010): 1335–44.

Benner, Katie. "Domestic Violence Has Increased during the Pandemic, Studies Show." *New York Times,* February 24, 2021.

Bennice, Jennifer A., Patricia A. Resick, Mindy Mechanic, and Millie Astin. "The Relative Effects of Intimate Partner Physical and Sexual Violence on Post-Traumatic Stress Disorder Symptomatology." *Violence and Victims* 18, no. 1 (2003): 87–94.

Bergen, Raquel Kennedy. *Marital Rape: New Research and Directions.* Harrisburg, PA: VAWnet, a Project of the National Resource Center on Domestic Violence, 2006.

———. "An Overview of Marital Rape Research in the United States: Limitations and Implications for Cross-Cultural Research." In *Marital Rape: Consent, Marriage, and Social Change in a Global Context,* edited by Kersti Yllö and M. Gabriela Torres, 19–28. New York: Oxford University Press, 2016.

———. *Wife Rape: Understanding the Response of Survivors and Service Providers.* Thousand Oaks, CA: Sage, 1996.

Bhattacharjee, Anannya. *Whose Safety? Women of Color and the Violence of Law Enforcement.* Philadelphia: American Friends Service Committee and the Committee on Women, Population, and the Environment, 2001.

Bhuptani, Prachi H., and Terri L. Messman-Moore. "Blame and Shame in Sexual Assault." In *Handbook of Sexual Assault and Sexual Assault Prevention*, edited by William T. O'Donohue and Paul A. Schewe, 309–35. Cham, Switzerland: Springer, 2019.

Bitch Media. "About Us." Accessed August 11, 2021. www.bitchmedia.org /about-us.

Black, Michele C., Kathleen C. Basile, Matthew J. Breiding, Sharon G. Smith, Mikel L. Walters, Melissa T. Merrick, Jieru Chen, and Mark R. Stevens. *The National Intimate Partner and Sexual Violence Survey (NISVS): 2010 Summary Report.* Atlanta, GA: National Center for Injury Prevention and Control, Centers for Disease Control and Prevention, 2011.

Blackburn, Ashley G., Janet L. Mullings, and James W. Marquart. "Sexual Assault in Prison and Beyond: Toward an Understanding of Lifetime Sexual Assault among Incarcerated Women." *Prison Journal* 88, no. 3 (September 2008): 351–77.

Bleiweis, Robin. "Quick Facts about the Gender Wage Gap." March 24, 2020. www.americanprogress.org/article/quick-facts-gender-wage-gap.

Boesch, Diane, and Shipla Phadke. "When Women Lose All the Jobs: Essential Actions for a Gender-Equitable Recovery." February 1, 2021. www .americanprogress.org/article/women-lose-jobs-essential-actions-gender -equitable-recovery.

Bonami, Amy E., Britton Trabert, Melissa L. Anderson, Mary A. Kernic, and Victoria L. Holt. "Intimate Partner Violence and Neighborhood Income: A Longitudinal Analysis." *Violence Against Women* 20, no. 1 (January 2014): 42–58.

Bonger, William Adrian. *Criminality and Economic Conditions.* Translated by Henry P. Horton. Boston: Little, Brown, 1916.

Brown, Brené. *I Thought It Was Just Me: Women Reclaiming Power and Courage in a Culture of Shame.* New York: Gotham Books, 2007.

Brownridge, Douglas. "Violence against Women Post-Separation." *Aggression and Violent Behavior* 11, no. 5 (2006): 514–30.

Bryant-Davis, Thema. *Thriving in the Wake of Trauma: A Multicultural Guide.* Lanham, MD: AltaMira Press, 2005.

Burnett-Zeigler, Inger. *Nobody Knows the Trouble I've Seen: The Emotional Lives of Black Women.* New York: Amistad, 2021.

Burton, Angela Olivia. "Toward Community Control of Child Welfare Funding: Repeal the Child Abuse Prevention and Treatment Act and De-Link Child Protection from Family Well Being." *Columbia Journal of Race and Law* 11, no. 3 (2021): 639–80.

Burton, Tracey. "'He's Always in My Head, Always in My Mind': A Psycho-Social Study into the Emotional Experience of Teaching a Child at Risk of Exclusion." Doctoral thesis, University of Essex, May 2019.

Campbell, Rebecca. "The Psychological Impact of Rape Victims' Experiences with the Legal, Medical, and Mental Health Systems." *American Psychologist* 63, no. 8 (2008): 702–17.

Campbell, Rebecca, Adrienne E. Adams, Sharon M. Wasco, Courtney E. Ahrens, and Tracy Sefl. "Training Interviewers for Research on Sexual Violence: A

Qualitative Study of Rape Survivors' Recommendations for Interview Practice." *Violence Against Women* 15, no. 5 (2009): 595–617.

———. "What Has It Been Like for You to Talk with Me Today? The Impact of Participating in Interview Research on Rape Survivors." *Violence Against Women* 16, no. 1 (2010): 60–83.

Campbell, Rebecca, Emily Dworkin, and Giannina Cabral. "An Ecological Model of the Impact of Sexual Assault on Women's Mental Health." *Trauma, Violence, & Abuse* 10, no. 3 (2009): 225–46.

Case, Anne, and Angus Deaton. *Deaths of Despair and the Future of Capitalism*. Princeton, NJ: Princeton University Press, 2020.

Catalano, Shannan, Erica Smith, Howard Snyder, and Michael Rand. *Female Victims of Violence*. Washington, DC: Bureau of Justice Statistics, US Department of Justice, Office of Justice Programs, September 2009. NCJ 228356.

Chemaly, Soraya. *Rage Becomes Her: The Power of Women's Anger*. New York: Atria Books, 2018.

Chou, Rosiland S. *Asian American Sexual Politics: The Construction of Race, Gender, and Ethnicity*. Lanham, MD: Rowman and Littlefield, 2005.

Chzhen, Yekateria, Annan Gromada, and Gwyther Rees. *Are the World's Richest Countries Family Friendly? Policy in the OECD and EU*. Florence, Italy: United Nation's Children's Fund (UNICEF) Office of Research, 2019.

Clear, Todd R. *Imprisoning Communities: How Mass Incarceration Makes Disadvantaged Neighborhoods Worse*. New York: Oxford University Press, 2009.

Coker, Donna. "Shifting Power for Battered Women: Law, Material Resources, and Poor Women of Color." *U.C. Davis Law Review* 33, no. 4 (Summer 2000): 1009–55.

Coker, Donna, and Ahjané D. Macquoid. "Why Opposing Hyper-Incarceration Should Be Central to the Work of the Anti-Domestic Violence Movement." *University of Miami Race & Social Justice Law Review* 5 (2015): 585–618.

Collins, Chuck. "U.S. Billionaire Wealth Surged by 70 Percent, or $2.1 Trillion, during Pandemic." Institute for Policy Studies. October 18, 2021. https://ips -dc.org/u-s-billionaire-wealth-surged-by-70-percent-or-2-1-trillion-during -pandemic-theyre-now-worth-a-combined-5-trillion.

Collins, Patricia Hill. *Black Feminist Thought: Knowledge, Consciousness, and the Politics of Empowerment*. Boston: Unwin Hyman, 1990.

———. "Shifting the Center: Race, Class, and Feminist Theorizing about Motherhood." In *Mothering: Ideology, Experience, and Agency*, edited by Evelyn Nakano Glenn, Grace Chang, and Linda Rennie Forcey, 371–89. New York: Routledge, 1994.

Collins, Patricia Hill, and Sirma Bilge. *Intersectionality*. Cambridge, UK: Polity Press, 2016.

Connell, Raewyn. *Gender and Power: Society, the Person and Sexual Politics*. Stanford, CA: Stanford University Press, 1987.

———. *Masculinities*, 2nd ed. Berkeley: University of California Press, 2005.

———. "Masculinity Research and Global Change." *Masculinities and Social Change* 1, no. 1 (2012): 4–18.

Connell, Raewyn, and James W. Messerschmidt. "Hegemonic Masculinity: Rethinking the Concept." *Gender and Society* 19, no. 6 (2005): 829–59.

Connell, Raewyn, and Rebecca Pearse. *Gender: In World Perspective,*. 3rd ed. Cambridge, UK: Polity Press, 2014.

Conner, Kenneth R., Catherine Cerulli, and Eric D. Caine. "Threatened and Attempted Suicide by Partner-Violent Male Respondents Petitioned to Family Violence Court." *Violence and Victims* 17, no. 2 (2002): 115–25.

Cook, Katy. *The Psychology of Silicon Valley: Ethical Threats and Emotional Unintelligence in the Tech Industry*. Cham, Switzerland: Palgrave Macmillan, 2020.

Cox, Robin. "The Ruthless Overlords of Silicon Valley." *Newsweek*, March 12, 2012. www.newsweek.com/ ruthless-overlords-silicon-valley-63639.

Crary, David. "Growing Number of Southern Baptist Women Question Roles." *ABC News*, March 24, 2021, https://abcnews.go.com/US/wireStory/doubts -southern-baptists-limits-womens-roles-76651536.

Creative Interventions. Home page. Accessed March 9, 2022. www.creative -interventions.org.

Crenshaw, Kimberlé. "Mapping the Margins: Intersectionality, Identity Politics, and Violence against Women of Color." *Stanford Law Review* 43, no. 6 (July 1991): 1245.

Critical Resistance. "The Prison Industrial Complex." Accessed February 23, 2022. http://criticalresistance.org/ about/not-so-common-language.

Crompton, Rosemary, and Michael Mann, eds. *Gender and Stratification*. Cambridge, UK: Polity Press, 1986.

Crosset, Todd W., James Ptacek, Mark A. McDonald, and Jeffrey R. Benedict. "Male Student-Athletes and Violence against Women: A Survey of Campus Judicial Affairs Offices." *Violence Against Women* 2, no. 2 (June 1996): 163–79.

Currie, Elliott. "Market, Crime and Community: Toward a Mid-Range Theory of Post-Industrial Violence." *Theoretical Criminology* 1, no. 2 (1997): 151–52.

Daniels, Arlene. "Invisible Work." *Social Problems* 34, no. 5 (1987): 403–15.

Davis, Angela Y., Gina Dent, Erica R. Meiners, and Beth Richie. *Abolition. Feminism. Now*. Chicago: Haymarket Books, 2022.

Davis, Fania E. *The Little Book of Race and Restorative Justice: Black Lives, Healing, and US Social Transformation*. New York: Good Books, 2019.

Deckard, Natalie Delia, Irene Browne, Cassaundra Rogriguez, Marisela Martinez-Cola, and Sofia Gonzalez Leal. "Controlling Images of Immigrants in the Mainstream and Black Press: The Discursive Power of the 'Illegal Latino.'" *Latino Studies* 18 (2020): 581–602.

DeGue, Sarah, Katherine A. Fowler, and Cynthia Calkins. "Deaths Due to Use of Lethal Force by Law Enforcement." *American Journal of Preventive Medicine* 51, no. 5, supp. 3 (2016): S173–87.

DeKeseredy, Walter S., and Marilyn Corsianos. *Violence against Women in Pornography*. New York: Routledge, 2016.

DeKeseredy, Walter S., Molly Dragiewicz, and Martin D. Schwartz. *Abusive Endings: Separation and Divorce Violence against Women*. Oakland: University of California Press, 2017.

DeKeseredy, Walter S., and Martin D. Schwartz. *Male Peer Support and Violence against Women*. Boston: Northeastern University Press, 2013.

Desmond, Matthew. *Evicted: Poverty and Profit in the American City.* New York: Crown, 2016.

Devries, Karen M., Joelle Y. Mack, Loraine J. Bacchus, Jennifer C. Child, Gail Falder, Max Petzold, Jill Astbury, and Charlotte H. Watts. "Intimate Partner Violence and Incident Depressive Symptoms and Suicide Attempts: A Systematic Review of Longitudinal Studies." *PLoS Medicine* 10, no. 5 (May 2013), https://doi.org/10.1371/journal.pmed.1001439.

Dobash, R. Emerson, and Russell P. Dobash. *Violence against Wives.* New York: Free Press, 1979.

Dunn, Jennifer L. *Judging Victims: Why We Stigmatize Survivors, and How They Reclaim Respect.* Boulder, CO: Lynne Rienner, 2010.

Dworkin, Andrea. *Pornography: Men Possessing Women.* New York: Penguin, 1981.

Ehrenreich, Barbara. *Fear of Falling: The Inner Life of the Middle Class.* New York: Harper Perennial, 1989.

Elliott, Diana B., and Tavia Simmons. *Marital Events of Americans: 2009.* Washington, DC: US Census Bureau, August 2011.

Enander, Viveka. "'A Fool to Keep Staying': Battered Women Labeling Themselves Stupid as an Expression of Gendered Shame." *Violence Against Women* 16, no. 5 (2010): 5–31.

———. "Leaving Jekyll and Hyde: Emotion Work in the Context of Intimate Partner Violence." *Feminism & Psychology* 21, no. 1 (2011): 29–48.

Enander, Viveka, and Carin Holmberg. "Why Does She Leave? The Leaving Process(es) of Battered Women." *Health Care for Women International* 29, no. 3 (2008): 200–226.

Ferraro, Kathleen. *Neither Angels nor Demons: Women, Crime, and Victimization.* Boston: Northeastern University Press, 2006.

Finkelhor, David, and Kersti Yllö. *License to Rape: Sexual Abuse of Wives.* New York: Henry Holt, 1985.

Fiske, Susan T. *Envy Up, Scorn Down: How Status Divides Us.* New York: Russell Sage Foundation, 2011.

Fitzpatrick, Petya, and Rebecca E. Olson. "A Rough Road Map to Reflexivity in Qualitative Research into Emotions." *Emotion Review* 7, no. 1 (2014): 49–54.

Fortune, Marie. *Is Nothing Sacred?* Eugene, OR: Wipf & Stock, 1999.

———. "Justice-Making in the Aftermath of Woman-Battering." In *Domestic Violence on Trial*, edited by Daniel Jay Sonkin, 237–48. New York: Springer, 1987.

Gaarder, Emily. "Lessons from a Restorative Circles Initiative for Intimate Partner Violence." *Restorative Justice: An International Journal* 3, no. 3 (2017): 342–67.

Gallagher, Rachel J. "Welfare Reform's Inadequate Implementation of the Family Violence Option: Exploring Dual Oppression of Poor Domestic Violence Victims." *American University Journal of Gender, Social Policy, and the Law* 19, no. 3 (2011): 987–1007.

Gilens, Martin. *Why Americans Hate Welfare.* Chicago: University of Chicago Press, 1999.

Gilligan, James, and Bandy Lee. "The Resolve to Stop the Violence Project: Reducing Violence in the Community through a Jail-Based Initiative." *Journal of Public Health* 27, no. 2 (2005): 143–48.

Glass, Nancy, Kathryn Laughon, Jacquelyn Campbell, Anna D. Wolf, Carolyn Rebecca Block, Ginger Hanson, Phyllis W. Sharps, and Ellen Taliaferro. "Non-Fatal Strangulation Is an Important Risk Factor for Homicide of Women." *Journal of Emergency Medicine* 35, no. 3 (2008): 329–35.

Glynn, Sarah Jane, and Jane Farrell. "The United States Needs to Guarantee Paid Maternity Leave." Center for American Progress, March 8, 2013. www.americanprogress.org/article/the-united-states-needs-to-guarantee-paid-maternity-leave.

Gómez, Jennifer M., and Robyn L. Gobin. "Black Women and Girls & #MeToo: Rape, Cultural Betrayal, & Healing." *Sex Roles* 82, nos.1–2 (2020): 1–12.

Gondolf, Edward. *The Future of Batterer Programs: Reassessing the Future of Evidence-Based Practice.* Boston: Northeastern University Press, 2012.

Goodman, Lisa, Mary Ann Dutton, Kevin Weinfurt and Sarah Cook. "The Intimate Partner Violence Strategies Index: Development and Application." *Violence Against Women* 9, no. 2 (2003): 163–86.

Goodmark, Leigh. *Decriminalizing Domestic Violence: A Balanced Policy Approach to Intimate Partner Violence* Berkeley: University of California Press, 2018.

———. "Politics, Safety, and Officer-Involved Intimate Partner Violence." In *The Politicization of Safety: Critical Perspectives on Domestic Violence Responses,* edited by Jane K. Stoever, 227–45. New York: NYU Press, 2019.

Gordon, Linda. *Heroes of Their Own Lives: The Politics and History of Family Violence.* New York: Viking, 1988.

Graf, Nikki. "Key Findings on Marriage and Cohabitation in the U.S." Pew Research Center, November 6, 2019. www.pewresearch.org/fact-tank/2019/11/06/key-findings-on-marriage-and-cohabitation-in-the-u-s.

Green, Bonnie L., Priscilla Dass-Brailsford, Alejandra Hurtado de Mendoza, Mihriye Mete, Shannon M. Lynch, Dana D. DeHart, and Joanne Belknap. "Trauma Experiences and Mental Health among Incarcerated Women." *Psychological Trauma: Theory, Research, Practice, and Policy* 8, no. 4 (2016): 455–63.

Guadalupe-Diaz, Xavier L. *Transgressed: Intimate Partner Violence in Transgender Lives.* New York: NYU Press, 2019.

Hacker, Andrew. *Two Nations: Black and White, Separate, Hostile, Unequal.* New York: Scribner, 2003.

Hamilton, Leah. *Welfare Doesn't Work: Promises of Basic Income for a Failed American Safety Net.* Cham, Switzerland: Palgrave Macmillan, 2020.

Harper, Shannon B. "Exploring the Relationship between Intimate Partner Sexual Assault, Severe Abuse, and Coercive Control." In *Handbook of Sexual Assault and Sexual Assault Prevention,* edited by William T. O'Donohue and Paul A. Schewe, 813–31. Cham, Switzerland: Springer, 2019.

Harris, Angela P. "Heteropatriarchy Kills: Challenging Gender Violence in a Prison Nation." *Washington University Journal of Law & Policy* 37 (2011): 13–65.

Harris-Perry, Melissa V. *Sister Citizen: Shame, Stereotypes, and Black Women in America*. New Haven, CT: Yale University Press, 2011.

Haselschwerdt, Megan L., and Jennifer L. Hardesty. "Managing Secrecy and Disclosure of Domestic Violence in Affluent Communities." *Journal of Marriage and Family* 79 (April 2017): 562.

Hattery, Angela J., and Earl Smith. *Gender, Power, and Violence: Responding to Sexual and Intimate Partner Violence in Society Today*. Lanham, MD: Rowman and Littlefield, 2019.

Hawkins, Robert B., Eric J. Charles, and J. Hunter Mehaffey. "Socio-Economic Status and COVID-19–Related Cases and Fatalities." *Public Health* 189 (December 2020): 129–34.

Heggeness, Misty L., Jason Fields, Yazmin A. García Trejo, and Anthony Schulzetenberg. "Tracking Job Losses for Mothers of School-Age Children during a Health Crisis." *Moms, Work, and the Pandemic* (blog), US Census Bureau, March 3, 2021. www.census.gov/library/stories/2021/03/moms-work-and-the-pandemic.html.

Henry, Nicola, and Anastasia Powell, eds. *Preventing Sexual Violence: Approaches to Overcoming a Rape Culture*. London: Palgrave Macmillan, 2014.

Herman, Judith. "Justice from the Victim's Perspective." *Violence Against Women* 11, no. 5 (2005): 571–602.

———. *Trauma and Recovery*. New York: Basic Books, 1992.

Hess, Cynthia, and Alona Del Rosario. *Dreams Deferred: A Survey on the Impact of Intimate Partner Violence on Survivors' Education, Careers, and Economic Security*. Washington, DC: Institute for Women's Policy Research, 2018.

Hochschild, Arlie Russell. "Emotion Work, Feeling Rules, and Social Structure." *American Journal of Sociology* 85, no. 3 (1979): 551–75.

———. "The Sociology of Feeling and Emotion: Selected Possibilities." In *Another Voice: Feminist Perspectives on Social Life and Social Science*, edited by Marcia Millman and Rosebeth Moss Kanter, 280–307. Garden City, NY: Anchor, 1975.

Hochschild, Arlie Russell (with Anne Machung). *The Second Shift: Working Parents and the Revolution at Home*. New York: Viking, 1989.

Holcomb, Stephanie, Laura Johnson, Andrea Hetling, Judy L. Postmus, Jordan Steiner, Larry Braasch, and Annette Riordan. "Implementation of the Family Violence Option 20 Years Later: A Review of State Welfare Rules for Domestic Violence Survivors." *Journal of Policy Practice* 16, no. 4 (2017): 415–31.

Holy See. "Letter to the Bishops of the Catholic Church on the Collaboration of Men and Women in the Church and in the World." *Daily Bulletin of the Holy See Press Office*. Accessed June 9, 2021. www.vatican.va/roman_curia/congregations/cfaith/documents/rc_con_cfaith_doc_20040731_collaboration_en.html.

hooks, bell. *Feminism Is for Everybody*. 2nd ed. New York: Routledge, 2014.

Horkheimer, Max. "Authority and the Family." In *Critical Theory: Selected Essays*, translated by Matthew J. O'Connell, 47–128. New York: Continuum, 1972. Originally published 1936.

Hudson, Christopher G. "Socioeconomic Status and Mental Illness: Tests of the Social Causation and Selection Hypotheses." *American Journal of Orthopsychiatry* 75, no. 1 (2005): 3–18.

Human Rights Watch. "US: Look Critically at Widespread Use of Solitary Confinement." June 18, 2012. www.hrw.org/news/2012/06/18/us-look-critically-widespread-use-solitary-confinement.

Hunnicut, Gwen. "Varieties of Patriarchy and Violence against Women." *Violence Against Women* 15, no. 5 (May 2009): 553–73.

Hunt, Swanee. "#MeToo Women Punished in Ways They Feared." *Boston Globe*, October 12, 2019.

Ipsos/NPR. *Sexual Assault: A New and Divided Era of Understanding.* Washington, DC: Ipsos, October 31, 2018.

Jack, Dana Crowley. "The Anger of Hope and the Anger of Despair: How Anger Relates to Women's Depression." In *Situating Sadness: Women and Depression in Social Context*, edited by Janet M. Stoppard and Linda M. McMullen, 62–87. New York: NYU Press, 2003.

Jack, Dana Crowley, and Alisha Ali, eds. *Silencing the Self across Cultures: Depression and Gender in the Social World.* Oxford: Oxford University Press, 2010.

Jane Doe, Inc.: The Massachusetts Coalition Against Sexual Assault and Domestic Violence. "Transformative and Restorative Justice for Survivors of Sexual and Domestic Violence in Massachusetts." Conference sponsored by Jane Doe, Inc., Boston, December 20, 2020. https://janedoeinc.wildapricot.org/event-396846.

Jasinski, Jana. "Pregnancy and Domestic Violence: A Review of the Literature." *Trauma, Violence, & Abuse* 5, no. 1 (2004): 47–64.

Jones, Charisse, and Kumea Shorter-Gooden. *Shifting: The Double Lives of Black Women in America.* New York: Harper Perennial, 2004.

Kelly, Liz. "The (In)credible Words of Women: False Allegations in European Rape Research." *Violence Against Women* 16, no. 12 (2010): 1345–55.

———. "Standing the Test of Time? Reflections on the Concept of the Continuum of Sexual Violence." In *Handbook on Sexual Violence*, edited by Jennifer M. Brown and Sandra L. Walklate, xviii–xxxvi. London: Routledge, 2012.

———. *Surviving Sexual Violence.* Minneapolis: University of Minnesota Press, 1988.

Kim, Mimi. "Alternative Interventions to Violence: Creative Interventions." *International Journal of Narrative Therapy and Community Work* 4 (2006): 45–52.

Kirkwood, Katherine. *Leaving Abusive Partners.* London: Sage, 1993.

Koss, Mary P. "Restorative Justice for Acquaintance Rape and Misdemeanor Sex Crimes." In *Restorative Justice and Violence against Women*, edited by James Ptacek, 218–38. Oxford: Oxford University Press, 2010.

———. "The RESTORE Program of Restorative Justice for Sex Crimes: Vision, Process, and Outcomes." *Journal of Interpersonal Violence* 29, no. 9 (2014): 1623–60.

Krienert, Jessie L., and Jeffrey A. Walsh. "An Examination of Intimate Partner Sexual Violence: Comparing Marital and Nonmarital Incidents Employing NIBRS Data, 2008–2012." *Partner Abuse* 9, no. 1 (2018): 41–57.

Kuhn, Annette. *Family Secrets: Acts of Memory and Imagination.* London: Verso, 1995.

Lafrance, Michelle N. *Women and Depression: Recovery and Resistance.* London: Routledge, 2009.

Lafrance, Michelle N., and Janet M. Stoppard. "Constructing a Non-Depressed Self: Women's Accounts of Recovery from Depression." *Feminism & Psychology* 16, no. 3 (2006): 307–25.

Lee, Bandy, and James Gilligan. "The Resolve to Stop the Violence Project: Transforming an In-House Culture of Violence through a Jail-Based Programme." *Journal of Public Health* 27, no. 2 (2005): 149–55.

Leonhardt, David, and Kevin Quealy. "The American Middle Class Is No Longer the World's Richest." *New York Times,* April 22, 2014.

Levin, Andrew P., Stuart B. Kleinman, and John S. Adler. "DSM-5 and Posttraumatic Stress Disorder." *Journal of the American Academy of Psychiatry and the Law* 42, no. 2 (2014): 146–58.

Lewis, Andrea L., and Sara L. Sommervold. "Death, But Is It Murder? The Role of Stereotypes and Cultural Perceptions in the Wrongful Convictions of Women." *Albany Law Review* 78, no. 3 (2014–2015): 1035–58.

Lisak, David, Lori Garinier, Sarah C. Nicksa, and Ashley M. Cote. "False Allegations of Sexual Assault: An Analysis of Ten Years of Reported Cases." *Violence Against Women* 16, no. 12 (2010): 1318–34.

Lonsway, Kimberly A. "Trying to Move the Elephant in the Living Room: Responding to the Challenge of False Reports." *Violence Against Women* 16, no. 12 (2010): 1356–71.

Lorde, Audre. *Sister Outsider: Essays & Speeches by Audre Lorde.* Trumansburg, NY: Crossing Press, 1984.

Lubiano, Wahneema. "Black Ladies, Welfare Queens, and State Minstrels: Ideological Wars by Narrative Means." In *Race-ing Justice, En-gendering Power: Essays on Anita Hill, Clarence Thomas and the Construction of Social Reality,* edited by Toni Morrison, 323–63. New York: Pantheon Books, 1992.

Lutgendorf, Monica A. "Intimate Partner Violence and Women's Health." *Obstetrics & Gynecology* 134, no. 3 (2019): 470–80.

Lynch, Shannon M., Dana D. Dehart, Joanne E. Belknap, Bonnie L. Green, Priscilla Dass-Brailsford, Kristine A. Johnson, and Elizabeth Whalley. "A Multisite Study of the Prevalence of Serious Mental Illness, PTSD, and Substance Use Disorders of Women in Jail." *Psychiatric Services* 65, no. 5 (May 2014): 670–74.

MacDaniels-Wilson, Cathy, and Joanne Belknap. "The Extensive Sexual Violation and Sexual Abuse Histories of Incarcerated Women." *Violence Against Women* 14, no. 10 (2008): 1090–1127.

Martin, Sandra L., Jennet Arcara, McLean D. Pollock, and Lonna Davis. *Domestic Violence during Pregnancy and the Postpartum Period.* Harrisburg, PA: VAWnet, a Project of the National Resource Center on Domestic Violence, 2012.

Massachusetts Department of Public Health. *Guidelines and Standards for the Certification of Intimate Partner Abuse Education Programs*. Boston: Massachusetts Department of Public Health, 2015.

Massachusetts General Laws. "Rape, Generally." Chapter 265, Section 22. N.d.

Massey, Douglas S., and Nancy A. Denton. *American Apartheid: Segregation and the Making of the Underclass*. Cambridge, MA: Harvard University Press, 1993.

Mateer, Erin Street. "Compelling Jekyll to Ditch Hyde: How the Law Ought to Address Batterer Duplicity." *Howard Law Journal* 48, no. 1 (2004): 525–70.

Mauer, Marc, and Meda Chesney-Lind, eds. *Invisible Punishment: The Collateral Consequences of Mass Imprisonment*. New York: New Press, 2002.

McCarter, Stephanie. "The Bad Wives: Misogyny's Age-Old Roots in the Home." *Eidolon*, April 9, 2018.

McOrmond-Plummer, Louise, ed. *Intimate Partner Sexual Violence*. London: Jessica Kingsley, 2014.

Messerschmidt, James. *Crime as Structured Action: Doing Masculinities, Race, Class, Sexuality, and Crime*. Lanham, MD: Rowman and Littlefield, 2014.

———. *Gender, Heterosexuality, and Youth Violence: The Struggle for Recognition*. Lanham, MD: Rowman and Littlefield, 2012.

———. *Masculinities and Crime: Critique and Reconceptualization of Theory*. Lanham, MD: Rowman and Littlefield, 1993.

Messinger, Adam M. *LGBTQ Intimate Partner Violence*. Oakland: University of California Press, 2020.

Messner, Steven F., and Richard Rosenfeld. *Crime and the American Dream*. 4th ed. Belmont, CA: Wadsworth, 2007.

Metropolitan Milwaukee Fair Housing Council. *City of Milwaukee Impediments to Fair Housing*. Milwaukee, WI: Metropolitan Milwaukee Fair Housing Council, 2005.

Miller, Elizabeth, Beth Jordan, Rebecca Levenson, and Jay G. Silverman. "Reproductive Coercion: Connecting the Dots between Partner Violence and Unintended Pregnancy." *Contraception* 81, no. 6 (2010): 457–59.

Miller, Susan L. *After the Crime: The Power of Restorative Justice Dialogues between Victims and Offenders*. New York: NYU Press, 2011.

Mogul, Joey L., Andrea J. Ritchie, and Kay Whitlock. *Queer (In)Justice: The Criminalization of LGBT People in the United States*. Boston: Beacon Press, 2012.

Moore, Angela. "Intimate Violence: Does Socioeconomic Status Matter?" In *Violence between Intimate Partners: Patterns, Causes, and Effects*, edited by Albert P. Cardarelli, 90–100. Boston: Allyn and Bacon, 1997.

Moore-Lobban, Shavonne J. and Robyn J. Gobin. *The Black Woman's Guide to Overcoming Domestic Violence*. Oakland: New Harbinger Publications, 2022.

Morgan, David. "Class and Masculinity." In *Handbook of Studies on Men & Masculinities*, edited by Michael S. Kimmel, Jeff Hearn, and R. W. Connell, 165–77. Newbury Park, CA: Sage, 2005.

Munshi, Soniya, Bhavana Nancherla, and Tiloma Jayasinghe. "Building towards Transformative Justice at Sakhi for South Asian Women." *University of Miami Race & Social Justice Law Review* 5, no. 2 (2015): 421–35.

National Institute of Justice. "Overview of Intimate Partner Violence." October 23, 2007. https://nij.ojp.gov/topics/articles/overview-intimate-partner -violence.

National Institutes of Health. "NCI Study Highlights Pandemic's Disproportionate Impact on Black, American Indian/Alaska Native, and Latino Adults." News release, October 4, 2021. www.nih.gov/news-events/news-releases /nci-study-highlights-pandemics-disproportionate-impact-black-american -indian-alaska-native-latino-adults.

National Women's Law Center. *A Year of Strength & Loss: The Pandemic, the Economy, and the Value of Women's Work.* Washington, DC: National Women's Law Center, March 2021. https://nwlc.org/wp-content/uploads /2021/03/Final_NWLC_Press_CovidStats.pdf.

New York Times. "Search the New York Times." Accessed August 4, 2021. www .nytimes.com/search.

Ogawa, Brian. *Walking on Eggshells: Practical Counsel for Women in or Leaving an Abusive Relationship.* Dubuque, IA: Kendall Hunt, 2009.

Oremus, Will. "The Ruthless Tactics Keeping Amazon on Top." *OneZero,* July 25, 2020. https://onezero.medium.com/the-ruthless-tactics-keeping-amazon-on -top-fa6bd2e91117.

Organisation for Economic Co-Operation and Development (OECD). "Employment: Time Spent in Paid and Unpaid Work, by Sex." Accessed August 11, 2021. https://stats.oecd.org/index.aspx?queryid=54757.

Ortner, Sherry B. *Anthropology and Social Theory.* Durham, NC: Duke University Press, 2006.

Padnick, Steven. "What Everyone Gets Wrong about Jekyll and Hyde." Tor.com. June 22, 2012. www.tor.com/2012/06/22/what-everybody-gets-wrong-about -jekyll-and-hyde.

Parker, Kim, and Renee Stepler. "As U.S Marriage Rate Hovers at 50%, Education Gap in Marital Status Widens." Pew Research Center, September 14, 2017, www.pewresearch.org/fact-tank/2017/09/14/as-u-s-marriage-rate-hovers-at -50-education-gap-in-marital-status-widens.

Pauly, Madison. "It's 2019, and States Are Still Making Exceptions for Spousal Rape." *Mother Jones,* November 21, 2019.

Pease, Bob. *Facing Patriarchy.* London: Zed Books, 2019.

Pence, Ellen, and Michael Paymar. *Education Groups for Men Who Batter: The Duluth Model.* New York: Springer, 1983.

Pennell, Joan, Gale Burford, Erika Sasson, Hillary Packer, and Emily L. Smith. "Family and Community Approaches to Intimate Partner Violence: Restorative Programs in the United States." *Violence Against Women* 27, no. 10 (2021): 1608–29.

Petrosky, Emiko, Janet M. Blair, Carter J. Betz, Katherine A. Fowler, Shane P. D. Jack, and Bridget H. Lyons. "Racial and Ethnic Differences in Homicides of Adult Women and the Role of Intimate Partner Violence—United States, 2003–2014." *Morbidity and Mortality Weekly Report* 66, no. 28 (July 21, 2017): 741–46.

Phifer, Hanna. "For Angela Davis and Gina Dent, Abolition is the Only Way." *Harper's Bazaar,* January 14, 2022. www.harpersbazaar.com/culture/art

-books-music/a38746835/angela-davis-gina-dent-abolition-feminism-now
-interview.

Postmus, Judy L., Sarah-Beth Plummer, and Amanda Sytlianou. "Measuring Economic Abuse in the Lives of Survivors: Revising the Scale of Economic Abuse." *Violence Against Women* 22, no. 6 (2016): 692–703.

Potter, Hillary. *Battle Cries: Black Women and Intimate Partner Abuse.* New York: NYU Press, 2008.

Ptacek, James. *Battered Women in the Courtroom: The Power of Judicial Responses.* Boston: Northeastern University Press, 1999.

———, ed. "Feminism, Restorative Justice, and Violence against Women." Special issue of *Violence Against Women* 11, no. 5 (May 2005).

———. "Hidden Dramas of Masculinity: Women's Perspectives on Intimate Violence in Different Social Classes." *Violence Against Women* 27, no. 5, (April 2021): 666-87.

———. "Rape and the Continuum of Sexual Abuse in Intimate Relationships: Interviews with US Women from Different Social Classes." In *Marital Rape: Consent, Marriage and Social Change in Global Context,* edited by Kersti Yllö and Gabriela Torres, 123-38. New York: Oxford University Press, 2016.

———. "Resisting Co-Optation: Three Feminist Challenges to Antiviolence Work." In *Restorative Justice and Violence against Women,* edited by James Ptacek, 5–36. Oxford: Oxford University Press, 2010.

———, ed. *Restorative Justice and Violence against Women.* Oxford: Oxford University Press, 2010.

———. "Why Do Men Batter Their Wives?" In *Feminist Perspectives on Wife Abuse,* ed. Kersti Yllö and Michele Bograd, 133–57. Newbury Park, CA: Sage, 1988.

Puri, Lakshmi. "Fear of Violence Affects the Everyday Lives of Women and Girls." UN Women, March 16, 2016. www.unwomen.org/en/news/stories /2016/3/lakshmi-puri-at-habitat-iii-agenda-and-gender-equality.

Quadagno, Jill. *The Color of Welfare: How Racism Undermined the War on Poverty.* New York: Oxford University Press, 1994.

Ragin, Charles C., Joane Nagel, and Patricia White. *Workshop on Scientific Foundations of Qualitative Research.* Arlington, VA: National Science Foundation, 2004.

Raj, Anita, Jennifer Rose, Michele R. Decker, Cynthia Rosengard, Megan R. Hebert, Michael Stein, and Jennifer G. Clarke. "Prevalence and Patters of Sexual Assault across the Life Span among Incarcerated Women." *Violence Against Women* 14, no. 5 (2008): 528–41.

Ramazanoglu, Caroline. *Feminism and the Contradictions of Oppression.* London: Routledge, 1986.

Reay, Diane. "Beyond Consciousness? The Psychic Landscape of Social Class." *Sociology* 39, no. 5 (2005): 911–28.

Reiter, Keramet A. *Mass Incarceration.* New York: Oxford University Press, 2017.

Renzetti, Claire M. "Economic Issues and Intimate Partner Violence." In *Sourcebook on Violence against Women,* 2nd ed., edited by Renzetti, Jeffrey L. Edleson, and Raquel Kennedy Bergen, 171–87. Los Angeles, CA: Sage, 2011.

Resko, Stella M. *Intimate Partner Violence and Women's Insecurity.* El Paso, TX: LFB Scholarly Publishing, 2010.

Richardson, Olivia. "The Story of the First Black-Owned Home in Wauwatosa." WUWM Radio, February 4, 2020. www.wuwm.com/podcast/lake -effect-segments/2020-02-24/the-story-of-the-first-black-owned-home-in -wauwatosa.

Richie, Beth. *Arrested Justice: Black Women, Violence, and American's Prison Nation.* New York: NYU Press, 2012.

Ritchie, Andrea. *Invisible No More: Police Violence against Black Women and Women of Color.* Boston: Beacon Press, 2017.

Roberts, Dorothy E. "Critical Race Feminism." In *Research Handbook on Feminist Jurisprudence*, edited by Robin West and Cynthia G. Bowman, 112–26. Cheltenham, UK: Edward Elgar, 2019.

———. "Prison, Foster Care, and the Systemic Punishment of Black Mothers." *UCLA Law Review* 59, no. 6 (2012): 1474–1500,

———. *Torn Apart: How the Child Welfare System Destroys Black Families— and How Abolition Can Build a Safer World.* New York: Basic Books, 2022.

Ross, Luana. *Inventing the Savage: The Social Construction of Native American Criminality.* Austin: University of Texas Press, 1998.

Ruglass, Lesia M., and Kathleen Kendall-Tackett. *Psychology of Trauma 101.* New York: Springer, 2015.

Russell, Brenda, ed. *Intimate Partner Violence and the LGBT+ Community.* Cham, Switzerland: Springer, 2020.

Russell, Diana E. H. *Rape in Marriage.* Bloomington: Indiana University Press, 1990.

Saar, Malika Saada, Rebecca Epstein, Lindsay Rosenthal, and Yasmin Vafa. *The Sexual Abuse to Prison Pipeline: The Girls' Story.* Washington, DC: Human Rights Project for Girls, Georgetown Law Project on Poverty and Inequality, and the Ms. Foundation for Women, 2015.

Sabo, Don, Terry A. Kupers, and Willie London, eds. *Prison Masculinities.* Philadelphia: Temple University Press, 2001.

Sayer, Andrew. *The Moral Significance of Class.* Cambridge, UK: Cambridge University Press, 2005.

Schochet, Leila. "The Child Care Crisis Is Keeping Women out of the Workforce." Center for American Progress, March 28, 2019. www.americanprogress.org /article/child-care-crisis-keeping-women-workforce.

Schwartz, Martin D. "Ain't Got No Class: Universal Risk Theories of Battering." *Contemporary Crises* 12 (1988): 373–92.

Scott, Allison, Freada Kapor Klein, and Uriridiakoghene Onovakpuri. "Tech Leavers Study." Kapor Center, April 27, 2017. www.kaporcenter.org/wp -content/uploads/2017/08/TechLeavers2017.pdf.

Semuels, Alana. "The End of Welfare as We Know It." *Atlantic*, April 1, 2016. www.theatlantic.com/business/archive/2016/04/the-end-of-welfare-as-we -know-it/476322.

Sentencing Project. *Fact Sheet: Incarcerated Women and Girls.* Washington, DC: The Sentencing Project, 2020.

Sered, Danielle. *Until We Reckon: Violence, Mass Incarceration, and a Road to Repair*. New York: NYU Press, 2019.

Sered, Susan, and Maureen Norton-Hawk. *Can't Catch a Break: Gender, Jail, Drugs, and the Limits of Personal Responsibility*. Oakland: University of California Press, 2014.

Shepard, Melanie F., and James A. Campbell. "The Abusive Behavior Inventory: A Measure of Psychological and Physical Abuse." *Journal of Interpersonal Violence* 7, no. 3 (1992): 291–305.

Smith, Sharon G., Xinjian Zhang, Kathleen C. Basile, Melissa T. Merrick, Jing Wang, Marcie-jo Kresnow, and Jieru Chen. *The National Intimate Partner and Sexual Violence Survey (NISVS): 2015 Data Brief—Updated Release*. Atlanta, GA: National Center for Injury Prevention and Control, Centers for Disease Control and Prevention, 2018.

Southern Baptist Convention. "The Baptist Faith and Message 2000." Accessed May 27, 2021. https://bfm.sbc.net/ bfm2000/#sviii-the-family.

SpearIt. "Gender Violence in Prison & Hyper-Masculinities in the 'Hood': Cycles of Destructive Masculinity." *Washington University Journal of Law & Policy* 37 (2011): 89–147.

Stark, Evan. *Coercive Control: How Men Entrap Women in Personal Life*. New York: Oxford University Press, 2007.

Steinmetz, Suzanne K., and Murray A. Straus. *Violence and the Family*. New York: Harper and Row, 1974.

Stevenson, Robert Louis. *Strange Case of Dr. Jekyll and Mr. Hyde*. London: Longman, Greens, 1886.

Stoever, Jane K., ed. *The Politicization of Safety: Critical Perspectives on Domestic Violence Responses*. New York: NYU Press, 2019.

Tangney, June Price, and Ronda L. Daring. *Shame and Guilt*. New York: Guilford Press, 2003.

Taylor, Charles. "The Politics of Recognition." In *Multiculturalism: Examining the Politics of Recognition*, edited by Amy Gutman, 25–74. Princeton, NJ: Princeton University Press, 1994.

Temin, Peter. *The Vanishing Middle Class*. Cambridge, MA: MIT Press, 2017.

Tonry, Michael. *Punishing Race: A Continuing American Dilemma*. New York: Oxford University Press, 2011.

Traister, Rebecca. "The Toll of #MeToo: Assessing the Costs for Those Who Came Forward." *New York Magazine*, October 25, 2019.

Ullman, Sarah E. *Talking about Sexual Assault: Society's Response to Survivors*. Washington, DC: American Psychological Association Press, 2010.

UN Women. *Progress of the World's Women 2019–2020: Families in a Changing World*. New York: UN Women, 2019.

United Nations. "Gender Statistics." United Nations Department of Economic and Social Affairs. Accessed August 11, 2021. https://unstats.un.org/unsd/gender/vaw.

United States. "Sexual Assault." 10 U.S. Code § 920, Art. 120 (2012).

Upadrashta, Pranava. "Recent Developments: Child Exclusion Provisions; The Harmful Impacts on Domestic Violence Survivors." *Berkeley Journal of Gender, Law & Justice* 27, no. 1 (2012):113–41.

US Bureau of the Census. "Income and Poverty in the United States: 2020." Last modified September 14, 2021. www.census.gov/library/publications/2021/demo/p60-273.html.

US Commission on Civil Rights. *Women in Prison: Seeking Justice behind Bars.* Washington, DC: United States Commission on Civil Rights, 2020.

US Department of Commerce. *Middle Class in America.* Washington, DC: US Department of Commerce, 2010.

US Department of Justice. "What Is Domestic Violence?" Accessed August 11, 2021. www.justice.gov/ovw/domestic-violence.

U.S. News & World Report. "How Much Does a Lawyer Make?" and "How Much Does a Physician Make?" Accessed August 9, 2021. https://money.usnews.com/careers/best-jobs/lawyer/salary and https://money.usnews.com/careers/ best-jobs/physician/salary.

Venezia, Todd. "The Terrifying 'Psychopath' Who Inspired 'Dr. Jekyll and Mr. Hyde.'" *New York Post,* November 6, 2016.

Vick, Branndon, Khristine Jones, and Sophie Mitra. "Poverty and Severe Psychiatric Disorder in the U.S.: Evidence from the Medical Expenditure Panel Survey." *Journal of Mental Health and Economics* 15, no. 2 (2012): 83–96.

Walby, Sylvia. "Gender, Class and Stratification." In *Gender and Stratification,* edited by Rosemary Crompton and Michael Mann, 23–39. Cambridge, UK: Polity Press, 1986.

———. *The Future of Feminism.* Cambridge, UK: Polity Press, 2011.

———. "Theorising Patriarchy." *Sociology* 23, no. 2 (May 1989): 213–34.

———. *Theorizing Patriarchy.* Oxford: Basil Blackwell, 1990.

Wang, Leah. "The U.S. Criminal Justice System Disproportionately Hurts Native People: The Data, Visualized." Prison Policy Initiative, October 8, 2021. www.prisonpolicy.org /blog/ 2021/10/08/indigenouspeoplesday.

Wang, Wendy. "The Link Between a College Education and a Lasting Marriage." Pew Research Center, December 4, 2015. www.pewresearch.org/fact-tank/2015/12/04/education-and-marriage.

Washington State Coalition Against Domestic Violence (WSCADV). *Fatal Police Shootings Related to Intimate Partner Violence.* Seattle WA: WSCADV, December 28, 2020.

Webster, Elizabeth. "Gendering and Racing Wrongful Conviction: Intersectionality, Normal Crimes and Women's Experience of Miscarriage of Justice." *Albany Law Review* 78, no. 3 (2014–2015): 973–1033.

Weissman, Deborah M. "In Pursuit of Economic Justice: The Political Economy of Domestic Violence Laws and Policies." *Utah Law Review* 1, no. 1 (2020): 1–67.

West, Carolyn M., and Kalimah Johnson. *Sexual Violence in the Lives of African American Women.* Harrisburg, PA: VAWnet, a Project of the National Resource Center on Domestic Violence, 2013.

West, Traci C. *Wounds of the Spirit: Black Women, Violence, and Resistance Ethics.* New York: NYU Press, 1999.

Wilson, William Julius. *The Truly Disadvantaged: The Inner City, the Underclass, and Public Policy,* 2nd ed. Chicago: University of Chicago Press, 2012.

Wolff, Nancy, Jing Shi, and Jane A. Siegel. "Patterns of Victimization among Male and Female Inmates: Evidence of an Enduring Legacy." *Violence and Victims* 24, no. 4 (2009): 469–84.

Wright, Erik Olin, and Joel Rogers. *American Society: How It Really Works.* New York: W. W. Norton, 2010.

Wysong, Earl, Robert Perrucci, and David Wright. *The New Class Society.* 4th ed. Lanham, MD: Rowman and Littlefield, 2014.

Yllö, Kersti. "Prologue: Understanding Marital Rape in Global Context." In *Marital Rape: Consent, Marriage, and Social Change in a Global Context*, edited by Yllö and M. Gabriela Torres, 1–6. New York: Oxford University Press, 2016.

———. "Rape, Marital." In *Encyclopedia of Victimology and Crime Prevention*, edited by Bonnie S. Fisher and Steven P. Lab, 720–23. Thousand Oaks, CA: Sage, 2010.

———. "Wife Rape: A Social Problem for the 21st Century." *Violence Against Women* 5 , no. 9 (1999): 1059–63.

Yllö, Kersti, and M. Gabriela Torres, eds. *Marital Rape: Consent, Marriage, and Social Change in a Global Context.* New York: Oxford University Press, 2016.

Yuan, Nicole P., Mary P. Koss, and Mirto Stone. *The Psychological Consequences of Sexual Trauma.* Harrisburg, PA: VAWnet, a Project of the National Resource Center on Domestic Violence, 2006.

Zinsstag, Estelle, and Marie Keenan, eds. *Restorative Responses to Sexual Violence.* London: Routledge, 2017.

Zweig, Michael. *The Working Class Majority: America's Best Kept Secret.* Ithaca, NY: Cornell University Press, 2012.

Index

Founded in 1893,
UNIVERSITY OF CALIFORNIA PRESS
publishes bold, progressive books and journals
on topics in the arts, humanities, social sciences,
and natural sciences—with a focus on social
justice issues—that inspire thought and action
among readers worldwide.

The UC PRESS FOUNDATION
raises funds to uphold the press's vital role
as an independent, nonprofit publisher, and
receives philanthropic support from a wide
range of individuals and institutions—and from
committed readers like you. To learn more, visit
ucpress.edu/supportus.